AIA Guide to the Architecture of Atlanta

Text by Isabelle Gournay
Photographs by Paul G. Beswick
Foreword by Dana F. White
Edited by Gerald W. Sams

The University of Georgia Press
Athens and London

© 1993 by the University of Georgia Press
Athens, Georgia 30602
All rights reserved

Designed and produced by the staff of the
University of Georgia Press
Set in Optima by Tseng Information Systems, Inc.
Printed and bound by Maple-Vail
The paper in this book meets the guidelines for
permanence and durability of the Committee on
Production Guidelines for Book Longevity of the
Council on Library Resources.

Printed in the United States of America
97   96   95   94   93   C   5   4   3   2   1
97   96   95   94   93   P   5   4   3   2   1

Library of Congress Cataloging in Publication Data
Gournay, Isabelle.
    AIA guide to the architecture of Atlanta / text by
Isabelle Gournay ; photographs by Paul G. Beswick ;
foreword by Dana F. White ; edited by Gerald W.
Sams.
        p.   cm.
    Includes bibliographical references and indexes.
    ISBN 0-8203-1439-0 (alk. paper). — ISBN
0-8203-1450-1 (pbk. : alk. paper)
        1. Architecture—Georgia—Atlanta—Guidebooks.
2. Atlanta (Ga.)—Buildings, structures, etc.   I.
Beswick, Paul G.   II. Sams, Gerald W.
III. American Institute of Architects.   IV. Title.   V.
Title: Guide to the architecture of Atlanta.
NA735.A83G68   1993
720'.9758'231–dc20   92-12694
                                             CIP

British Library Cataloging in Publication Data available

Note

AIA Atlanta dedicates this book to its Executive Director,
Dorothy P. Spence, Honorary AIA,
for her endearing nature, loyal dedication, and immense contribution
to the practice of architecture in Atlanta
and the profession of architecture in general.

Contents

Abbreviations ix
Preface xi
Acknowledgments xv
Sponsors xvii
Foreword xix
 The Dogwood and the Dollar
 Dana F. White
Introduction xxv
 Urbanism and Architecture in Atlanta,
 A Personal View
 Isabelle Gournay
Regional Map xxviii
Central City Map xxx

Area 1 Downtown South (DS) 1
Area 2 Five Points (FP) 19
Area 3 Peachtree Center (PC) 45
Area 4 Downtown West (DW) 63
Area 5 Sweet Auburn (SA) 71
Area 6 Lower Midtown (LM) 85
Area 7 Upper Midtown (UM) 111
Area 8 Ansley Park (AP) 137
Area 9 Georgia Tech (GT) 147
Area 10 West End (WE) 161
Area 11 South East (SE) 173
Area 12 Inman Park (IP) 185
Area 13 Virginia-Highland (VH) 195
Area 14 Druid Hills (DH) 207
Area 15 Emory University (EU) 217
Area 16 Buckhead Residential (BR) 235
Area 17 Buckhead, Lenox Square (BL) 263
Area 18 Cumberland Mall (CM) 281
Area 19 Perimeter Mall (PM) 295
Area 20 Roswell (RS) 307
Area 21 Decatur (DC) 315
Area 22 South Side (SS) 325

Works Cited 333
Glossary 335
General Index 339
Index to Buildings and Places 355
Additional Resources 365

Abbreviations

See the Preface for further information about the designations listed below.

AIA   American Institute of Architects
ASLA   American Society of Landscape Architects
FAIA   Fellow, American Institute of Architects
GAAIA   Georgia Association of the American Institute of Architects
HB   City of Atlanta Historic Buildings
HL   City of Atlanta Honorary Landmark Building
LB   City of Atlanta Landmark Buildings
NHL   National Historic Landmark
NR   National Register of Historic Places
SARC   South Atlantic Regional Conference of the American Institute of Architects
UDC   Urban Design Commission

Preface

AIA Atlanta, a chapter of the American Institute of Architects, is proud to offer this *AIA Guide to the Architecture of Atlanta* in response to requests from residents and visitors alike. The *Guide* has been more than six years in the making and represents the dedicated efforts of many individuals who have seen the need for this publication and devoted their time and resources to making it a reality.

As the AIA's designated editor, I must first give special thanks to Isabelle Gournay, the author, for her tireless efforts in researching each building and writing lively, readable, and insightful descriptions and critiques. Although no guidebook could function without photographs, I am sure those who use this volume will agree that the ones supplied by Paul G. Beswick, AIA, for this publication are exceptional works of art. His dedication to the project and his desire to photograph every building featured rather than to rely on historic or existing promotional photographs gives the *Guide* an artistic unity that few guidebooks can claim. Also important to this guidebook has been the input of Dana F. White, whose foreword sets the historic groundwork for the building entries that follow. Working with him has been a pleasure and an honor.

One of the most essential elements of any successful guidebook is the cartography. In this volume the maps have been expertly produced by the Georgia State University Department of Geography under the direction of Jeff McMichael, whose personal involvement and commitment to this endeavor have resulted in clear, accurate, and easy to use maps. My personal thanks go out to him for his enthusiasm and cooperation.

To establish the contents of this guidebook and review its early progress, AIA Atlanta formed an advisory committee of professional architects and scholars. This group consisted of Merrill Elam, AIA; Richard Rothman, AIA; Joseph N. Smith, FAIA; Eugene L. Surber, AIA; Timothy Crimmins, professor of history at Georgia State University; Richard Cloues, National Register Coordinator, Parks and Historic Sites Division of the Georgia Department of Natural Resources; Thomas Lyman, professor of art history at Emory University; and Douglas Allen, ASLA, professor of landscape architecture at Georgia Institute of Technology. Isabelle Gournay and I assembled lists of buildings for possible inclusion in the book and submitted them to this committee for consideration. Criteria for selection were based on a combination of factors: historic, architectural, and cultural significance were key considerations. Other factors included awards received, predominance on the skyline, and uniqueness of style, design, or building type. Once the maps were established which included all the major buildings selected, additional entries were added to the list based on their proximity to those originally chosen and their possible general interest to visitors and students of architecture.

The text is written in essay form, describing either single buildings or groups of buildings that share a common feature or location. Generally the first building discussed in each passage of the text is featured with a photograph, though this is not always the case. Occasionally, because of a building's location and its numbered sequence on a map, the primary building described in the text and illustrated with a photograph occurs later in the passage. The buildings are consistently discussed in the order in which they appear on the area map, which is intended to establish a reasonable walking or driving tour of each area and to facilitate locating individual buildings for those who wish to create their own tours.

The maps themselves are named for areas of the city they encompass, although one should not assume that they define those areas exclusively. For instance, the map entitled Virginia-Highland contains the historic Virginia-Highland area, but not all the buildings described in this section are in that legally defined district. We have also created new names for some areas, strictly for the convenience of this guidebook—Upper Midtown and Lower Midtown, for example. The entire area is generally known as Midtown, but because it is too large to represent on a single map, we have divided the area. Each of the twenty-two maps has a two-letter abbreviation for ease of cross referencing and indexing.

Commercial and institutional entries are listed by their current names, with their historic or original names in parentheses. Private residences are listed by the names of their original owners unless they have been given estate names, such as Knollwood and Callanwolde. The date listed is generally the date of construction. A range of dates (such as 1969–1980 for the Atlanta-Fulton County Public Library) indicates the span of years from the building's design to its final construction. This sort of listing is confined to projects where such a range is significant in the study of the project's history. If only one date is listed it can usually be assumed that the building was designed shortly before it was constructed.

Because it is common for an architectural firm to change its name or merge with another firm, credit for the design of each entry is given to the firm as it was known at the time the building was constructed. We have also attempted to list individual designers, project architects, and principals-in-charge when that information was available, especially in instances where individuals have later made names for themselves in their own practices. Philip Shutze's work under Hentz, Reid and Adler is a prime example. Unless otherwise noted, the design firm cited is based in Atlanta.

Many buildings in this guidebook have been recognized by official organizations as worthy of special attention because of their historic or architectural significance. These are indicated in heading notes by the following abbreviations: **NR** for buildings and historic sites on the National Register of Historic Places, **NHL** for National Historic Landmarks, **LB** for City of Atlanta Landmark Buildings, **HB** for City of Atlanta Historic Buildings, and **HL** for City of Atlanta Honorary Landmark. These designations afford the buildings or sites various degrees of protection against development and demolition. The city designations carry statutory restrictions along with the mostly honorary status associated with the national labels. Those interested in pursuing the specifics of these designations should consult the Atlanta Historical Society or the Urban Design Commission. Addresses and telephone numbers for these and other sources of additional information can be found at the end of this guidebook.

Design awards and recognition are also listed in the heading notes by initials. The **UDC Award** indicates that the project has been recognized by Atlanta's Urban Design Commission for excellence in some aspect of improving the built environment: architectural design, rehabilitation, or historic preservation, for example. **GAAIA Awards** are presented annually to Georgia architects and project owners for design excellence by the Georgia Association of the American Institute of Architects, a statewide association of local AIA chapters. Projects are submitted for consideration to a jury of distinguished practitioners from outside the state. **SARC Awards** are presented biannually at the South Atlantic Regional Conference of the American Institute of Architects. AIA chapters in Georgia, North Carolina, and South Carolina make up the South Atlantic Region and awards for "Excellence in Architecture" are selected by nationally assembled juries from entries submitted from all three states. **AIA Awards** are given annually at the American Institute of Architects National Convention, which recognizes design excellence world-wide. The nine projects in Atlanta that have been singled out for this prestigious award are included in the guidebook: High Museum of Art at Georgia-Pacific Center (FP 21); North and East Wings, Georgia Baptist Medical Center (SA 17); Professional Building, Georgia Baptist Medical Center (SA 18); High Museum of Art (UM 20); Emory University Museum of Art and Archeology (EU 5); Trinity School (BR 18); Lenox Square (BL 10); John Knox Presbyterian Church (CM 14); and Clayton County Headquarters Library (SS 1). Unfortunately, not every recipient of the other awards could be included, most often because of their location or because their appearance has been altered to the point that they no longer manifest the design qualities that won them recognition.

We hope that future editions of this book can expand the somewhat arbitrary geographical limits imposed in order to manage the number of buildings initially proposed for this volume. We trust the reader will find, however, that this guidebook offers a commendable variety of buildings, spanning Atlanta's history from the Civil War to the present day, and covering its various geographical and cultural districts in as complete a form as may be expected of such a survey. We welcome comments from users of this guidebook on projects that they feel should be included in future editions.

Finally, I would like to add a personal note on my involvement with this book. Nothing in my background has made me more qualified to edit this volume than any other active AIA member. In fact, I feel I am far less qualified than many members who could have been chosen. My job as editor has been to orchestrate a relatively small ensemble of players (researchers, advisors, authors, photographers, cartographers, and publishers) and to deal with the public's and the architectural profession's expectations for this *Guide* while keeping an eye on the ever-present budgetary constraints imposed on its production. I could not have done this alone, and I must extend my personal gratitude to those who lent moral as well as physical support: to Dorothy Spence, Honorary AIA, Executive Director of the Atlanta Chapter and the Georgia Association AIA, to whom this book is dedicated, for her continued reassurances and support in this and other endeavors; to Richard Taylor, FAIA, past president of the Atlanta Chapter, AIA and my employer, who originally appointed me to this position (under the premise that all good deeds should not go unpunished), for allowing me the time to fulfill obligations of the position and contributing advice and encouragement when needed; and to Karen Orchard, Executive Editor of the University of Georgia Press, who initiated me to the publishing business and contributed immeasurably to the actual production of the book. I have thoroughly enjoyed the experience of working with all those involved with this project and look forward to what I am sure will be several future editions.

Gerald W. Sams, AIA
Editor

Acknowledgments

The author, photographer, and editor wish to extend their gratitude to the following individuals for their invaluable assistance in the preparation of this guidebook.

Elizabeth Dowling, AIA
Georgia Institute of Technology
Guidebook Conception

Douglas Allen, ASLA
Georgia Institute of Technology
Advisory Committee Member

Richard Clouse
Georgia Department
    of Natural Resources
Advisory Committee Member

Timothy J. Crimmins
Georgia State University
Advisory Committee Member

Thomas Lyman
Emory University
Advisory Committee Member

Merrill Elam, AIA
Scogin Elam & Bray, Architects
Advisory Committee Member

Richard Rothman, AIA
Richard Rothman & Associates
Advisory Committee Member

Joseph N. Smith, FAIA
Architect
Advisory Committee Member

Eugene L. Surber, AIA
Surber & Barber, Architects
Advisory Committee Member

Pat Connell
Georgia Institute of Technology
Historical Research

Elliott Pavlos
Georgia Institute of Technology
Historical Research and Editing

Charlotte Ramsay
Georgia Department
    of Natural Resources
Historical Research

Joan Williamson
Text Review and Editing

Jeff McMichael
Georgia State University
Cartography Design

Alisa Pengue Solomon
Georgia State University
Computer Cartography

Jill Kirn
Georgia State University
Computer Cartography

Jim Larkin, AIA
Emory University
Research and Project Information

Eleanor Wright
Thompson Ventulett Stainback
    & Associates
Project Information

Lori Stainback
Thompson Ventulett Stainback
    & Associates
Preview Booklet for
    International Olympic Committee

Carla McClone
AIA Chapter Office
Fund Raising

Barbara Forbes
AIA Chapter Office
Administrative Assistance
and Research

Henry Teague, AIA
Atlanta Chapter, AIA President,
1986

Richard Hall, AIA
Atlanta Chapter, AIA President,
1987

Brian Gracey, AIA
Atlanta Chapter, AIA President,
1988

Richard L. Taylor, FAIA
Atlanta Chapter, AIA President,
1989

Ben Darmer, AIA
Atlanta Chapter, AIA President,
1990

Richard Rothman, AIA
Atlanta Chapter, AIA President,
1991

G. Geddes Dowling, AIA
Atlanta Chapter, AIA President,
1992

Shawn Stickney
Photography

Paula Soowal Brown
Photographic Assistance

P. Christopher Beswick
Photographic Assistance

Jana Lowe
Photographic Assistance

Orman L. Stanfill
Photographic Assistance

Emily Minton
Photography Lab Assistance

Sue Ann Kuhn-Smith
Photography Lab Assistance

Sponsors

The publication of this book was made possible by a liberal grant from the American Institute of Architects' College of Fellows and the generous contributions of the firms and individuals listed below. AIA Atlanta gratefully acknowledges their support of this project and their commitment to both the AIA and the City of Atlanta.

Firms

Albion Design Associates
Allain and Associates
Appel Associates
Bilbro, Spangler & Manley
Niles Bolton Associates
Bradfield, Richards, and Associates, Architects
Bull, Brown and Kilgo, Architects
BWS Architects & Engineers
Cooper Carry and Associates
Donaldson/Architects
Dowling Architects and Associates
EDAW
Marshall Erdman and Associates
Gardner, Spencer, Smith & Associates
Greenberg Farrow Architecture
Gresham Architecture
Heery Architects & Engineers
Howell Rusk Dodson-Architects
Hunt/Enloe/MacKinnon
Jova/Daniels/Busby, Architects
Lord, Aeck & Sargent
Lyman + Davidson
Tipton Masterson Associates
Moore/Architecture
Nichols Carter Grant Architects
Nix, Mann and Associates
George Novak Company
John Portman & Associates
Priegel & Ludwig
Rabun Hatch and Associates
Rondeau and Associates
Rosser Fabrap International
Richard Rothman & Associates
Ruys & Company
SAE/Carlson
Sizemore/Floyd, Architects

Slater-Paull & Associates
Smallwood, Reynolds, Stewart, Stewart and Associates
Henry Howard Smith, Architect
Stang & Newdow
Stevens & Wilkinson
Thompson, Ventulett, Stainback & Associates
Warner, Summers, Ditzel & Associates

Individuals

Marc Bigley, AIA
Elizabeth Harris Blackburn, AIA
David G. Cavender, AIA
J. Hollis Dorsey Jr., AIA
G. Geddes Dowling III, AIA
William S. Edwards, AIA
Steven Elmets, AIA
Pam Game
Ann Gerondelis, AIA
John B. Gesbocker, AIA
Brian H. Gracey, AIA
Lois M. Grant, AIA
James C. Haigler, AIA
J. Ted Hall, AIA
Jeffrey Tanner Hendrick, AIA
David H. Hicks, AIA
Geoffrey O. Horn, AIA
Jerry Huie
Wes Jennings, AIA
Gary Johnson, AIA
Jake A. Jones III, AIA
Joseph R. Kordys Jr., AIA
Thomas J. Laccetti, Associate Member AIA
Melissa M. Ludwig, AIA
Paul G. Ludwig, AIA
Mark R. Lysett, AIA

Robert D. McKerrow, AIA
William R. McNeel, AIA
George P. Melas, AIA
Matteo P. Moore, AIA
Charles H. Potts, AIA
Jack H. Pyburn, AIA
Mark A. Reece, AIA
Garland M. Reynolds, FAIA
Charles J. Robisch, AIA

Bernard B. Rothschild, FAIA
Alex Roush, AIA
William Russell, AIA
Pete Ruys, AIA
Andrew J. Singletary Jr., AIA
Brian Bethea Smith, AIA
Dorothy P. Spence, Honorary AIA
Jim Stewart, AIA

Foreword

The Dogwood and the Dollar

Dana F. White

Atlanta, the thriving city within the green forest, brings to mind another culture, similarly defined by two contrasting forces that shaped its eventual character. In *The Chrysanthemum and the Sword,* a classic analysis of immediate post–World War II Japan, Ruth Benedict described a seemingly schizoid culture which, simultaneously, "lavishes art upon the cultivation of chrysanthemums" and "is devoted to the cult of the sword and the top prestige of the warrior." Japan's aesthetic (the chrysanthemum) and aggressive (the sword) drives have their parallels in Atlanta's environmental (the dogwood) and commercial (the dollar) impulses. Moreover, as the warrior stood as the mythic hero for Imperial Japan, the entrepreneur-developer stands as the counterpart for modern Atlanta. The reasons for these cultural imperatives are, quite literally, built into the city's very being.

The Business of Atlanta

Commerce is the city's sole reason for being. Atlanta possesses no natural "locational advantages"—such as a site along a navigable river, access to a harbor, or proximity to mineral deposits or agricultural hinterland. Nor was it established as an administrative center—its designation as state capital came later in its history.

The city came into being during the mid-1830s as a railroad center, a "Terminus" (so it was first called) for a regional rail network. It was this function that, quite literally, put Atlanta on the map and that during the Civil War made it the staging point for William Tecumseh Sherman's 1864 "March to the Sea."

Born as a railroad town, Atlanta has grown progressively as a transfer point—rail, during its first century of growth; automotive and air, over the past half-century. Throughout its history, Atlanta has had only one thing in its favor: a confident assertion of self that is embodied in the so-called Atlanta Spirit. This spirit manifested itself, for example, during the 1960s when this biracial, segregated community distinguished itself from other municipalities in the region by proclaiming itself "The City Too Busy to Hate" and in the process garnered the image of being the Civil Rights capital of the South. (Rival cities in the region have been known to mock the city's self-promotion. A Savannah proverb reads: "If Atlanta could suck as hard as it blows, it could bring the ocean to it and become a seaport.") Whatever else may be said of the city's celebration of self, there is no denying the centrality of that tradition in Atlanta's history and its manifestation in the structures that express the Atlanta Spirit.

Underground Atlanta, the festival marketplace for the contemporary city, marks the center of the historic city, that confluence of railroads that shaped, in turn, Terminus, then briefly, Marthasville, and finally, Atlanta. The railroad town that developed in the vicinity of Old Alabama and Pryor streets during the half-century punctuated by the Civil War was representative of its age. Its modest skyline of two- to five-story buildings was that of a heterogeneous, mixed-use, dense, pedestrian-oriented city that grew from a population of about ten thousand at the start of the Civil War to nearly ninety thousand by the turn of the century. Its most impressive structures, save two, were likely to have been the "lettable office blocks" or "business blocks," which typically contained four to five stories with shops at ground level, offices for professionals (doctors and lawyers) on the second floor, public rooms (a lodge hall, assembly room, or library) on the third, and rooms to let (or flats) at the top. More modest in height—and more common in view—were one- to three-story shops, homes, stables, and businesses, which constituted the bulk and the heart of the city.

In this modest setting, two structures stood out. The first was the Georgia State Capitol, constructed during the late 1880s, virtually solitary in its grandeur for decades to come. The Capitol would eventually become the focal point for a government center—state and municipal offices— that would define a new eastern edge of the old commercial center. The second was the Kimball House—constructed in 1871, rebuilt during the mid-1880s, and demolished in 1959—which offered an innovative approach to hotel living. No mere local inn or hostelry, this establishment attracted a national clientele and its message was that travelers required more than just comfort and convenience, that they also sought urbanity, and that hotel-living should become a memorable and entertaining experience. The Kimball House tradition, itself a manifestation of the Atlanta Spirit, permeates Atlanta's resurgence over the past three decades.

As business expanded, traffic increased, and families moved out, the commercial core shifted northward to the area defined as Five Points. The multi-use, sprawling horizontal town was giving way to a single-function, compact central business district. The city's center— its Downtown—was in the process of becoming clearly separate and easily distinguishable from other urban districts. A "Regional City" was taking shape.

The distinctive mark of the new Downtown developing around Five Points was its verticality. The multistory office building, symbolized in Atlanta by the 1892 Equitable Building (since demolished), was economical in its use of valuable ground space, profitable in its appeal to specialized renters (a new "office industry"), and inspirational in its creation of a dramatic skyline. It seemed to symbolize Atlanta's economic "take off," its population explosion from 90,000 to almost 155,000 inhabitants during the first decade of the new century.

As the city's economy flourished during the first quarter of the twentieth century, Five Points became Atlanta's major financial district, its version of Wall Street. At the northern edge stood the Candler Building (1906), its ship's prow pointing toward the modest hotel-theater district beyond and an ill-defined area of auto showrooms, surviving homes, and shops that would, some thirty years later, mushroom into a self-proclaimed new "center" for Atlanta.

In the early years of the century, downtown Atlanta was predominantly white. As a result of the race riot of 1906, most black-owned businesses, as well as black professionals, fled the city's center and relocated along the eastern edge of the commercial core, creating what would become known as the Sweet Auburn business district. Earlier still, between 1869 and 1893, the American Missionary Association had purchased some seventy acres of land to house the city's first center for higher learning. That institution, Atlanta University, came to represent more than just a campus. It also served as the focal point for the teachers, students, and citizens who resided in this second "Black Side of Atlanta," as those in the area called it. This university-focused district would develop eventually into the largest concentration of predominantly black institutions of higher education in the world.

As white Atlanta moved north, black Atlanta moved east and west, and segregation fostered increasing racial distance. Still, for nearly three decades, stasis, not movement, best described the city's condition. During the 1930s, 1940s, and 1950s, Atlanta languished. The Great Depression, which manifested itself early in the region, World War II, which absorbed the nation's energies into the late 1940s, and two technological revolutions, automobility and atomic power, halted downtown building nationwide. Many came to question whether cities were defensible either in terms of their concentration of people, which the automobile revolution could disperse, or in their providing population targets for a nuclear age, a world immersed in the Cold War. In Atlanta, for those and other purely local reasons, only three major structures were built between 1930 and 1962 in the Five Points district: the Fulton National Bank Building (now the Bank South Building), the National Bank of Georgia Building (now First American Bank), and the Atlanta Chamber of Commerce Building.

With the construction of two major buildings in 1962—the Atlanta Merchandise Mart and the nearby Georgia Power building (since vacated for a newer structure across the expressway)—notice was served not only that the inner city would undertake revitalization, but also that its "downtown" would gravitate "uptown." The Merchandise Mart was the beginning point for John Portman's ambitious Peachtree Center— a virtual city-within-a-city. Over the years the ever-expanding Portman empire served to anchor such immediate commercial neighbors as the Atlanta Center Limited, Peachtree Summit complex, the new Georgia Power Headquarters, and, along its southern edge, the Ritz-Carlton Hotel, the Georgia-Pacific Center, and One-Ninety-One Peachtree Tower. In time, with some glaring vacancies still apparent, the three successive commercial cores of the city—Underground (referred to as Downtown South in this guidebook), Five Points, and Peachtree Center—became a single linear extension stretching north along Peachtree Street. In one sense, Downtown is now complete; in another, it points ever northward.

The City in a Forest

As the city built up, it also grew out. As residences gave way to businesses within the city's core, new communities were created along its rings, and urbanization begat suburbanization. Here, aesthetics and commerce—the dogwood and the dollar—were married. Although Atlanta possesses no natural locational advantages, it boasts many advantages of nature. Situated astride the verdant southern Piedmont, where lush forests provide both amenity and natural screening, and elevated atop a thousand-foot ridge line, where prevailing western winds moderate sultry southern summers, the Atlanta area proved an ideal setting for suburban development.

The creation of new suburban communities became big business in turn-of-the-century Atlanta, and the developmental schemes proposed were often innovative, comprehensive, and sometimes even breathtaking. Developer Joel Hurt, for one, planned a total commuting pattern by linking his downtown Equitable Building to his planned suburb of Inman Park (begun in 1887) by way of his Atlanta and Edgewood Street Railway Company (1888). In 1890, moreover, Hurt engaged the services of America's genius of landscaped amenity, Frederick Law Olmsted, to design the unique "parkway suburb" of Druid Hills, a project carried to completion in the next decade by Olmsted's sons (1908). During the same period, on the city's near north side, Edwin Ansley developed the concept of "twin parks," the public Piedmont Park and his private suburb of Ansley Park (1904) as related amenities. Other suburbs developed earlier to the city's south (Grant Park) and contemporaneously to the west (West End), but the trend was mainly due north, ultimately to lush, suburban, and posh Buckhead.

During the 1920s, black entrepreneur Heman Perry promoted his Washington Park suburban community in conjunction with the adjacent (and public) Washington Park and nearby Booker T. Washington High School, thereby breaking the "color line" that had previously blocked black suburbanization. What tied all of these ventures together—black and white, westside and northside—was the concept of clustering, with the residential suburb providing stability and serving as a take-off point for future expansion.

The "Piedmont Picturesque" suburban development gave residential Atlanta a distinctive character—that of a city in a forest. North from the central business district, the major path of white suburbanization, an observer will discover repeated reminders of Druid Hills or Ansley Park—all the way to the Perimeter and beyond; so, too, traveling west, the path of black suburbanization, the viewer sees hints of Washington Park—again, all the way to the Perimeter and beyond.

The City without Limits

In 1949 William B. Hartsfield, who would serve as the city's mayor for more than twenty years, announced a "Plan of Improvement," an annexation scheme to transform the municipality into a metropolis. Upon the plan's implementation on January 1, 1952, approximately 100,000 citizens were added to the city's population and the area bounded by the city limits was expanded from 37 to 118 square miles. By 1970 the city's population, which had fluctuated near the 300,000 mark since 1930, stood at a highpoint of just under 500,000. More dramatic still were changes in the standard metropolitan statistical area (the economic, as opposed to political region). Population metro-wide exploded from just over 1 million in 1960 to nearly 1.4 million in 1970, reaching 2.5 million in 1990.

The preponderance of this growth stemmed from the post–World War II transportation revolution that transformed modern urban America. In Atlanta the federal interstate highway system imprinted a rim-and-spoke pattern that describes metro Atlanta's current spatial dimensions. The Perimeter, Interstate 285, which circumscribes the area, and Interstates 75, 85, and 20, the radials that run in six directions from the city's center, form a web of roads across which Atlanta has spread rapidly and, it would seem, chaotically.

Commercially, this expansion began with the "malling" of Atlanta. A beginning point was the building in 1939 of Briarcliff Plaza, a shopping center with off-street parking, along the western edge of suburban Druid Hills. The take-off point was the building in 1959 of Lenox Square, the region's bellwether mall, some eight miles due north of the new Downtown.

Exurban expansion over the past quarter century (especially the past decade) produced a need for an innovative nomenclature: "inside" or "outside" the Perimeter thus came into being. This convenient classification provided a ready measure for physical distance, accessibility, style of life, class, and race. The Perimeter became, in the process, metropolitan Atlanta's "Main Street." Outside the Perimeter, specifically beyond its northern borders, there has developed a new community form and style of life—variously termed the exurban, the suburban city, or "edge city." In contrast with older, closer in, more traditional suburbs that were extensions of the city proper, these new configurations are independent of the old Downtown and are self-sufficient communities unto themselves. Inside the Perimeter seems to be almost the mirror opposite of outside. Outside, the population is three-quarters white. Inside, it is two-thirds black. Outside is a new Atlanta. Inside, the old—but not the same.

Recent trends suggest that the movement of people, businesses, and jobs will continue northward—along metropolitan Atlanta's new "Main Street," now designated the Inner Perimeter, or even beyond to a projected Outer Perimeter. One thing remains certain: as we do today, historians in the future will continue to read the history of Atlanta in its buildings. They are the structural record of our metropolitan culture—its wealth, its tastes, its distribution of power and resources.

Introduction

Urbanism and Architecture in Atlanta, A Personal View

Isabelle Gournay

Atlanta today has two distinct identities. On the one hand, Atlanta the "traditional city" tries to strike a balance between the preservation of its heritage and the challenge of modernization. This creative tension between the past and the future has led to the revitalization of the historic downtown area (the struggling Fairlie-Poplar Historic District and Underground Atlanta); the gentrification of several intown residential neighborhoods so conducive to a relaxed lifestyle; the construction of residential units near the downtown area, encouraged by tax incentives; and the completion, backed by hefty subsidies from the federal government, of two rapid-transit lines intersecting at Five Points. Hence Upper Midtown's rapid revitalization, which began with the construction of the Woodruff Arts Center and Colony Square in the late 1960s, was given a decisive boost in the late 1970s with the coming of MARTA, and in the early 1980s with the construction of the High Museum of Art and One Atlantic Center (the IBM Tower).

On the other hand, Atlanta the "invisible metropolis" (as Dutch architect Rem Koolhaas has called it), is a decentralized city in a state that until 1989 had no comprehensive land-use planning laws, a city shaped more by isolated capitalistic ventures than by public intervention. For the foreseeable future, Atlanta's complex centrifugal growth will most likely remain in the hands of ambitious developers—the worthy heirs of Richard Peters and Joel Hurt. More development occurs along expressways and the perimeter highway, Interstate 285 (the northern portion of which was completed in 1969), than around the suburban rapid transit stations strategically planned to control urban sprawl. While Perimeter Center and the Cumberland-Galleria area are among new self-sufficient "urban villages," the Buckhead–Lenox Square area is generally considered a "second downtown." The city's transportation engineers continue to spread the "gospel of the fast track," as exemplified by the monumental "gateway" on the northern intersection of Interstate 285 and Interstate 75. Interestingly enough, the city's greatest natural asset, its lush vegetation and gently rolling topography, which eighty years ago enabled Druid Hills to become one of the most beautiful Olmstedian garden suburbs in North America, distinguishes Atlanta's highway architecture from suburban office complexes in other boom towns like Houston and Tampa. Finally, there is the dramatic departure from existing urban morphologies and architectural types in recent residential subdivisions. The northern suburbs exhibit countless protected enclaves of inflated French chateaux and Georgian mansions covered in synthetic stucco. Paradoxically, the more high tech the workplaces become, the more traditional the homes remain!

Regrettably, Atlanta's commitment to protecting its past is at times ambivalent. Since the "Save the Fox" campaign in the mid-1970s, preservation issues have had broader public support, but the number of significant landmarks that have disappeared in the past three decades is appalling—among them, the Peachtree Arcade, Burnham and Root's Equitable Building (Atlanta's first skyscraper), Terminal Station, and the Carnegie Library. The preservation of Cabbage Town—whose textile factories and working-class housing bear precious witness to Atlanta's industrial life at the turn of the century—is not seen as a priority. As of this writing the rehabilitation of Auburn Avenue, bisected by the downtown connector, has not been implemented. Those sections of Downtown that have been renovated have not preserved the advantages of a traditional city. For all the attention it has brought the city, John Portman's introverted Peachtree Center may have had a long-term negative effect on the street life and fabric of the city.

As a newcomer to the city, I came to realize that a number of historical factors provide clues to defining and appreciating Atlanta's architecture. The city's relatively young age, even by North American standards, is remarkable. The oldest buildings in downtown Atlanta date from 1869. These are the Georgia Railroad Freight Depot (now significantly altered) and the nearby Shrine of the Immaculate Conception, designed by William H. Parkins (1836–1894), a New Yorker who, so far as we know, was the first practicing architect to reside in Atlanta. The first era to leave a sizable architectural legacy was the turn of the century, when Atlanta's small-town appearance gave way to a more metropolitan atmosphere, with the construction of eclectic skyscrapers near Five Points and period and Victorian homes in the West End and Inman Park.

Architecturally, Atlanta is not a particularly "southern" city. Many of the local landmarks could as easily have been erected in the East or the Midwest. Because Atlanta originated as a railroad town, rather than a patrician southern seaport like Savannah or Charleston, in the mid nineteenth century it looked more like a hasty frontier settlement than the epitome of Old South gentility depicted in the Hollywood version of *Gone with the Wind*.

Atlanta's architecture was, and to a certain extent still is, ruled by an alliance between privately controlled boosterism and traditionalist aesthetic tastes. The Herndons, Candlers, Woodruffs, and others who shaped the city at the turn of the century promoted radical growth and favored established architectural styles. The eclectic production of Gottfried L. Norrman (1846–1909), a prolific Swedish-born architect who came to Atlanta in the 1880s to design buildings for the Cotton States Exposition, is essentially conservative. The few Art Deco structures built in Atlanta in the 1920s and 1930s are understated, almost classical. Conservatism does, however, have its advantages: two of America's most talented revivalist architects were based in Atlanta. Alabama-born Neel Reid (1885–1926) and his successor Philip Shutze (1890–1982), a native of Columbus, Georgia, were well-grounded designers. Both studied at Columbia University in New York and in Europe (Shutze had won the coveted Rome Prize in 1915). Inspired by American colonial styles, Italian Mannerism, and English neo-Palladianism, they reinterpreted these sources with elegance and panache, and translated the aspirations of Atlanta's upper class into a reborn southern gentility.

Today, with an excellent architecture school at Georgia Tech (opened in 1908), Atlanta has a larger number of professional architectural firms than any other city of the same size. Although several firms were already well established in the Southeast, it was John Portman who in the 1960s placed Atlanta architecture in the national spotlight. His unorthodox blend of spectacular design and entrepreneurial skill was received with both awe and fascination by professionals. Today, as this guidebook demonstrates, Atlanta is home to a number of firms, some large corporate entities and other small partnerships, which have gained national recognition for their work in the metropolitan area and beyond.

Atlanta, shaped by its "complexity and contradiction," its positive and negative forces, and its struggle to be a "traditional city" within an "invisible metropolis," appears to be in a perpetual state of change. Highrise construction downtown, providing an increasingly exciting skyline, has been so prolific over the past two decades that the once commanding view from the revolving restaurant of the Hyatt Regency Atlanta Hotel is now obstructed by taller structures. One can even anticipate a soon-to-come fusion between the downtown and midtown skylines along Peachtree Street. Atlanta's incredible vitality forces us to look at the most recent "un-urban" developments with fresh eyes and new aesthetic criteria.

Regional Map

Areas 1 to 9	See Central City Map	xxx
Area 10	West End (WE)	161
Area 11	South East (SE)	173
Area 12	Inman Park (IP)	185
Area 13	Virginia-Highland (VH)	195
Area 14	Druid Hills (DH)	207
Area 15	Emory University (EU)	217
Area 16	Buckhead Residential (BR)	235
Area 17	Buckhead, Lenox Square (BL)	263
Area 18	Cumberland Mall (CM)	281
Area 19	Perimeter Mall (PM)	295
Area 20	Roswell (RS)	307
Area 21	Decatur (DC)	315
Area 22	South Side (SS)	325

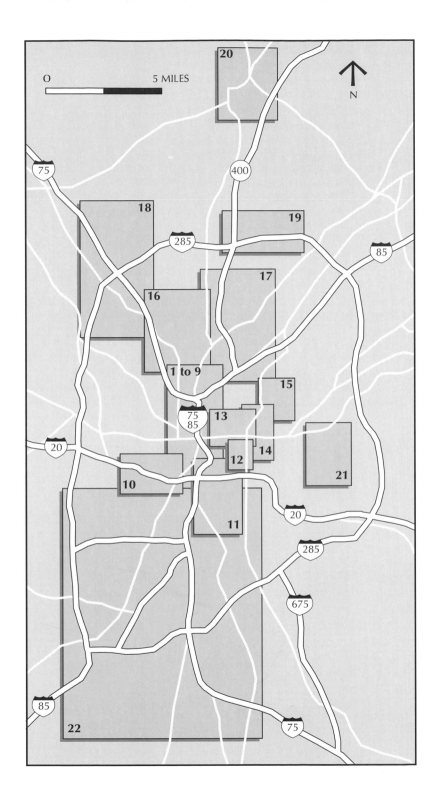

Central City Map

Area 1   Downtown South (DS)   1
Area 2   Five Points (FP)   19
Area 3   Peachtree Center (PC)   45
Area 4   Downtown West (DW)   63
Area 5   Sweet Auburn (SA)   71
Area 6   Lower Midtown (LM)   85
Area 7   Upper Midtown (UM)   111
Area 8   Ansley Park (AP)   137
Area 9   Georgia Tech (GT)   147

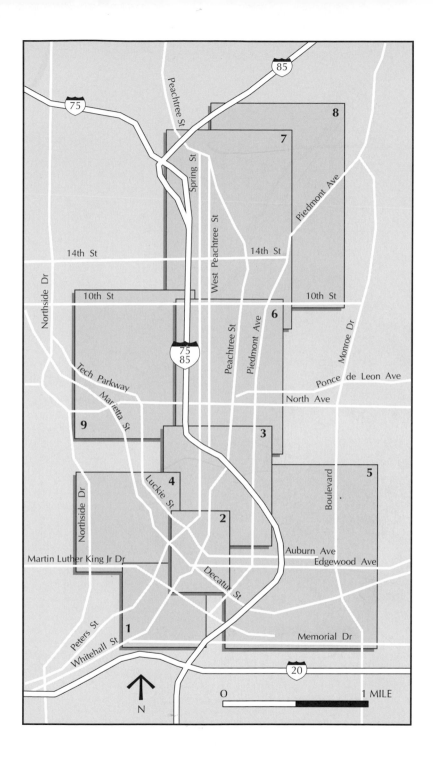

AIA Guide to the
Architecture of Atlanta

Downtown South (DS)

This walking tour takes the visitor directly south of Five Points, the historical hub of the city. Although this district lacks visual unity and is less lively than the northern section of Downtown, it nonetheless offers the largest concentration of late-nineteenth-century buildings of architectural interest in Atlanta. These landmarks vary in nature: modest, but finely detailed commercial structures stand as isolated reminders of the once-thriving district connected to the railroad tracks, an area that the redeveloped Underground Atlanta (DS 1) has partly succeeded in resurrecting; picturesque Victorian churches that testify to the former presence of an elegant residential neighborhood on the eastern side of the district; and the Georgia State Capitol (DS 9), which serves as the nucleus for the ever-expanding governmental district. Tours of Underground and the Capitol area are available through the Atlanta Preservation Center.

Area 1

Downtown South (DS)

1 Underground Atlanta
2 The Suite Hotel at Underground Atlanta
3 Block Building
4 Georgia Railroad Freight Depot
5 The World of Coca-Cola Pavilion
6 Shrine of the Immaculate Conception
7 Central Presbyterian Church
8 Campbell-Eagan Educational Building
9 Georgia State Capitol
10 Atlanta City Hall
11 Trinity Methodist Church
12 Fulton County Government Center
13 Fulton County Courthouse
14 The Counsel House
15 Cottongim Building
16 Concordia Hall
17 Martin Luther King Jr. Federal Building
18 Rich's Department Store
19 Rich's Bridge and Store for Homes
20 Rich's Store for Men
21 MARTA Five Points Station
22 MARTA Garnett Street Station
23 Garnett Station Place

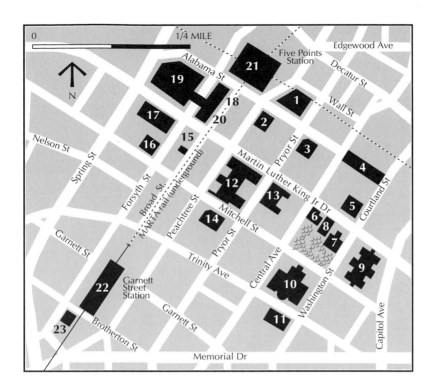

DS 1 **Underground Atlanta**
Peachtree Street at Alabama Street, S.W.
Adaptive Reuse and Additions 1986–1989: The Rouse Corporation, Master Planner; Cooper Carry and Associates with Turner Associates, Joint Venture Architects, Sanford Nelson, Principal-in-Charge; Roy Ashley and Associates, Landscape Architects; New South Design Associates, Graphic Designers; Richard Rothman and Associates, Master Plan and Urban Design Consultant to the Owner; UDC, GAAIA Awards

DS 2 **The Suite Hotel at Underground Atlanta (Connally Building)**
54 Peachtree Street, S.W.
1916: William L. Stoddart, Architect; NR. Addition 1990: AI Group, Architects; UDC Award

DS 3 **Block Building**
90 Pryor Street, S.W.
1882: Architect Unknown; NR

No other section of Atlanta has as long and eventful a history as the area in which **Underground Atlanta** now lies, which was the city's birthplace. Reduced to ruins during the Civil War, it became a thriving commercial district in the 1890s. By the late 1920s, a system of viaducts bridging the railroad gulch had been built to accommodate the expanding automobile traffic. As a result, building entrances on Alabama, Pryor, Central, Wall, and Whitehall streets were relocated to the level of these viaducts. In 1968 part of the lower level became an entertainment center, but this first incarnation of Underground Atlanta, after a few years of success, declined, and the last of its businesses closed in 1981. Encompassing the revitalization of six blocks, today's festival marketplace, which opened in June 1989, was developed in public/private partnership, and is managed by the Rouse Company, known for similar projects such as Faneuil Hall Marketplace (1976) in Boston and Harborplace (1979) in Baltimore. Aimed at attracting both conventioneers and Atlantans, its 223,000 square feet of leasable space (both above ground and in the enclosed Lower Alabama and Pryor streets) are devoted to upscale specialty shops and food and entertainment establishments. The design challenge resided in the need to provide good access to the complex and to remedy the apparent lack of visual identity and landmark structures (historic buildings and storefronts comprise only one third of the project). A sense of the area's history has been built into the project by a walking tour with markers, theme statues, wall murals, and a historical exhibit of great interest at Atlanta Heritage Row on Upper Alabama Street. Large public areas have been created from scratch, in particular the Peachtree Fountain Plaza across from the MARTA Five Points Station (DS 21), which is dominated by a 138-foot "high tech" landmark tower and framed by pavilions resembling train sheds. This plaza has become the emotional heart of the city, serving as the gathering place for such celebrations as the announcement of the selection of the site for the 1996 Olympic games, the annual lighting of Rich's Christmas tree, and a New Year's Eve extravaganza in the tradition of New York's Times

DS 1

Square. Upper Alabama Street is treated as a pedestrian mall, and its fine turn-of-the-century commercial structures, such as the **Suite Hotel at Underground Atlanta** (the original lower floors of which are sheathed in Atlantic terra-cotta made to resemble Tennessee marble while the well-executed brick tower above is a recent addition) and the **Block Building** have been authentically and beautifully restored. It is unfortunate that the contextualism of the rest of the project does not extend to the parking decks serving Underground Atlanta: these massive structures create barriers between the festival marketplace and the governmental district.

DS 4 **Georgia Railroad Freight Depot**
Central Avenue and Alabama Street, S.W.
1869: Corput and Bass, Engineers; NR

DS 5 **The World of Coca-Cola Pavilion**
55 Martin Luther King Jr. Drive, S.W.
1990: Thompson, Ventulett, Stainback and Associates, Architects;
UDC Award

For automobiles and tour buses, the primary drop-off point to Underground Atlanta (DS 1) is located near the **Georgia Railroad Freight Depot**. Built in 1869, this Italianate structure in red brick with stone accents was originally three stories high; it served as offices and a warehouse for the state-chartered Georgia Railroad. Severely remodeled after a fire in 1935, it is the oldest building in downtown Atlanta, along with the Shrine of the Immaculate Conception (DS 6), a block away. **The World of Coca-Cola Pavilion** is a welcome addition, defining the street corner and the entrance to Underground Atlanta. The pavilion was conceived as a lighthearted showcase for Coke memorabilia. Notice its bottle-shaped column along Martin Luther King Jr. Drive and the neoclassical "Coke frieze," a whimsical addition to its simple geometry below the roof line. The four-section, square-shaped building is divided into three rectangular pavilions topped by pyramids and connected by glass walls and a covered plaza. From its roof hangs a giant neon Coca-Cola sign, an updated version of the sign that towered above Margaret Mitchell Square (FP 17) on Peachtree Street from 1948 to 1981.

DS 6 Shrine of the Immaculate Conception

48 Martin Luther King Jr. Drive, S.W.
1873: William H. Parkins, Architect; NR. Restoration 1984: Henry
Howard Smith, Architect; UDC Award

The Shrine of the Immaculate Conception is Atlanta's oldest religious
establishment. The first church built on this site in 1848 was among
the few structures left standing by the Union army. There are varying accounts of why it was spared. One story is that General Sherman
had been warned by its priest, Father Thomas O'Reilly, that its demolition would entail mutiny of all Roman Catholics among his troops.
Nonetheless the original structure was badly damaged by the war, and
the construction of a new church was entrusted to William H. Parkins
(1836–1894). On the outside, Parkins designed two towers of unequal
height and different ornamentation, terminated by impressive finials; he
combined elements borrowed from French Gothic churches—the tripar-

DS 6

tite portal and rose window in particular—with the polychromatic use of materials that was so fashionable in English High Victorian Gothic architecture. The pristine interior is notable for the elegance of its slender iron columns and capitals, its unusual chandeliers, and clover-design paintings of the Apostles on the ceiling of the nave. In 1954 the church was rededicated as a diocesan shrine. Gutted by fire in 1982, it has since undergone a faithful restoration.

DS 7

DS 7 **Central Presbyterian Church**
201 Washington Street, S.W.
1884: Edmund G. Lind, Architect; NR, LB. Additions and Remodeling 1967: FABRAP, Architects

DS 8 **Campbell-Eagan Educational Building**
36 Martin Luther King Jr. Drive, S.W.
1926: Dougherty and Gardner, Architects (Nashville). Renovation 1989: Surber and Barber, Architects

Central Presbyterian Church holds an important place in the history of Atlanta because its congregation has long been at the forefront of social activism in the city. The first church on this site was completed in 1860 and survived the Civil War. The present building was designed by an English-born architect, Edmund G. Lind (1829–1909), who worked for about a decade in Atlanta and was also active in Baltimore, where a number of his buildings can still be seen. Its design is reminiscent of small parish churches in Victorian England. The unusual presence of twin openings on the Washington Street entrance facade, as opposed to the customary tripartite bay arrangement, enhances the vertical thrust of the nave. Located behind the main church building, the **Campbell-Eagan Educational Building** is a fine neo-Tudor structure in buff brick with terra-cotta spandrels. It houses a health clinic and two multilevel assembly spaces on its upper floors.

DS 9

DS 9 Georgia State Capitol
206 Washington Street, S.W.
1889: Edbrooke and Burnham, Architects (Chicago); NHL, HL

When Atlanta became the seat of government for the state in 1879, an architectural competition for the capitol was launched. The building's kinship to the neoclassical Capitol in Washington, D.C., demonstrated the state's allegiance to the Union. However, as architectural historian Elizabeth Lyon points out, "The capitol building's architectural vocabulary was classical, but the vertical thrust of its tall dome and the complexity of its massing mark it as a forcefully Victorian building" (*Atlanta Architecture, The Victorian Heritage, 1837–1918*, p. 38). The novelty of the design solution resided in the use of fireproof construction devices that had been recommended by the consulting architect, George B. Post of New York City. Facades are in Indiana limestone, while Georgia marble is extensively used for the lavish interior decoration. On Washington Street a projecting entrance pavilion has a four-story pedimented portico supported by columns set on large stone piers; the end pavilions feature matching Corinthian pilasters. The central dome was last gilded in 1981, with gold leaf from the North Georgia mining town of Dahlonega. The grounds are parklike, with a variety of monuments and markers. The underground parking facility across the street is well disguised as Georgia Plaza Park by landscape architects and planners Sasaki, Dawson, DeMay.

DS 10 **Atlanta City Hall**
68 Mitchell Street, S.W.
1930: G. Lloyd Preacher, Architect; NR, LB. Addition 1988 and
Renovation 1989: Muldawer + Moultrie with Jova/Daniels/Busby and
Harris and Partners, Joint Venture Architects; UDC Awards

DS 11 **Trinity United Methodist Church**
265 Washington Street, S.W.
1911: Walter T. Downing, Architect

Atlanta City Hall, a fourteen-story tower surmounted by a shallow
pyramidal roof, was erected on the site of the Neal Residence, which
served as General Sherman's headquarters during the Civil War. Un-

like the Art Deco setback skyscrapers of New York City which inspired its easily recognizable silhouette, the new municipal building featured relatively obsolete neo-Gothic decorative elements, each setback being enhanced with pinnacles and pointed arches (this type of ornamentation had known its heyday with the completion of the Woolworth Building in New York City in 1913). All exterior and interior materials were extracted or manufactured in Georgia. On top of a granite base, the reinforced concrete structure is covered with cream-colored tiles and olive green spandrels in terra-cotta (notice the Phoenix motif on the second-story spandrels, symbolizing the quick recovery of Atlanta after the Civil War). No money was spared on the main lobby, with its floors and walls in polished marble and ornate gilded-wood ceiling, entrance and elevator doors in heavy bronze, and brass fixtures. The exterior and all public spaces have recently been restored to their original grandeur concurrently with the addition on the south side. The lower addition houses a number of services and offices, including the mayor's office, which are distributed around an impressive skylit atrium. The form of the city council chamber is expressed on the Trinity Avenue entrance facade as a semicircular overhang. Across the street, constructed since the antebellum period in what used to be a fashionable residential district, is Walter T. Downing's **Trinity United Methodist Church** (its original building also survived the burning of Atlanta). The exterior ornamentation of this powerful brick structure resides solely in the rhythm of its massive buttresses. Inside, translucent stained-glass windows illustrate the history of the church as well as more traditional religious themes.

DS 10, addition

DS 12 **Fulton County Government Center**
141 Pryor Street, S.W.
1989: Rosser Fabrap International with Turner Associates, Joint Venture
Architects; Oscar Harris, Project Manager; Paul Friedberg, Landscape
Architect

DS 13 **Fulton County Courthouse**
136 Pryor Street, S.W.
1914: A. Ten Eyck Brown, Morgan and Dillon, Architects

The **Fulton County Government Center** occupies an entire city block,
defined by Peachtree, Mitchell, and Pryor streets and Martin Luther
King Jr. Drive. In order to match the scale of its surroundings, the building program was divided into several three- to ten-story units centered
around a glass atrium. The square shapes of the entrance pavilion on
Pryor Street and of the openings in the screen wall, the curved glass
curtain and gables, all standard devices of postmodernism, are meant to
soften the institutional character of the complex. After the Georgia State
Capitol (DS 9), the nine-story **Fulton County Courthouse** is the largest
public structure built in the classical idiom in Atlanta. The inset section
of six giant Corinthian semidetached columns overpowers the modest arched entrances, and looks tightly squeezed in a facade otherwise
punctured by utterly utilitarian openings. This arrangement contributes
to the general impression of heaviness and mismatched proportions.

DS 14 **The Counsel House (Bass Furniture Building)**
142 Mitchell Street, S.W.
1898: Architect Unknown; NR. Addition and Renovation 1924: A. Ten Eyck Brown, Architect. Restoration 1983: John Steinichen, Architect

DS 15 **Cottongim Building**
97 Broad Street, S.W.
Circa 1890: Architect Unknown

DS 16 **Concordia Hall**
201 Mitchell Street, S.W.
1893: Bruce and Morgan, Architects

The Counsel House is the finest structure in the Terminus District, a once thriving commercial area that has retained its turn-of-the-century appearance. At the beginning of the twentieth century, Mitchell Street was the main artery between the central business district and the affluent residential neighborhood of West End. With the completion of the nearby Terminal Station in 1905, this street attracted a number of small hotels as well. Built as a feed-and-grain store in 1898, the Counsel House has been host to a variety of businesses over the years. The original section, which has known several remodelings and enlargements, has three stories; the addition, which takes advantage of the slope of Mitchell Street, has four. The brick facades feature a homogeneous rhythm of arched windows with terra-cotta capitals and a continuous cornice, ornamented with an inverted pyramidal design in brick. The overall proportions and decorative effect are particularly successful, as is the treatment of the building corner at the intersection of Mitchell and Peachtree streets. Damaged by fire on several occasions, the Counsel House was recently restored with design and financial assistance provided through the city's Historic Facade Program. Inappropriate storefront additions dating from the 1950s gave way to attractive glass planes supported by slender columns. Other commercial structures of interest awaiting restoration in the Terminus District include the **Cottongim Building,** a fine example of mill construction with wood joists and cast-iron columns, and **Concordia Hall** (notice the terra-cotta ornaments on the Forsyth Street doorway—especially the lyre at the center of the pediment, which indicates that the building's first tenant was a literary and musical society).

DS 17

DS 17   **Martin Luther King Jr. Federal Building (United States Post Office)**
77 Forsyth Street, S.W.
1933: A. Ten Eyck Brown with Alfredo Barili Jr. and J. W. Humphreys, Architects

Originally built with funds from the Work Projects Administration to house Atlanta's central post office, this monumental structure was located in the vicinity of the now demolished Terminal Station. It was designed in the stripped-down classical style that prevailed for public structures in the 1930s not only in New Deal America but also throughout Europe. The highly symmetrical facades of this freestanding block feature a series of setbacks. They are sheathed in granite left plain and smooth with the exception of an occasional fluted "pilaster" and carved frieze. Vacated by the Postal Administration in 1980, the recently renamed Martin Luther King Jr. Federal Building now houses government offices.

DS 18   **Rich's Department Store**
45 Broad Street, S.W.
1924: Hentz, Reid and Adler, Architects; Philip Shutze, Designer

DS 19   **Rich's Bridge and Store for Homes**
1947: Toombs and Creighton, Architects

DS 20   **Rich's Store for Men**
1953: Stevens and Wilkinson, Architects; Eleanor LeMaire, Interior
Designer

Rich's Department Store, founded by Morris Rich and his brothers in
1867, had occupied three different locations on Whitehall Street (now
Peachtree Street) before it moved to what was, in the early 1920s, a
prime commercial site. Before the Great Depression, local competition
was so keen that Rich's decided to commission Hentz, Reid and Adler—
one of the best architectural firms in Atlanta—to design a "palazzo" in
the grand Italian manner. The two-story rusticated base features large

DS 18, *left;* DS 19, *right*

rectangular display windows and two lofty arcaded entrances on Broad Street. Pilasters articulate this stone base, as well as the four stories sheathed in buff brick above it. Coupled windows are left unadorned, with the exception of those directly above the Broad Street entrances. Unfortunately the prominent cornice that provided an elegant termination to the design was removed in the late 1930s. Built in the late 1940s and early 1950s, additions by local firms were among the first commercial designs in the International Style to be seen in Atlanta. The sleek steel-and-glass **Bridge** over Forsyth Street, which connected the new **Store for Homes** with the existing store, started the ongoing controversy over the right of individuals and corporations to build structures spanning public streets. Reached from Broad Street through a bold cantilevered aluminum canopy, the **Rich's Store for Men** used glass and aluminum extensively at a time when windowless elevations had become standard in department-store design. It also featured an innovative interior designed by Eleanor LeMaire. When it first opened, Rich's was one of the most impressive retail facilities in the Southeast, but in the 1970s and '80s the downtown store was eclipsed by the company's suburban stores, which led to its closing in the summer of 1991.

DS 21 MARTA Five Points Station

30 Alabama Street, S.W.
1979: Finch-Heery, Joint Venture Architects; Vincent Kling
(Philadelphia), Design Consultant to MARTA

Considering the decentralized character of Atlanta's metropolitan area, the MARTA rapid-transit system, which opened in 1979, should probably be regarded as a symbol of the city's self-esteem as well as a solution to traffic congestion problems. MARTA's stations were designed by Atlanta firms as highly visible civic monuments, generally uncluttered by advertising billboards and providing little public seating (in an effort to discourage loitering), rather than as understated but functional access points to the rapid-rail system. The stations are for the most part superstructures, sometimes raised well above ground with boldly designed roofs. Two MARTA rail lines intersect at the Five Points Station, which encloses 200,000 square feet of floor area. A grade-level landscaped plaza covered by a precast concrete canopy provides natural lighting to the underground concourse level. The selection of materials—marble and glass tiles for the walls, cast-in-place concrete with metal coffer liners for the ceilings—contributes to the stately character of the two train levels, which are reached by stairs and escalators sheathed in granite. A dramatic counterpoint to the rigorous overall geometry is brought to the design by three neoclassical arches, visible from the intermediate level at the end of the northbound track. The arches at one time crowned the Whitehall Street facade of the Eiseman Building (1901, Walter T. Downing), which was demolished to make way for MARTA. The pedestrian mall on Broad Street was planned as part of a promenade through Downtown. Unfortunately the monumental station and its modern surroundings divide rather than unite the southern and northern parts of the central district.

DS 21

DS 22 **MARTA Garnett Street Station**
Forsyth and Garnett Streets, S.W.
1981: Cooper Carry and Associates with Jones and Thompson, Joint
Venture Architects; GAAIA Award

DS 23 **Garnett Station Place (Southern Belting Company Building)**
236 Forsyth Street, S.W.
1915: Lockwood-Greene, Engineers; NR. Remodeling 1985: Stang and
Newdow, Architects; UDC Award

The **MARTA Garnett Street Station** was expected to act as a nucleus for
major redevelopment in the area. Exposed concrete columns support
the railway platform and upper public concourse. Glazed aluminum
frames are used as wind breaks and offer protection from the elements
for the predominantly open-air structure. Currently occupied by offices,
Garnett Station Place is an open-plan structure in brick with stone accents which was built by a manufacturer of belts for textile looms. Its
facade on Garnett Street is particularly well composed, with its stately
balconied entrance and windows of different widths (the center and
corners are marked by narrower glass panes).

Area 2

Five Points (FP)

This walking tour encompasses the National Register Fairlie-Poplar District and its immediate surroundings. With eclectic and Art Deco office towers as well as lower commercial structures of great architectural interest, the office district immediately north of Five Points has, to a large extent, preserved the urban and architectural physiognomy of the early twentieth century when businesses and financial institutions moved northward and away from the railroad tracks. Today it is the living memory of Atlanta's growth from the New South period of the 1890s to the Wall Street crash in 1929. A few International Style skyscrapers witness Atlanta's economic ascent in the late 1960s. The only major intervention in an otherwise tight and truly "urban" fabric has occurred with the creation of Woodruff Park along Peachtree Street in the early 1970s. If the Fairlie-Poplar District has failed to develop into a pedestrian mall as projected, it still allows for a pleasant walking tour. The visitor should take advantage of the fact that lobbies, some with interesting eclectic decor or nicely remodeled, have multiple entrances and provide for a varied pedestrian experience. Tours of the historic downtown area can be arranged through the Atlanta Preservation Center.

Area 2

Five Points (FP)

1 Wachovia Bank of Georgia Building
2 William-Oliver Building
3 NationsBank Building
4 Forty Marietta Building
5 Forty-One Marietta Building
6 Bank South Building
7 Walton Place
8 Healey Building
9 United States Eleventh District Court of Appeals
10 Grant Building
11 Muse's Building
12 Flatiron Building
13 Equitable Building
14 Rhodes-Haverty Building
15 Atlanta History Center, Downtown Office
16 Atlanta–Fulton County Public Library
17 Margaret Mitchell Square
18 Winecoff Hotel
19 Carnegie Building
20 Georgia-Pacific Center
21 High Museum of Art at Georgia-Pacific Center
22 Candler Building
23 AT&T Communications Building
24 Hurt Building
25 Trust Company Bank Building
26 Ten Park Place South Building
27 Olympia Building

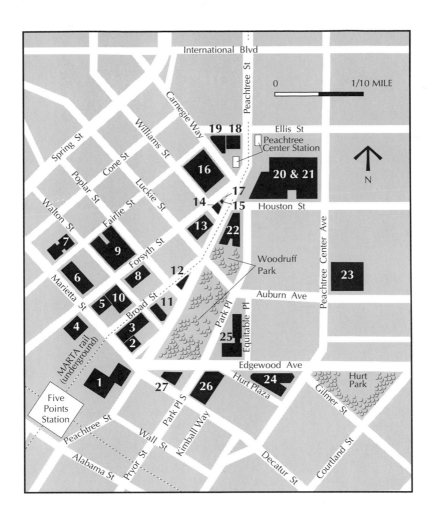

FP 1

FP 1 **Wachovia Bank of Georgia Building (First National Bank Building)**
2 Peachtree Street, N.W.
1966: FABRAP with Emory Roth and Sons (New York), Architects;
Cecil A. Alexander, Designer

Built on the site of the Peachtree Arcade, the forty-one-story Wachovia
Bank of Georgia Building was the tallest structure in the Southeast at the
time of its construction. Its slablike profile and abstract ornamentation is
characteristic of late International Style skyscraper design. Emphasizing
the vertical thrust of the tower, the unbroken marble columns provide
a sharp color contrast with the bronzed aluminum spandrels. A slight
horizontal recess defines the top, which houses two mechanical floors.
The project included the drastic remodeling of the existing bank building
built in 1903 (with floors added in 1928) at the corner of Peachtree and
Marietta streets. In order to allow for an unobstructed view from, and of,
the new office tower and to achieve stylistic "harmony," the height of
the old structure was reduced by half and refaced in white marble.

FP 2 William-Oliver Building

32 Peachtree Street, N.W.
1930: Pringle and Smith, Architects

This sixteen-story steel-frame office building was named for developer Thomas G. Healey's grandsons William and Oliver. The facade of the William-Oliver Building displays a tripartite arrangement. The base is clad in red granite, the larger openings of the first two floors expressing their design for commercial use. The shaft is sheathed in smooth limestone. In order to enhance its vertical thrust, windows at the corner and ends of the building are left unadorned while the six central bays, on Peachtree Street as well as on Marietta Street, are set between cast stone panels in low relief. Art Deco ornamentation is concentrated on the two upper floors, with friezes featuring geometric patterns of chevrons and waves as well as rosettes and other stylized floral arrangements. Characteristically, horizontal divisions are as "superficial" in the quasi-monolithic shaft of the William-Oliver Building as they are strongly marked in the adjoining NationsBank Building (FP 3), designed almost

FP 2

three decades earlier. On Peachtree Street, a delicate bronze awning leads to the off-center lobby, which has kept its original decoration, with inlaid marble patterns on the floors and fine brass floral ornamentation on the ventilating grilles and elevator doors.

FP 3

FP 3 NationsBank Building (Citizens and Southern National Bank Building, Empire Building)

35 Broad Street, N.W.

1901: Bruce and Morgan, Architects, NR. Remodeling of Lower Floors and Interiors 1929: Hentz, Adler and Shutze, Architects; Philip Shutze, Designer

Fourteen stories high, the NationsBank Building was the first steel-framed structure to be built in Atlanta. Its clear-cut silhouette, simple fenestration, and heavily decorated terra-cotta top bear the influence of the Chicago School. In 1929 the building became the headquarters of the Citizens and Southern National Bank, which asked Philip Shutze to redesign its three lower floors. Because the impression of load-bearing masonry was regarded as better suited for a banking establishment than large glass panes were, the original display windows were replaced by classical motifs apparently "carved out" of Indiana limestone. Philip Shutze was inspired by Italian Mannerism, and especially by the city gates of Verona by Michele Sanmicheli (1484–1559). As Henry Hope Reed points out, "the bold quoining and voluted keystones of the round-arched bays and the use of rustication and quoining inside the entrance bay result in a masterly play of light and shade and convey an imperial sense of scale" (*Classical America*, p. 18). Notice also how symmetry was restored to the Broad Street facade in spite of the presence of un-centered entrances. Reached from Marietta and Walton streets through lofty arcaded entryways and a more intimate elevator lobby in the early Renaissance style on Broad Street, the banking hall is a long nave ar-ticulated by colossal Corinthian pilasters. While its walls and floors feature several kinds of Georgia, Tennessee, and European marbles in a warm gold-brown color scheme, the ceiling, from which hang gigantic chandeliers, is left bare. The Pantheon, which Shutze had measured during his internship at the American Academy in Rome, served as a direct source for the pedimented niches (their bases house ventilation ducts) and for the floors with alternate square and circular patterns. Also of Roman inspiration are the bronze desks and the eagle motif found throughout the design. On the other hand, the officers' area, with its mahogany panels, is decorated in a cozier American Georgian style. In 1991 Citizens and Southern Bank merged with North Carolina National Bank to become NationsBank, which has moved its Atlanta corporate headquarters to its midtown property (see LM 8). Fortunately the banking hall, in which Shutze demonstrated a "great sense of correctness" and "meticulous attention to details" will remain as one of the greatest of its kind in the United States (Elizabeth Dowling, *American Classicist*, p. 51).

FP 3

FP 4 Forty Marietta Building (First Federal Savings and Loan Association Building)

40 Marietta Street, N.W.
1964: Tomberlin and Sheetz, Architects; Chastain and Tindel, Structural Engineers

An innovative structural solution gave birth to the unconventional exterior of the seventeen-story **Forty Marietta Building**. It is supported by six giant pentagonal columns, visible from the exterior of the building, with post-tensioned beams spanning its column-free interior. The exposed curved faces of the deep spandrel beams that ring each floor alternate with ribbon windows in grey-tinted glass. The elevator service tower toward the rear is partly of poured-in-place concrete to stiffen the structure.

FP 5 **Forty-One Marietta Building (Standard Federal Savings and Loan Building)**
41 Marietta Street, N.W.
1975: Toombs, Amisano and Wells, Architects; GAAIA Award

FP 6 **Bank South Building (Fulton National Bank Building)**
55 Marietta Street, N.W.
1958: Wyatt C. Hedrick (Dallas) with Wilner and Millkey, Architects

FP 7 **Walton Place (Georgia Railway and Power Building)**
75 Marietta Street, N.W.
1907: Morgan and Dillon, Architects. Restoration 1988: Stang and Newdow, Architects; UDC Award

On the opposite (northern) side of Marietta Street, notice the striking contrast in size and ornamentation between the **Forty-One Marietta** and the **Bank South** buildings with their marked horizontal rhythm of ribbon windows, and the brick-and-stone facade of **Walton Place** (encompassing an entire city block). The latter is an early example of the consolidation of all services in one location for a large utility company.

FP 6, *center;* FP 5, *right*

FP 8   **Healey Building**
        57 Forsyth Street, N.W.
        1913: Bruce and Morgan with Walter T. Downing, Architects; NR.
        Renovation 1988: Stang and Newdow, Architects; UDC Award

FP 9   **United States Eleventh District Court of Appeals (Federal Courthouse
        and Post Office)**
        56 Forsyth Street, N.W.
        1911: James Knox Taylor, Architect. Restoration and Renovation 1987:
        Robert and Company, Architects

FP 10   **Grant Building (Grant-Prudential Building)**
        44 Broad Street, N.W.
        1898: Bruce and Morgan; Architects. Renovation 1980: Toombs,
        Amisano and Wells, Architects; UDC Award

The **Healey Building** is an elegant office tower, which was named after
its developer, William T. Healey, and most likely designed by Walter T.
Downing. The vertical thrust of the uninterrupted piers is terminated by
a strong projecting cornice. At the time of its construction, the Gothic
style of the terra-cotta ornaments was considered the most fashionable
for skyscraper design. Notice the unusual design of the slightly projecting display windows on the two-story base in the English perpendicular
style, as well as the different width of the upper windows. A commercial
arcade once extended from Poplar Street completely through the block
to Walton Street. Its junction with the elevator lobby facing on Forsyth

Street is marked by a rotunda bathed in natural light. This rotunda was intended as a connection to a twin tower on Broad Street, the construction of which was abandoned due to the outbreak of World War I and the death of William T. Healey. The building started to decay when it was sold by the Healey family in 1972. After it was acquired by a Dutch consortium in the mid-1980s, the entire block was restored, with the construction of a well-integrated lobby facing on Broad Street as a continuation of the existing neo-Gothic rotunda. Two of the Healey Building's neighbors are worth mentioning: the monumental **United States Eleventh District Court of Appeals,** with its fairly heavy-handed Beaux-Arts ornamentation, and the **Grant Building,** with its neo-Renaissance exterior in limestone and terra-cotta.

FP 10

FP 11   **Muse's Building (George Muse Clothing Company Building)**
52 Peachtree Street, N.W.
1921: Hentz, Reid and Adler, Architects; Philip Shutze, Designer

This seven-story building was commissioned by the George Muse Clothing Company, which until 1992 operated a store there. The Muse's
Building occupies the site of a Confederate arsenal during the Civil War.
Since the creation of Woodruff Park, the need for a structure of equal
height to abut it to the north on Peachtree Street is all the more obvious.
Until that happens, its narrow silhouette will continue to look unex-
pectedly picturesque. Hentz, Reid and Adler exploited here the same
Italianate idiom they did in their design for Rich's Department Store (DS
18). The rusticated base in limestone features large display windows
with consoles as keystones, a motif that Shutze repeated in the nearby
NationsBank Building (FP 3). The entrance on Peachtree Street has since
been remodeled. Above this base, elaborate cartouches frame the corner
and end windows. The rest of the building is sheathed in plain beige
brick and terminated by a richly carved frieze and a cornice supported
by brackets.

Flatiron Building (English-American Building)
84 Peachtree Street, N.W.
1897: Bradford Gilbert, Architect (New York); NR. Renovation
1977–1987: Brisbin, Brook and Beynon, Architects (Toronto);
UDC Award

Since the unfortunate demolition of Burnham and Root's original Equitable Building in 1971, the eleven-story Flatiron Building is now the
oldest skyscraper still standing in Atlanta. Its designer, Bradford Gilbert,
was the supervising architect of the 1895 Cotton States Exposition. He
is credited with building the first steel-framed skyscraper in the United
States—the Tower Building in New York City (1889). The picturesque
and uncommon triangular shape of what was originally called the
English-American Building was imposed by its location on the narrow
corner of Broad and Peachtree streets. Complying with the traditional
tripartite composition of turn-of-the-century skyscrapers, the two lower
and the two upper floors are separated from the building's shaft by
strongly projecting horizontal bands. Above the colonnaded base, the
ornamentation relies on straightforward rhythms created by continuous
bay windows and unbroken piers (notice how these piers emphasize the
slenderness of the apex). Gilbert's design predates Daniel Burnham's

FP 12

New York Flatiron Building (1901) at the intersection of Broadway and Fifth Avenue. That landmark became so popular that its Atlanta predecessor adopted the same name between 1916 and 1920, and again during the past decade. Neither the exterior color scheme nor the current decoration of the entrance lobby is original.

FP 13 **Equitable Building**
100 Peachtree Street, N.W.
1968: Skidmore, Owings and Merrill, Architects (New York Office); FABRAP, Consulting Architects; James Wylie, Landscape Architect

The thirty-five-story Equitable Building occupies the site of the former Piedmont Hotel, which opened in 1903. The office tower's setback position from Peachtree Street allows for the presence of a small triangular piazza, and its dark mass, in sharp contrast with the silhouette of its older neighbors, is very noticeable in the Atlanta skyline. With a clear-cut composition stressing the horizontal rhythm of the girders, while

FP 13

strong vertical divisions are placed intentionally far apart, the Equitable Building closely resembles the Chicago Civic Center (1965) and belongs to the family of International Style skyscrapers inspired by Ludwig Mies van der Rohe's Seagram Building (1958) in New York City.

FP 14

FP 14   **Rhodes-Haverty Building**
134 Peachtree Street, N.W.
1929: Pringle and Smith, Architects; NR, LB

FP 15   **Atlanta History Center, Downtown Office (Hillyer Trust Company Building)**
140 Peachtree Street, N.W.
1911: Hentz, Reid and Adler, Architects; NR. Interior Remodeling 1987: Lord and Sargent, Architects; UDC Award

Named after its developers, furniture magnates A. G. Rhodes and J. J. Haverty, the twenty-one-story **Rhodes-Haverty Building** was the tallest structure in Atlanta until the construction of the Bank South Building

(FP 6) in 1954. The stern grey granite veneer of the three-story base and neoclassical store entrance are not original to the building, which once featured much larger display windows. In order to enhance the vertical thrust of the Peachtree Street facade, openings at the corner are left un-adorned while the four center bays have terra-cotta spandrels contrasting with the buff brick facing. A stringcourse with Art Deco chevron motifs isolates the last three floors from the building shaft. With its arcaded two-story bays, low gable, and corbelled arches punctuating the roofline, the top is reminiscent of Byzantine or early Romanesque architecture. The lobby incorporates walls and floors in travertine, elaborate carved ceilings, and delicately incised elevator doors. The **Atlanta History Center, Downtown Office** is located in the former headquarters of the Hillyer Trust Company, one of Atlanta's first banking institutions. Badly damaged by weather exposure, the upper six stories of what was conceivably one of the narrowest highrise office buildings in the United States were razed in 1978.

FP 16   **Atlanta–Fulton County Public Library**
1 Margaret Mitchell Square
1969–1980: Marcel Breuer and Hamilton Smith Associated Architects
(New York) with Stevens and Wilkinson, Architects; UDC Award

FP 17   **Margaret Mitchell Square**
1986: Joint Venture of Robert and Company with Williams Russell and Johnson, Architects; Kit Tin Snyder, Sculptor; UDC Award

The **Atlanta–Fulton County Public Library** occupies a full city block and replaced the Carnegie Library (1902), Atlanta's first and probably finest public building in the Beaux-Arts style. The design which was commissioned in 1969 took more than ten years to reach the construction stage and is reminiscent of one of Breuer's better-known compositions, the Whitney Museum in New York City. Both buildings have boldly cantilevered masses pierced by only a few large openings (in Atlanta, offices are grouped around a terrace so that their small windows do not disturb the monumental character of the Peachtree Street eleva-

FP 16

tion). Large precast concrete panels with diagonal striations sheath the exterior. Two floors were added at the back of the building when bids for the construction of the library came in below budget. Landscaped plazas, including **Margaret Mitchell Square,** have been designed on all sides of the complex street crossing, in order to define and enliven this prominent urban space.

FP 18

FP 18 **Winecoff Hotel**
176 Peachtree Street, N.W.
Circa 1913: William L. Stoddart, Architect

FP 19 **Carnegie Building (Wynne-Claughton Building)**
133 Carnegie Way, N.W.
1926: G. Lloyd Preacher, Architect; HB

The **Winecoff Hotel** was named after its builder and owner, William Fleming Winecoff. The base and top sheathed in limestone and crowned by a powerful dentiled cornice are in sharp contrast with the brick shaft

of this fourteen-story building. The structure's primary significance is that it led to a nationwide change in fire-safety regulations because of a fire in 1946 that killed 119 people, including Mr. Winecoff. In more recent years it has served as a retirement home and an office building. Completing the triangular city block is the **Carnegie Building,** which uses the same brick-and-stone color scheme and decor.

FP 20 **Georgia-Pacific Center**
133 Peachtree Street, N.E.
1982: Skidmore, Owings and Merrill, Architects (New York Office)

In 1978 Georgia-Pacific, a giant forest-products corporation, moved its headquarters to Atlanta from Portland, Oregon. In 1982, the Georgia-Pacific Center replaced Loew's Grand Theater (site of the world premiere of *Gone with the Wind*), which had recently been damaged by fire. This fifty-two-story, 1.36 million-square-foot skyscraper is clad in Texas granite pierced by narrow energy-efficient openings. In this highly visible downtown location where Peachtree Street changes the city's grid and bends to the north toward Midtown, its stepped-back silhouette on the east side makes the Georgia Pacific Center a distinctive landmark in the city's skyline. According to its designers, it was intended as a "design response to the site and varied heights of surrounding buildings." It offers the advantage of a large range of floor sizes with a conventional elevator system.

FP 20

FP 21   **High Museum of Art at Georgia-Pacific Center**
133 Peachtree Street, N.E.
1986: Parker and Scogin, Architects; UDC, SARC, AIA Awards

The downtown branch of the High Museum of Art at Georgia-Pacific
Center is intended for thematic displays of objects from the museum's
permanent collection, as well as for small- or medium-size traveling
exhibitions. It is reached through the main lobby of the Georgia-Pacific
Center (FP 20), which features a large white sculpture by Louise Nevelson. The museum itself is housed in a long and narrow glass-enclosed
space along Houston Street. Because this "greenhouse" did not comply with the fire, climate, and security regulations proper to museum
spaces, a self-sufficient environment was created within what was originally designed as an exhibition space for Georgia-Pacific products. A
freestanding steel-frame structure is clad with an exotic wood veneer
of African anigree, remarkable for its fine grain and golden tone. Upon
entering, visitors descend a ramp, which provides dramatic vistas of
both the museum and the cityscape. Exhibits are held in two large superimposed galleries and in narrower lateral display spaces, totaling five
thousand square feet. Most impressive is the pristine Upper Gallery, with
its translucent barrel vault and floor inlaid with glass blocks. The High
Museum at Georgia-Pacific Center, which was recognized for design
excellence by the American Institute of Architects in 1988, demonstrates
that a rigorous geometrical order can convey a serene atmosphere,
enhancing art works and welcoming the visitor.

Candler Building
127 Peachtree Street, N.E.
1906: Murphy and Stewart, Architects; NR, LB, UDC Award

Set on a triangular lot at the corner of Peachtree, Pryor, and Houston streets, the seventeen-story neo-Renaissance Candler Building, entirely covered in white North Georgia marble, was the tallest and the best-equipped office building in Atlanta at the time of its construction. In this speculative venture, the founder of the Coca-Cola Company, philanthropist Asa Griggs Candler (1851–1929), built a monument to his own success, spending lavishly on the ornamentation, which was supervised by the sculptor F. B. Miles. On the outside, decorative sculpture flourishes on the two-story base and on the top three floors, which are terminated by a powerful cornice supported by brackets in the shape of lions. At the street level, each bay features in its center a medallion reproducing the profiles of famous men, among them Shakespeare, Raphael, Buffalo Bill Cody, and Cyrus McCormick. The recessed

FP 22

FP 22

entrance on Houston Street, which originally gave access to a banking hall, is no longer in use. It is through one of the lateral arched entryways framed by term-supported brackets that the visitor proceeds to the lobby. This space features an extraordinarily free and playful assemblage of early Renaissance motifs. The monumental staircase is supported by bronze birds and fabulous animals crowd its marble banister; a frieze of putti and foliage frames busts of local politicians and literati, such as Sidney Lanier and Joel Chandler Harris, as well as those of Asa Candler's parents, Samuel and Martha. Notice also the letterbox boasting the Candler family coat-of-arms and motto, *ad mortem fidelis* [faithful until death] and the marble alligators above the drinking fountain.

FP 23   AT&T Communications Building (Southern Bell Telephone Company Building)

51 Peachtree Center Avenue, N.E.
1929: Marye, Alger and Vinour, Architects; NR

In the prosperous 1920s the Southern Bell Telephone Company envisioned a twenty-five-story setback skyscraper, which would have been by far the tallest building in Atlanta, as its new southeastern headquarters. Such an ambitious undertaking was consistent with the Bell

Company's philosophy that a strong design policy was the best means of boosting its corporate image. Unfortunately, with the depression in the 1930s, the building was scaled down to only six floors (subsequent additions in 1947, 1948, and 1963 resulted in a building that is now fourteen stories). The base of what is now called the AT&T Communications Building in smooth-faced limestone features Art Deco flutings in very low relief and panels with intricate floral and geometric patterns. The elongated and sharply contoured entrance portal on Peachtree Center Avenue is surmounted by an elaborate keystone motif and flanked by stylized human figures (notice also the sharp eagle profiles and metal torchères on the side). The ornamentation of the AT&T Communications Building was not particularly advanced for the late 1920s, when more colorful and abstract features had become the fashion in New York City.

FP 23

FP 24 **Hurt Building**
50 Hurt Plaza, S.E.
1913, 1926: J. E. R. Carpenter, Architects (New York); NR, LB.
Renovation 1985: Associated Space Design, Architects and Interior
Designers; UDC Award

FP 25 **Trust Company Bank Building**
25 Park Place, N.E.
Tower 1969, Banking Hall 1973: Carson, Lundin and Shaw, Architects
(New York City). Columns from the original Equitable Building, 1892:
Burnham and Root, Architects (Chicago)

FP 26 **Ten Park Place South Building (Thornton Building)**
10 Park Place South, S.E.
1932: A. Ten Eyck Brown, Architect; LB

FP 27 **Olympia Building**
23 Peachtree Street, S.E.
1937: Ivey and Crook, Architects; LB

The **Hurt Building** was named after Joel Hurt (1850–1926), the enlight-
ened developer who commissioned Frederick Law Olmsted to lay out

Druid Hills and Burnham and Root to design Atlanta's first skyscraper, the Equitable Building, whose columns have been kept on the building's original site in the **Trust Company Bank Building** plaza. Originally trained as an engineer, Hurt made preliminary drawings for his seventeen-story speculative office tower before entrusting its final design to J. E. R. Carpenter, a New York architect whose eclectic practice included many posh apartment houses on Park and Fifth avenues. The Hurt Building occupies an elongated triangular site. Its front part was erected in 1913, with an apex cut back thirty feet in order to allow a greater window area and more visibility from the heart of Downtown. Begun in 1924, its two wings were completed two years later. The monumental stone base is articulated by stern pilasters, the rotunda at the apex by engaged Corinthian columns. The shaft, in light grey porcelain brick with ocher and green terra-cotta spandrels, is surmounted by an elaborate cornice, also in terra-cotta. The domed ceiling of the entrance rotunda, which is supported by marble columns, has been beautifully restored, the lobby dramatically enlarged and remodeled. Two small commercial structures of the 1930s with a restrained but elegant ornamentation complete this tour of the financial district: the **Ten Park Place South Building** and the **Olympia Building** (named after Olympia Beach in Florida, a previous venture of its developer Frank Hawkins).

FP 25

Area 3

Peachtree Center (PC)

Originally lined with mansions, the section of Peachtree Street directly
north of the financial district attracted some of Atlanta's largest retail
facilities in the 1920s. In 1961 this district's slow decline was reversed
by the opening of the Atlanta Merchandise Mart (PC 9). Designer and
developer John Portman's concept of wholesale services proved successful, and Atlanta's rapid development as a major trade center called
for the creation of a new hotel and business district (apartment buildings
are also planned). This snowballing phenomenon explains the rapid
growth of Peachtree Center, which by 1990 covered twelve city blocks.
Financed entirely by private funds, Peachtree Center's major buildings illustrate Portman's no-nonsense approach to design, expressed
by straightforward contrasts of volumes and materials. However, his
self-proclaimed desire "to involve people in [his] architecture both as
spectators and participants," has paradoxically resulted in a reversal of
the traditional components of street life from an outward to an inward
orientation. His developer's view of buildings as marketable objects is
exemplified by the deliberate and frequent alterations imposed on the
interior spaces. Peachtree Center is frequently referred to as Atlanta's
new downtown. Its dense fabric, however, has not spread, as demonstrated by the isolation of these buildings on the northern edge of this
district.

Peachtree Center (PC)

1 MARTA Peachtree Center Station
2 Macy's Department Store
3 One-Ninety-One Peachtree Tower
4 Westin Peachtree Plaza Hotel
5 209 Peachtree Street Building
6 Cornerstone Building
7 Peachtree Center Tower   .
8 Peachtree Center Mall
9 Atlanta Merchandise Mart
10 Atlanta Apparel Mart
11 Inforum
12 Atlanta Gift Mart
13 Capital City Club
14 Hyatt Regency Atlanta Hotel
15 Atlanta Marriott Marquis Hotel
16 Marquis One and Marquis Two Towers
17 One Peachtree Center
18 Sacred Heart Church
19 First United Methodist Church of Atlanta
20 Peachtree Summit
21 MARTA Civic Center Station
22 Georgia Power Company Corporate Headquarters
23 Atlanta Civic Center

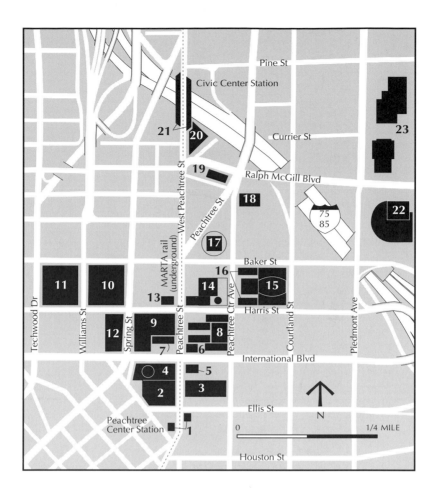

Pine St

Civic Center Station

Currier St

21 **20**

23

West Peachtree St

19

Ralph McGill Blvd

Peachtree St

18

75
85

22

MARTA rail (underground)

17

Baker St

16

11 **10**

14

15

13

Harris St

Techwood Dr

Williams St

Spring St

12 **9**

Peachtree St

8

Peachtree Ctr Ave

Courtland St

Piedmont Ave

7

6

International Blvd

4

5

2

3

Ellis St

N

Peachtree
Center Station

1

0   1/4 MILE

Houston St

PC 1

PC 1   **MARTA Peachtree Center Station**
Peachtree Street at Ellis Street
1982: Toombs, Amisano and Wells, Architects; Joseph Amisano,
Designer; UDC, GAAIA Awards

At the MARTA Peachtree Center Station, trains arrive in a vault 44 feet
high and 770 feet long, tunneled through solid rock 100 feet below
grade. The existing striated granite, reinforced with steel rods placed in
drilled holes, was used as both structural support and natural architectural finish. During the excavation, engineers devised special blasting
controls and drilling patterns in order to create a rough-hewn textured
surface. The overhead part of the rock arch, which had to be protected
with a thin concrete shell, is covered by aluminum acoustical panels
with integral lights. Here Piranesi meets high tech, and the contrast between awesome natural elements and sleek man-made materials is very
successful.

PC 2   **Macy's Department Store (Davison-Paxon Department Store)**
180 Peachtree Street, N.W.
1927: Hentz, Adler and Shutze, Architects; Starrett and Van Vleck,
Contractors (New York)

In 1925 the southern department-store chain of Davison-Paxon was
bought out by R. H. Macy and Company, but in an attempt to maintain
the goodwill of the local clientele, the Macy's name was not adopted
until the 1980s. The design of the new Macy's Department Store in

Atlanta was entrusted to local architect Philip Shutze and to Starrett and Van Vleck, a New York contracting firm that had been involved in the design of a number of department stores. Shutze's mark is evident on the exterior. With its base of two-story arched openings (the present canopies are not original to the design), unadorned upper floors, and prominent cornice, the massive block closely follows the prototype of the Italian Renaissance palazzo. Economic constraints dictated the lack of expensive materials and elaborate ornaments. The walls in rough dark brick (marble facing was intended but never installed) are enhanced by limestone trim. On the Peachtree Street facade, uniformity is broken by niches on either side of the entrances and reinforced by the window pattern above.

PC 2

PC 3

PC 3 One-Ninety-One Peachtree Tower
191 Peachtree Street, N.E.
1990: John Burgee Architects with Philip Johnson, Architects

A free interpretation of turn-of-the-century neoclassical skyscrapers, this fifty-story granite-clad office tower is a welcome addition to the downtown skyline. Derived from Johnson's AT&T Building in New York City, its monumental arched entryway on Peachtree Street leads into a six-story skylit atrium surrounded by retail space on the ground level. One-Ninety-One Peachtree Tower is set well back from Peachtree Street in order to be more respectful of the scale of Macy's Department Store (PC 2) across the street. The center of the shaft is recessed to give the impression of two slender towers, which are notched in order to provide for twelve corner offices on each floor and crowned by identical columned aediculae.

PC 4 Westin Peachtree Plaza Hotel

210 Peachtree Street, N.W.
1976, Renovation 1986: John Portman and Associates, Architects

On a relatively small site, where the first mansion for the governor
once stood, followed by the Henry Grady Hotel, John Portman built
the Westin Peachtree Plaza Hotel, a 1078-room, seventy-story concrete
structure, which remains (to this date) the tallest hotel in America. A
taut cylinder, sheathed entirely in reflective glass, is set above a massive
concrete base. Transparent elevators leading to a revolving restaurant
and cocktail lounge (which provide spectacular views of the city) run
in a glass-walled tube attached to the circular guest tower. The Westin
Peachtree Plaza Hotel epitomizes the way in which John Portman has
turned the traditional components of street life inward. Its blockhaus-
like entrance on Peachtree Street (the auto entrance is in back, on Spring
Street) leads to a five-story atrium surrounding the circular elevator core.
This atrium was transformed in the late 1980s when the indoor lake and

PC 4, *left*; PC 7, *right*

cocktail lounge "lily pads" were superseded by a postmodern stage set. Described by Portman's publicists as "a modern interpretation of a classic Venetian piazza," the new design lacks the honesty and playfulness of its predecessor. The hotel's massing suggests Portman's later and more elaborate designs, such as the Bonaventure Hotel in Los Angeles and Renaissance Center in Detroit.

PC 6

PC 5   **209 Peachtree Street Building (Regenstein's Department Store)**
209 Peachtree Street, N.E.
1930: Architect Unknown

PC 6   **Cornerstone Building (J. P. Allen Building)**
215 Peachtree Street, N.E.
1928: Morgan, Dillon and Lewis, Architects; NR. Renovation 1989: Turner Associates, Architects

Built by retailers whose large stores were originally located in the Whitehall Street area (the area south of Alabama Street along what has since been renamed Peachtree Street in an effort to encourage development), these two low commercial structures exemplified the move of commercial enterprises to the north that took place in the 1920s. While its base has been altered, the **209 Peachtree Street Building** retains the fine Art Deco ornamentation of its upper floors. Notice the monogram of its builder, the Peters Land Company, in the two center spandrels. The contrast between the smooth stone veneer of the piers and the black spandrels, "capitals," and roundels, ornate with stylized floral motifs is quite striking but is not original (the black paint is a recent addition).

Across International Boulevard, the recently renovated **Cornerstone Building** features the same general organization as the 209 Peachtree Street Building, with more conservative, stripped-down classical details.

PC 7 **Peachtree Center Tower**
230 Peachtree Street, N.W.
1965: Edwards and Portman, Architects

PC 8 **Peachtree Center Mall**
231 Peachtree Street, N.E.
1973, Addition 1979, Renovation 1986: John Portman and Associates, Architects; UDC Award

After its hotel atriums, Peachtree Center is best known to architects and the general public for its cluster of office towers. The first to be built was the **Peachtree Center Tower,** completed in 1965. Its precast concrete panels, which hang from the steel skeleton and frame narrow floor-to-ceiling openings, were duplicated with minor variations in six

PC 8

other towers, ranging in height from twenty-five to thirty-five stories and oriented east to west in an arrangement inspired by New York City's Rockefeller Center (Hofmeister, Corbett and Hood, 1931–1939). Instead of being distributed among the office towers, shops and other amenities have been centralized in **Peachtree Center Mall,** which connects four towers below grade (John Portman's offices are located above the mall, in a space originally constructed to house a dinner theater). Of the design features that make reference to Rockefeller Center (the integration of pedestrian outdoor and indoor spaces and a unified facade treatment), the most important, the narrow public promenade opening on Peachtree Street, has lost a significant part of its appeal. In 1986 the drastic renovation of the lower-level food court and retail spaces included enclosure of the sunken garden courtyard (where employees once ate their brown-bag lunches under bright yellow parasols) and installation of a transparent canopy along Peachtree Street, which has visually cut off the mall space from the street.

PC 9 **Atlanta Merchandise Mart**
240 Peachtree Street, N.W.
1961, Addition 1968: Edwards and Portman, Architects. Addition 1986: John Portman and Associates, Architects

PC 10 **Atlanta Apparel Mart**
250 Spring Street, N.W.
1979, Addition 1989: John Portman and Associates, Architects

PC 11 **Inforum**
250 Williams Street, N.W.
1989: John Portman and Associates, Architects

PC 12 **Atlanta Gift Mart**
230 Spring Street, N.W.
1992: John Portman and Associates, Architects

Along with the Decorative Arts Center in Buckhead (351 Peachtree Hills Avenue, N.E.), Peachtree Center's wholesale facilities form the Atlanta Market Center, which is operated and partly owned by John Portman. The requirement for ample and flexible space dictated their gigantic scale. The **Atlanta Merchandise Mart,** in which John Portman's new concept of wholesale services was first embodied, has more than tripled in size since its original phase was constructed in 1961. The **Atlanta Apparel Mart** has no fewer than 2.1 million square feet of showroom and exhibition space for the apparel industry. Its concrete exterior conceals a five-story skylit atrium in the shape of a hemicycle, with balconies patterned after those in the Hyatt Regency Atlanta Hotel (PC 14). Reflective glass minimizes the bulk of **Inforum,** a marketing center for computer and information-processing products and the only one of the above mentioned facilities open to the general public. The latest addition to the Atlanta Market Center is the **Atlanta Gift Mart,** which sits atop a parking garage designed by Portman in the late 1960s.

PC 10

PC 11

PC 13 **Capital City Club**
7 Harris Street, N.W.
1911: Donn Barber, Architect (New York); NR

Founded in 1883, the Capital City Club is the oldest private club in
Atlanta. It remains a popular (and exclusive) gathering place for the
city's business and professional leaders. The four-story building (the
floor above the dentiled cornice is a later addition) was designed by the
Beaux-Arts-trained architect Donn Barber (1871–1925) in the dignified
and rather severe mode that characterizes prestigious New York City
clubs such as the Colony Club (McKim, Mead and White, 1906). Projecting twin porches topped by an elegant balustrade provide a stately
base to the entrance facade on Harris Street. Located on prime real
estate, the club site has long been coveted by developers.

PC 14 **Hyatt Regency Atlanta Hotel (Regency Hyatt House Hotel)**
265 Peachtree Street, N.E.
1967: Edwards and Portman, Architects. Additions 1971, 1982: John
Portman and Associates, Architects

The 800-bedroom Hyatt Regency Atlanta Hotel was the first major hotel
to be built in downtown Atlanta since the 1920s. Since its dramatic
opening in 1967, the hotel has added 550 additional bedrooms in two
adjacent towers: one is cylindrical and served as a design precursor for
the Westin Peachtree Plaza Hotel (PC 4); the other imitates the original

exterior expression. Outside, the concrete mass is crowned by the sci-fi
blue dome of the revolving lounge, which once provided a commanding
view of the downtown skyline but is now boxed in by more recent highrise construction. The deliberately low entrance canopy and vestibule
give no hint of the spectacular full-height atrium inside. In addition to
the traditional registration area, the twenty-two-story skylit courtyard
(a design that required changes in the local life safety codes) includes
a gigantic aviary, an open cocktail lounge covered by a suspended
canopy, the 120-foot sculpture "Flora Raris" by Richard Lipphold, and
the exposed glass-enclosed "bubble" elevators that have become Portman's trademark. Dining areas on a more intimate scale are connected
to the central "piazza," and meeting and banquet facilities are located
on the lower levels. On the guest-room floors, instead of the customary
bleak corridors, rooms open onto plant-lined balconies. In effect, John
Portman expanded to an unprecedented scale the grand hotel lobbies of
such Gilded-Age caravansaries as the Brown Palace in Denver and the
Palmer House in Chicago. Eliciting a tremendous public response, Portman's design launched a new formula that he exploited in other hotels
for the Hyatt chain and that has been widely imitated.

PC 15   **Atlanta Marriott Marquis Hotel**
265 Peachtree Center Avenue, N.E.
1985: John Portman and Associates, Architects

PC 16   **Marquis One and Marquis Two Towers**
245 and 285 Peachtree Center Avenue, N.E.
1985, 1989: John Portman and Associates, Architects

With 1,674 guest rooms, the **Atlanta Marriott Marquis Hotel** is the largest convention hotel in the Southeast. Its exterior envelope in poured concrete consists of a low-rise podium and a tower with tapered walls on the north and south sides. The swelling atrium rises forty-eight stories, a height of 515 feet, with a volume of 9.5 million cubic feet. Its gigantic proportions overwhelm Portman's traditional hotel lobby features, including the hanging fabric sculpture by French artist Daniel Graffin. Each balcony, with its metal railing, looks like the rib of some fabulous prehistoric animal. The **Marquis One and Marquis Two Towers** flank the entrance to the north and south, and as with most of Portman's Peachtree Center buildings, their lobbies interconnect with the hotel for easy pedestrian movement without venturing outside.

PC 17   **One Peachtree Center**
303 Peachtree Street, N.E.
1992: John Portman and Associates, Architects

The sixty-story One Peachtree Center office tower, which includes 32,000 square feet of retail space, was designed as an anchor for the northern end of Peachtree Center. Stressing broad vertical divisions, its exterior in granite of different shades of grey and its faceted pyramid top in reflective glass are in sharp contrast to the concrete slabs of Portman's earlier office towers. The two-story lobby can be entered on any of the four sides through granite pavilions that bridge a circular reflecting pool.

PC 17

PC 18 **Sacred Heart Church (Church of the Sacred Heart of Jesus)**
335 Peachtree Center Avenue, N.E.
1897: Walter T. Downing, Architect; NR

PC 19 **First United Methodist Church of Atlanta**
360 Peachtree Street, N.E.
1903: Willis F. Denny, Architect

A highly visible and well-preserved landmark, the **Sacred Heart Church** enabled the Marist fathers to centralize their educational and religious facilities in Atlanta. Its exterior, in warm red brick with terra-cotta and marble accents, epitomizes Walter T. Downing's eclectic approach to architectural design. Elements of the decor—the triple arched-doorway surmounted by a low-pitched gable, the twin octagonal towers resting on square bases—are loosely patterned after Romanesque precedents, but the verticality is unmistakably Gothic in character. Built of Stone Mountain granite, the Gothic Revival **First United Methodist Church of Atlanta** hosts the oldest organized congregation in the city. Its pulpit, iron fence, and stained-glass windows are part of the original church of 1847.

PC 18

PC 20, PC 21

PC 20 **Peachtree Summit**
401 West Peachtree Street, N.E.
1975: Toombs, Amisano and Wells, Architects; Joseph Amisano and
Ronald Sineway, Designers; UDC, GAAIA Awards

PC 21 **MARTA Civic Center Station**
West Peachtree Street at Interstate 75/85
1979: M. Garland Reynolds and Partners, Architects; Welton Becket,
Associate Architects (Los Angeles)

Of a planned three-building complex, only the thirty-story **Peachtree
Summit** tower has been built. The form of its faceted base was dictated
by the irregular shape of the site. The facades, in cast-in-place concrete
and reflective glass, are a straightforward expression of the columnar
structure: on three of the corners, triangular "prows" or "handles" serve
as balconies; above the twenty-third floor, where the corner buttresses
are no longer needed to take wind stresses, they have been glazed and
turned into prestigious offices. The three-story public lobby relates to
both the lower street level that existed at the time of construction and the
new level of West Peachtree Street that resulted from the construction of
the **MARTA Civic Center Station** over the interstate highway.

PC 22

PC 22 **Georgia Power Company Corporate Headquarters**
333 Piedmont Avenue, N.E.
1976–1981: Heery and Heery, Architects; Mack Scogin, Design
Coordinator; Merrill Elam, Senior Project Designer; GAAIA Award

PC 23 **Atlanta Civic Center**
395 Piedmont Avenue, N.E.
1968: Robert and Company, Architects

Located on a twenty-three-acre parcel in the Bedford-Pine Redevelopment Area, the **Georgia Power Company Corporate Headquarters**
complex consolidates the operations of the company and symbol-
izes its commitment to energy conservation. The three-level sweeping
brick-and-granite structure, for special use and twenty-four-hour-a-
day functions, has on its roof a solar collector field. The highly visible
twenty-four-story tower, which houses executive and general office
space, features a curtain wall of insulated glass windows and reflective nonvision glass (the black color led to its being nicknamed "Darth
Vador"); the angle of its stepped-back southern facade is precisely con-
figured so that direct entry of the sun's rays is completely eliminated at
the summer solstice. Across Ralph McGill Boulevard is the **Atlanta Civic
Center,** whose striated ocher brick walls accented with white concrete
balconies and colonnades houses the city's theatrical auditorium and
exhibition space. The latter is now used as a hands-on science museum
known as SciTrek, designed by Rosser Fabrap International.

Downtown West (DW)

This nationally important convention and sporting events district had its origin in the early 1960s when Atlanta developer Tom Cousins decided to lease air rights above the open railroad tracks of the now demolished Terminal Station (there were also a few warehouses in the vicinity) and construct a multiuse "megastructure" adjacent to the newly completed Omni (DW 1). In spite of their economic importance to Atlanta and their undeniable public significance, these compatible but self-contained behemoths, whose design integrity as a unit owes mainly to the fact that they were entrusted to the same architectural firm, have not drawn other projects capable of spanning the gap that continues to divide Downtown from the West Side. They have, however, attracted other "megastructures" (entrusted to the same design team), which have made Atlanta and this district into the convention capital it is. Because of their proximity to one another, the buildings in this area will be discussed in order of their construction.

Area 4

Downtown West (DW)

1 The Omni
2 CNN Center
3 Georgia World Congress Center
4 Georgia Dome

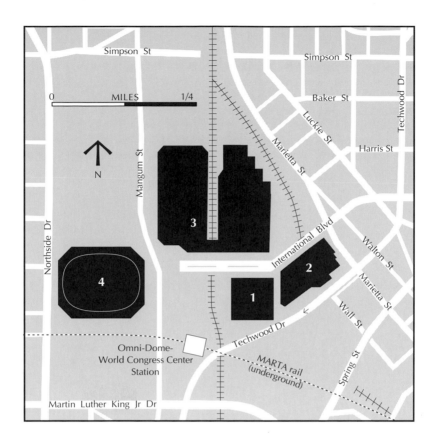

DW 1 **The Omni**
100 Techwood Drive, N.W.
1968–1972: Thompson, Ventulett and Stainback, Architects;
Prybylowski and Gravino, Structural Engineers; GAAIA Award

Jointly owned by city and county, the 377,000-square-foot multipurpose Omni seats 16,500 spectators and was originally built as home to both the Atlanta Flames, a professional ice-hockey team now based in Calgary, and the Atlanta Hawks, the city's professional basketball team. The arena allows flexible seating arrangements for other types of events, including the 1988 Democratic National Convention and numerous rock concerts. The seating bowl is placed on the diagonal axis of a 360-foot square, which improves visibility and increases the number of premium seats. Walls are sheathed in Cor-Ten weathering steel with large glass planes alleviating the corners. Spanning the entire space, four cantilevered wall trusses support an unusual roof structure (an "ortho-quad truss" system), which conspicuously incorporates evenly spaced truncated pyramids. The interior plan is successful, but the design suffers from unfortunate siting, which complicates ground-level access and confounds the visitor trying to reach the coliseum through a maze of poorly planned streets.

DW 2 **CNN Center (Omni International)**
190 Marietta Street, N.W.
1976: Thompson, Ventulett and Stainback, Architects; Marvin Housworth, Associate in Charge; GAAIA Award

The components of the CNN Center are differentiated on the outside: two fourteen-story office buildings and a five-hundred-room hotel form massive blocks of Alabama limestone, while the full-height atrium, in weathering steel and bronze glass, dramatically slopes toward the Omni (DW 1). Placed on a diagonal, a bridge connects the megastructure with the large parking deck erected in 1966. Omni International, which originated while the arena was under construction, was intended as a family recreation center. Its atrium featured not only a breathtaking eight-story escalator (at that time the world's longest), but also an Olympic-size indoor ice-skating rink. When the enterprise first opened, it housed a number of posh retail stores, restaurants, and an indoor amusement park. Unable to bring families back to the central city or compete with shopping and entertainment centers in the suburbs, the venture was nearly abandoned until T.V. mogul Ted Turner bought the property, renamed it CNN Center, and moved his broadcasting studios and headquarters there.

DW 2

DW 3 **Georgia World Congress Center**
285 International Boulevard, N.W.
1976, 1985: Thompson, Ventulett and Stainback, Architects

A convention and trade-fair facility financed by the state, the Georgia
World Congress Center was built in two phases. The eastern portion,
with its two long sides entrenched between the railroad tracks, was
built in the 1970s. Its 350,000-square-foot exhibition hall was at the
time the largest single-floor exhibition hall in the United States. Adding
one-and-a-half times the original square footage, the 1985 addition includes an entrance pavilion on International Boulevard with a stepped
down atrium in glass and weathered steel and a concrete frame pedestrian concourse. As of this writing new additions to the Georgia World
Congress Center are in the planning stage.

DW 4 **Georgia Dome**
285 International Boulevard, N.W.
1989–1992: Heery / Rosser Fabrap International / Thompson, Ventulett, Stainback and Associates, Joint Venture Architects; Scott Braley, Project Director. Weidlinger Associates (New York) and Harrington Engineers, Structural Engineers

Enclosing thirty-seven acres of floor space, the Georgia Dome boasts not only a 70,500-seat stadium designed to accommodate the Atlanta Falcons football franchise, but also 120,000 square feet of exhibition space, which is created from sections of the playing field. The Georgia Dome (the third largest domed stadium in North America in terms of seating capacity) will be the site of the 1994 Super Bowl and various venues of the 1996 Summer Olympics, as well as serve as an extension of the nearby Georgia World Congress Center (DW 3). On the outside, this double purpose is reflected in the superimposition of the world's largest rigid cable-supported oval dome, with a translucent roofing membrane made of Teflon-coated fiberglass on a corporate-looking base, with metal panels and a five-story glazed atrium at each of the four corners. In the stadium, the 850-foot clear span allows close views of the game from any seat. Construction started in March 1990 was completed in August 1992: the accelerated timetable was made possible by overlapping the design and construction phases of the project.

Sweet Auburn (SA)

Two landmark districts of great historical significance, the Sweet Auburn district and Martin Luther King Jr. National Historic Site, mark this area. Formerly called Wheat Street, Auburn Avenue got its present name in 1893, and by the early twentieth century had become the main artery of the most affluent black neighborhood in Atlanta. "Sweet Auburn" (a name coined by politician John Wesley Dobbs in the 1930s) is the home of nationally known black businesses and financial institutions, as well as cultural and fraternal organizations. In its prime, the avenue was lined by retail space, hotels, and popular nightclubs. The most famous resident of its predominantly residential western part was civil rights activist Dr. Martin Luther King Jr. (1929–1968), whose memorial and grave site are located in the district. The migration of the black middle class to the west side in the 1940s marked the beginning of the decline of Sweet Auburn, which was further aggravated by the construction in the 1960s of the downtown connector (Interstates 75 and 85), which now bisects the district. The revitalization of this center of African-American culture is under way and has met with a great deal of public support under the direction of the Auburn Avenue Revitalization Committee. Tours can be arranged through the Atlanta Preservation Center.

Area 5

Sweet Auburn (SA)

1 First Congregational Church
2 Baptist Student Center, Georgia State University
3 Atlanta Life Insurance Company Building
4 Herndon Plaza
5 John Wesley Dobbs Building
6 Odd Fellows Building
7 Big Bethel A.M.E. Church
8 Georgia Hall, Grady Memorial Hospital
9 Steiner Building, Grady Memorial Hospital
10 Grady Memorial Hospital
11 Martin Luther King Jr. Center for Nonviolent Social Change
12 Ebenezer Baptist Church
13 Martin Luther King Jr. Birth Home
14 Fire Station No. 6
15 Wigwam Apartments
16 West Wing, Georgia Baptist Medical Center
17 North and East Wings, Georgia Baptist Medical Center
18 Professional Building, Georgia Baptist Medical Center
19 East Professional Building, Georgia Baptist Medical Center

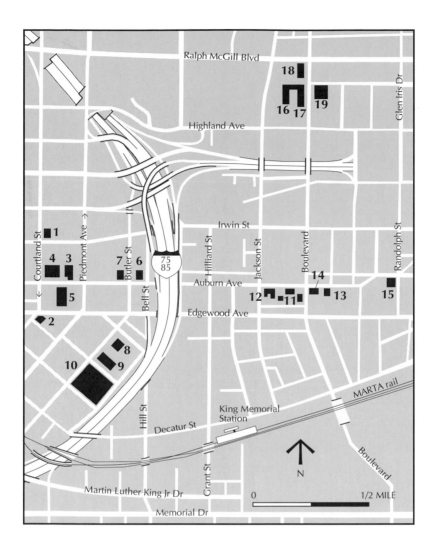

Map labels:
Ralph McGill Blvd
Highland Ave
Glen Iris Dr
Irwin St
Courtland St
Piedmont Ave →
Hilliard St
Jackson St
Boulevard
Randolph St
Butler St
Bell St
Auburn Ave
Edgewood Ave
MARTA rail
Hill St
Decatur St
King Memorial Station
Grant St
Boulevard
N
Martin Luther King Jr Dr
Memorial Dr
0   1/2 MILE

75
85

SA 1 First Congregational Church
105 Courtland Street, N.E.
1908: Bruce and Everett, Architects; LB

First Congregational Church, founded on the present site in 1867, has
always had a congregation deeply committed to social activism and
the well-being of the black community. Its corner location makes the
1908 structure, in tan brick with white accents resting on a rough-hewn
granite base, appear monumental. The treatment of the entrance facade
on Houston Street, the "side elevation" on Courtland Street, and a corner tower anchoring the design contribute to its grandeur. Although
the consistent use of arched openings acts as a unifying device, the
ornamentation is eclectic and full of fantasy. The entrance porch looks
Romanesque at first glance, but it is supported by coupled Ionic columns
and topped by a Spanish Mission motif; the belvedere atop the tower
is directly inspired by those of Italian Renaissance villas; and the large
stained-glass window on Courtland Street is straightforwardly Victorian.

SA 2   **Baptist Student Center, Georgia State University (Dixie Coca-Cola Bottling Company)**
125 Edgewood Avenue, S.E.
1891: Architect Unknown; NHL, LB. Addition 1988: Interior Remodeling and Facade Restoration 1989: Cavender Associates, Architects; UDC Award

The establishment of the Dixie Coca-Cola Bottling Company in 1900 marked the first application of the franchise concept to the soft-drink industry. This modest structure, which served as the first bottling plant of the Coca-Cola Company for just over a year, became a National Historic Landmark in 1977. Characteristic of the Queen Anne style, the building features a complex roof, with hipped sections and stepped Flemish gables, a square wood-shingled turret addressing the street corner (the second floor originally was used as a residence), and materials and textures combined in a picturesque fashion. In 1966 it became the Baptist Student Center for Georgia State University, which necessitated the recent nonintrusive addition built on Courtland Street.

SA 3 **Atlanta Life Insurance Company Building**
148 Auburn Avenue, N.E.
Date and Builder Unknown. Renovation and Facade 1927: Aiken and
Faulkner, Builders

SA 4 **Herndon Plaza**
100 Auburn Avenue, N.E.
1980: Thompson, Ventulett, Stainback and Associates, with J. W.
Robinson and Associates, Architects

SA 5 **John Wesley Dobbs Building (Southern Schoolbook Depository
Building)**
135 Auburn Avenue, N.E.
Circa 1910: Hentz and Reid. Renovation 1988: E. R. Mitchell
Construction Company

Founded by Alonzo F. Herndon in 1905, the Atlanta Life Insurance
Company is one of the largest black-owned business enterprises in the
country. The facade of its first headquarters, the **Atlanta Life Insurance
Company Building** at 148 Auburn Avenue (originally a YMCA building), was given a facelift in 1927: old-fashioned colossal neoclassical
columns and pilasters supporting a wide entablature were intended to
express the stability of the insurance business. Classical as well, but
more restrained, is the facade of the annex built next to the original
building in the 1930s. In contrast, the abstract masses of the Atlanta Life
Insurance Company's current headquarters, **Herndon Plaza,** with its
boldly cantilevered executive floor, bear witness to an aggressive and
dynamic entrepreneurial vision. Across from it is the **John Wesley Dobbs
Building,** one of the finest commercial structures in red brick with stone
accents remaining in this area. This building (restored with the support

of the Historic Facade Program) houses the first phase of the APEX (African American Panoramic Experience) Museum. Funds are being raised to initiate the second phase, a research library for African-American history.

SA 6

SA 6 **Odd Fellows Building**
250 Auburn Avenue, N.E.
Tower 1912, Auditorium Addition 1914: William A. Edwards, Architect; NR. Tower Restoration 1988: Stang and Newdow, Architects; UDC Award. Auditorium Restoration 1991: Perkins and Partners, Architects; UDC Award

SA 7 **Big Bethel A.M.E. Church**
220 Auburn Avenue, N.E.
1891: Architect Unknown

As indicated on its doorway, the **Odd Fellows Building** was completed in 1912 and served as the regional headquarters of the Grand United Order of Odd Fellows, a major trade and social organization. The six-story structure housed a number of black businesses. Its lower annex, completed in 1914, incorporated a concert hall and theater. For the most part, the picturesque brick-and-stone detailing was inspired by early English "Jacobean" precedents, while the highly stylized African-American heads ornamenting the facade were intended to celebrate the Sweet Auburn community. Damaged by fire in 1923, the nearby **Big Bethel A.M.E. Church** lost most of its fine Romanesque Revival detailing in the subsequent reconstruction. This historic structure also served as the first school for black children in Atlanta.

SA 8

SA 8   **Georgia Hall, Grady Memorial Hospital**
        36 Butler Street, S.E.
        1892: Eugene Clarence Gardner and Sons, Architects (Springfield, Massachusetts); NR, LB, UDC Award

SA 9   **Steiner Building, Grady Memorial Hospital (Albert Steiner Ward)**
        62 Butler Street, S.E.
        1923: Hentz, Reid and Adler, Architects; Neel Reid, Designer; HB

SA 10   **Grady Memorial Hospital**
        80 Butler Street, S.E.
        1958: Robert and Company, Architects. Goddard Chapel 1956: Philip Shutze, Architect

Atlanta's first publicly supported hospital, **Georgia Hall** (often referred to as Old Grady Hospital) opened in 1892. The institution was named after Atlanta Constitution editor and New South advocate Henry W. Grady (1851–1889). Both its historical significance and its architectural distinction justify the nomination of this three-story structure, in red brick resting on a granite base, to the National Register of Historic Places. Georgia Hall has a Romanesque Revival arched entrance portico topped by a carved frieze that incorporates the name of the hospital. The bracketed eaves of the hipped roofs of both the main building and the side tower as well as the scaled down window pattern make the structure look more residential than institutional. Originally a porte cochère was attached to the right end of the Butler Street facade and wards were placed at the back. (These were subsequently demolished in 1959 to make way for a parking lot.) Notice on the same block Neel Reid's **Steiner Building,** a palazzo-like structure covered in buff brick, which was built as a cancer ward but now houses offices for faculty members from Emory University. In sharp contrast to these modest structures, the twenty-one-story main building of **Grady Memorial Hospital** stands on the next block across Armstrong Street. The visitor is surprised to find in this modern structure the jewel-like neoclassical Goddard Chapel, designed by Philip Shutze. Grady Memorial Hospital is one of the largest health-care facilities in the Southeast, in terms of both square footage (1.2 million) and number of patients treated annually. An ambitious campaign of renovation and additions to Grady Memorial Hospital is scheduled to be completed by the end of 1995.

SA 10

SA 11 **Martin Luther King Jr. Center for Nonviolent Social Change (King Memorial Center)**
449 Auburn Avenue, N.E.
Memorial 1977, Freedom Hall 1981: Bond and Ryder, Architects (New York), UDC Award

SA 12 **Ebenezer Baptist Church**
407 Auburn Avenue, N.E.
1922: Architect Unknown

The **Martin Luther King Jr. Center for Nonviolent Social Change** was established in 1968 and is visited by more than a million individuals each year. Approaching the Center from Downtown along Auburn Avenue, the visitor passes the Victorian red brick facade of **Ebenezer Baptist Church,** where Dr. King, his father, and his grandfather each served as pastor. At the Center, a progressive visual sequence of architectural spaces gradually leads the visitor to a meditative space focused on the entombment of the civil-rights leader: rows of trees planted on lawns along the avenue, a narrow bright blue reflecting pool (symbolizing the life giving nature of water), a Chapel of All Faiths (receiving a soft reflected light from the underside of its vault), and the Freedom Walkway (a vaulted colonnade stepping the length of the site, with niches designed for future murals of King's leadership in the civil-rights movement). The simple white marble block of the tomb was placed dramatically at the center of the pool on a circular brick platform. Much more understated is the brick cylinder hosting the eternal flame, placed directly on axis with the crypt. At the eastern end, enclosure is provided by the two-story Freedom Hall, where the information center is located and placed at a right angle to the three-story Memorial Hall, an administration, program, and archives building, complete with a large exhibition area. The repetitive concrete barrel vaults with brick infills, which characterize all of these buildings, are reminiscent of Le Corbusier's Maisons Jaoul near Paris (1955) and respect the quiet red and grey harmony of the memorial ground.

SA 13

SA 13 **Martin Luther King Jr. Birth Home**
501 Auburn Avenue, N.E.
Circa 1893: Architect Unknown; UDC Award

SA 14 **Fire Station No. 6**
39 Boulevard, N.E.
1894: Bruce and Morgan, Architects; UDC Award

SA 15 **Wigwam Apartments**
587–591 Auburn Avenue, N.E.; 44–50 Randolph Street, N.E.
1940: Vincent Daley, Architect

The **Martin Luther King Jr. Birth Home** was owned by the civil-rights leader's maternal grandfather. The King family lived there until 1941. A two-story frame house with clapboard siding, its irregular massing,

porch ornaments, and gable are derived from the Queen Anne style. The National Park Service began restoring the site in 1974. The Park Service has purchased and restored several houses in the area to the time period 1929–1941, which is when Dr. King lived in the neighborhood. Among these are several two-story Victorian homes along Auburn Avenue as well as more modest "shotgun" houses that were built around 1905 (these are among the last examples remaining in Atlanta of this residential type so common in southern cities at the turn of the century). They form an interesting residential ensemble with their aligned projecting gables oriented to the street. Of both historical and architectural interest across Boulevard from the King Center is the still operating **Fire Station No. 6,** a flat brick structure graced with fine Romanesque Revival detailing. At the intersection of Randolph Street and Auburn Avenue, the **Wigwam Apartments** are a rare example of Streamlined Moderne apartment houses in Atlanta. The flat-roofed, stucco exterior is animated by wrapping corner windows and setback stairs and terraces.

SA 16 **West Wing, Georgia Baptist Medical Center**
300 Boulevard, N.E.
1925: Burge and Stevens, Architects

SA 17 **North and East Wings, Georgia Baptist Medical Center**
300 Boulevard, N.E.
1951: Stevens and Wilkinson, Architects; SARC, AIA Awards

SA˙18 **Professional Building, Georgia Baptist Medical Center**
300 Boulevard, N.E.
1951: Stevens and Wilkinson, Architects; AIA Award

SA 19 **East Professional Building, Georgia Baptist Medical Center**
315 Boulevard, N.E.
1974: Stevens and Wilkinson, Architects; GAAIA Award

The original 1925 portion of the Georgia Baptist Medical Center, currently known as the **West Wing,** is now hidden from view by the 1951 **North and East Wings** on Boulevard. This addition, in the International Style, received the American Institute of Architects' Award of Merit in Hospital Architecture. Its street facade enhanced by a regular grid of concrete and aluminum sun-shades significantly reduces air-conditioning costs. The asymmetrically placed entrance is marked by a large concrete awning characteristic of the 1950s. The **Professional Building** to its north was also recognized by the AIA with an Award of Merit in 1957. Across Boulevard, the **East Professional Building** is a four-story block with an elegant window pattern that alleviates the corners. The hospital complex has the unusual distinction of having had almost all of its recent structures designed by the same architectural firm, Stevens and Wilkinson.

Area 6

Lower Midtown (LM)

This area encompasses Peachtree Street and its surroundings, between the MARTA Civic Center (PC 21) and Tenth Street stations. It originated as an elegant district developed by farsighted entrepreneurs, the first among them being Richard Peters, who in 1849 bought 405 acres of land between North Avenue and Eighth Street. Although the area has lost its intricate fabric, with the exception of its residential eastern edge, it features a great variety of fine commercial structures dating from the second and third decades of the twentieth century, when the downtown retail, entertainment, and tourist activities spread northward along Peachtree and West Peachtree streets. With the exodus to the suburbs after World War II, the area deteriorated. The vicinity of Tenth and Peachtree streets was already quite run-down in the 1960s when it became the center of the counterculture. Today's rejuvenation of lower Midtown remains quite sporadic, with development focused, for the time being, at the major intersection of Peachtree Street and North Avenue. Prospects look bright for development further north because of the interest of Swedish developer G. Lars Gullstedt, who recently purchased the Biltmore Hotel (LM 22) and adjacent tracts of land.

Area 6

Lower Midtown (LM)

1 Baltimore Row
2 Peachtree-Pine Building
3 W. W. Orr Building
4 Rufus M. Rose House
5 Rio Shopping Mall
6 The Mansion Restaurant
7 North Avenue Presbyterian Church
8 NationsBank Plaza
9 Fire Station No. 11
10 All Saints Episcopal Church
11 One Georgia Center
12 The Varsity
13 The Ponce
14 Fox Theater
15 Southern Bell Center
16 Georgian Terrace Apartments
17 Days Inn Hotel—Peachtree
18 Saint Mark United Methodist Church
19 First Baptist Church
20 Evangelical Lutheran Church of the Redeemer
21 Crum and Foster Building
22 Biltmore Hotel
23 Biltmore Inn
24 Hotel Peachtree Manor
25 Shellmont Bed and Breakfast Lodge
26 Howard Johnson Hotel—Atlanta/Midtown
27 Academy of Medicine
28 Palmer House
29 Phelan Apartments

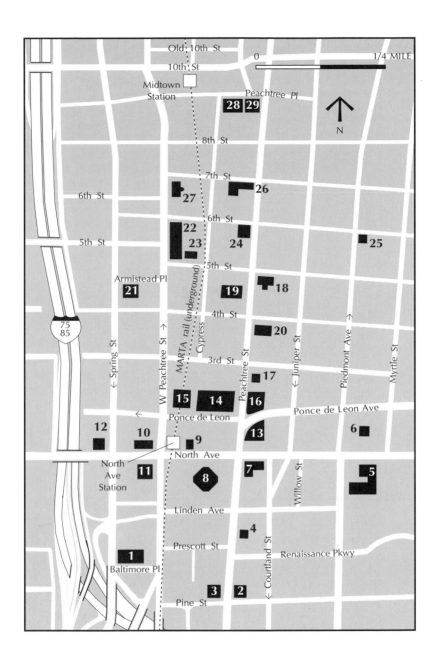

LM 1

LM 1 Baltimore Row (Baltimore Block)

5 to 19 Baltimore Place, N.W.

1886: Atlanta Land and Annuity Company, Builder; NR. Restoration and
Addition 1989: James Patterson Associates, Architects

Atlanta's first row-house development, now known as Baltimore Row,
was the inspiration of J. S. Rosenthal, a native of Baltimore, Maryland,
where this type of house was particularly popular. A specific feature of
Baltimore residential architecture, the stoop running straight from the
door to the sidewalk, was emulated in the block. Placed under the same
heavy cornice supported by decorative brackets, the fourteen original
single-family units, once known as Baltimore Block, are defined by
slight variations in ornamentation and openings (notice, for instance, the
different shapes of the glass transom lights above the doors). The row
houses introduced state-of-the-art amenities to Atlanta, including central
heating and independent sewage systems. When commercial development encroached on the neighborhood, Baltimore Block saw its wealthy

occupants move to more secluded precincts. Many of the units were subsequently divided into apartments. In the 1930s, Baltimore Block attracted artists in search of inexpensive studio space, housed several antique shops and a tearoom, and became one of the centers of Atlanta's intellectual life. Over time six of the outlying units were demolished and several others vandalized. In 1989, however, the old block was renovated into office space and is now joined by a glass-roofed atrium to an addition in the back featuring several floors of offices and sixteen penthouse apartments.

LM 2

LM 2   **Peachtree-Pine Building (United Motors Service Building)**
        477 Peachtree Street, N.E.
        Circa 1921: A. Ten Eyck Brown, Architect

LM 3   **W. W. Orr Building**
        478 Peachtree Street, N.E.
        1930: Pringle and Smith, Architects; LB

LM 4   **Rufus M. Rose House**
        537 Peachtree Street, N.E.
        Circa 1900: Architect Unknown; LB

This section of Peachtree Street is reminiscent of the years before the second world war, when single family homes and commercial structures comfortably coexisted. It presents a continuous streetscape and harmonious scale that echoes the once tightly knit fabric of the historic artery that has since been lost. The proximity to Downtown made it an attractive location for car dealerships and salesrooms, such as the **Peachtree-Pine Building,** which now houses several businesses. Its facade, however, still bears witness to the original occupants. An original decorative treatment gives this modest two-story block a distinctive character: an inset colonnade is framed by a colorful geometric frieze in terra-cotta. The rosette motifs that interrupt this frieze are also found on the metallic spandrels at the center of each bay. The opposite corner of Peachtree Street is well defined by the **W. W. Orr Building,** which interrupts the low profile of the area. This eleven-story structure in buff brick with stone accents adopts the same general massing and restrained Art Deco style as the earlier William-Oliver Building (FP 2), which was also designed by Pringle and Smith. Its initial use as medical and dental offices explains why caducei motifs are present in the spandrels between the first and second floors. Windows of various shapes and sizes punctuate the red-brick facade of the **Rufus M. Rose House** located farther north on Peachtree Street. A narrow oval opening echoes the motif defining the raised doorway. Notice the dignified treatment of the stone steps, which establish the proper Victorian distance between the private home and the public sidewalk.

LM 5

LM 5 Rio Shopping Mall

535 Piedmont Avenue, N.E.
1989: Arquitectonica, Architects (Miami); Marta Schwartz, Landscape Architect (San Francisco); Debra Baker, Graphic Designer; UDC Award

The 25,000-square-foot Rio Shopping Mall, a neighborhood retail and entertainment center, is a joint venture of Charles Ackerman and two nonprofit organizations, Central Atlanta Progress and the Bedford-Pine

Development Corporation. It was, overall, a risky and challenging venture, considering its location, the edge of commercial Midtown, and its designers, an unconventional Miami-based firm known for playful and glamorous beachside condos. On the outside, with its apparently randomly applied decoration of red tubes and yellow ladders, the U-shaped structure sheathed in blue corrugated steel answers Robert Venturi's definition of the "decorated shed." Inside, two levels of storefronts open onto a partially covered patio. It is in the treatment of this central space, oriented toward Piedmont Avenue, that the originality of the parti lies. A rotated square supporting freestanding elements as apparently mismatched as a video wall (a grid of twenty-five television screens), an elevator shaft, a gazebo bar, and a round bamboo pad seems to float on a black pond lighted by submerged fiber-optic strips. Along Piedmont Avenue, a huge tubular sphere stands atop a short slope, spraying mist at regular intervals. The most intriguing ornaments are the 350 golden frogs regularly spread on the pond and slope. Are they supposed to be reminiscent of old baroque fountains, such as the Pond of Latona in Versailles? Do they comment ironically on the purpose of the place?

LM 6   The Mansion Restaurant (Edward C. Peters House)
179 Ponce de Leon Avenue, N.E.
1883: Gottfried L. Norrman, Architect; NR, LB. Restoration and Additions 1973: Allan Salzman, Architect; UDC Award

The Edward C. Peters House, now the Mansion Restaurant, was built for the son of civic leader and land developer Richard Peters (1810–1889). Of all the mansions that lined major arteries north of Downtown, the Peters House is one of the most well preserved. It is also the finest illustration of the Queen Anne style remaining in Atlanta. A free interpretation of English domestic architecture of the late sixteenth and early

LM 6

seventeenth centuries, this style was introduced in the United States by
Henry Hobson Richardson and other East Coast designers in the late
nineteenth century. The Peters family's Philadelphia ancestry may ex-
plain why they embraced this new domestic trend, which soon became
fashionable among Atlanta's business elite and middle class. With its
porte cochere and deep porches, prominent half-timbered gables and
high chimney stacks, the exterior of the Peters House exhibits a picturesque massing and juxtaposes building materials (brick, terra-cotta,
wood shingles, and slate) of contrasting textures and colors. It also features Japanese-influenced wood balustrades and screen-porch railings.
Threatened with demolition upon the death of Edward Peters's daughter-
in-law in 1970, the house was transformed into a restaurant three years
later. The major rooms in the house, in which most of the original decorative features have been preserved, have been turned into intimate
dining areas and furnished with appropriate period pieces. Respectful of
the original structure, a gingerbread gazebo, which serves as a cocktail
lounge, was added to the North Avenue facade.

LM 7

LM 7 North Avenue Presbyterian Church
607 Peachtree Street, N.E.
1901: Bruce and Morgan, Architects; NR

At the turn of the century, North Avenue Presbyterian Church stood
among stately Victorian mansions. Asymmetrical, but well balanced,
the original Peachtree Street facade is composed of a central porch projecting from the gabled nave, which is framed by a turret and a square
crenellated tower addressing the intersection of Peachtree Street and
North Avenue. The addition on the right end was built in 1950. The

Romanesque Revival ornamentation is greatly simplified and relies on the use of coarse grey granite stonework and the alternation of arched and rectilinear openings to achieve its Old World appeal.

LM 8 **NationsBank Plaza**
600 Peachtree Street, N.E.
1992: Kevin Roche, John Dinkeloo and Associates, Architects (Hamden, Connecticut)

NationsBank Plaza is a joint venture of Atlanta-based developer Cousins Properties and the former Citizens and Southern Corporation, now NationsBank, which will consolidate its Atlanta headquarters in the tower. The design for the fifty-three-story skyscraper was unveiled in October 1989. With its granite cladding, arcade base, and pyramidal roof, NationsBank Plaza emulates Philip Johnson's eclectic One Atlantic

LM 8

Center (UM 12), while its spire alludes to the mooring mast crowning the Empire State Building in New York City. The shaft's vertical thrust is enhanced by the presence of setback beveled corners, which provide for eight corner offices per floor. Eight "super columns" on the exterior of the tower alleviate the need for internal supports. Surrounded by a large public park, the skyscraper faces bordering streets at 45-degree angles. Such placement provides, according to architect Kevin Roche, undisturbed views and a more "dramatic addition" to the skyline. It may also set a precedent for other monumental structures to break traditional alignments in this part of Midtown as Colony Square (UM 9) did in upper Midtown. A low freestanding structure at the southern end of the site has been designed to house an auditorium and restaurants.

LM 9

LM 9 Fire Station No. 11
30 North Avenue, N.E.
1907: Morgan and Dillon, Architects; NR

Of all the small fire stations built in the city at the turn of the century, Fire Station No. 11 is the most elaborate and well preserved. Like Fire Station No. 7 (1910, 535 West Whitehall Street, S.W.), which was designed by the same firm, the North Avenue facility is a two-story rectangular structure whose upstairs living quarters are accessible from a small side entrance. Its front facade is sheathed in glazed white brick. The moldings framing the twin truck bays on the ground floor—notice their authentic metal awning—create, on the upper level, the illusion of pilasters ended by brackets, which, in turn, seem to support the dentiled stringcourse.

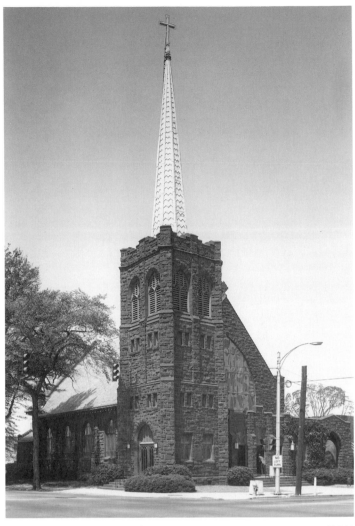

LM 10

LM 10 **All Saints Episcopal Church**
634 West Peachtree Street, N.W.
1906: Bruce and Morgan, Architects. Addition and Remodeling 1970:
Smith and Jones, Architects

LM 11 **One Georgia Center (Life of Georgia Building)**
600 West Peachtree Street, N.W.
1968: Lamberson, Plunkett, Shirley and Wooddall, Architects

Built on a property deeded to the church by developer Richard Peters's
wife in 1901, **All Saints Episcopal Church** is freely patterned after
English parish churches. The busy intersection of West Peachtree Street
and North Avenue is very successfully addressed by an asymmetri-

cally placed square tower. The copper of the slender octagonal steeple provides a striking contrast to the red Virginia sandstone of the rough-hewn masonry wall and dark roofing slates of the nave. Seven of the stained-glass windows are the work of the Tiffany Studio of New York. A modern canopy links the church to the Parish House, which was built in 1916. Across North Avenue is the monolithic **One Georgia Center,** a twenty-four-story tower, highly articulated in white Georgia marble. Originally built as corporate headquarters for the Life of Georgia Insurance Company, which later chose the larger floor plate made possible on a suburban site (see CM 7, Georgia U.S. Corporate Center), the building was the first skyscraper to break the bounds of the downtown skyline and start the inexorable northward expansion of the city's business community.

LM 12 **The Varsity**
61 North Avenue, N.W.
1940, 1959, 1965: Jules Grey, Architect

An Atlanta institution, the Varsity originated in the late 1920s as a small grill that catered to Georgia Tech students. It soon became a popular drive-in eating place. Its owner, Frank Gordy, is credited with originating the system of placing numbered placards on the cars and installing awnings to protect patrons from the blazing sun. With its dark horizontal accents, piano curve on the southwest corner, ocean-liner porthole, sleek enameled paneling, and steel window frames, the Varsity's elevation on North Avenue, begun in 1940, is characteristic of the commercial brand of Art Deco known as Streamlined Moderne. The same materials and motifs can be found in the central area, where hot dogs, chili steaks, and onion rings are produced and sold on an "assembly line." The slender neon sign on top of the main entrance was redesigned in the 1960s, but is still reminiscent of movie theater entrances of the Jazz Age. Notice the mock folded effect created by the enameled steel panels on the Spring Street facade, built in 1959. To meet popular demand, the Varsity has been enlarged many times. It has parking for six hundred cars and several T.V. dining rooms. Fortunately, it has preserved its "post–Art Deco" features and deserves to be regarded as an important landmark in its own right.

LM 12, *foreground;* LM 15, *background*

LM 13 The Ponce (Ponce de Leon Apartments)

75 Ponce de Leon Avenue, N.E.
1913: William L. Stoddart, Architect (New York); NR, LB

Built by the George A. Fuller Company of New York City, the Ponce de Leon Apartments was the first large highrise luxury apartment building in Atlanta. As such it aimed to express this new residential lifestyle in a strikingly dignified manner. The eleven-story building included shops on the ground floor and basement, and units ranging from one to ten rooms on the upper floors (the larger apartments had balconies). The unusual curve of the main facade, espoused by the entrance colonnade supported by coupled columns and the elegant stone balustrade crowning the cornice, was intended as a monumental urban gesture toward both Peachtree Street and Ponce de Leon Avenue. Its convex plane is abutted by two rectilinear blocks topped by Italianate aediculae concealing mechanical equipment. Classical detailing clearly defines the three-story stone base (notice the elegant marquee protecting the entrance) and the top floor with its elaborate decor of cartouche and swags in terra-cotta.

LM 14 Fox Theater
660 Peachtree Street, N.E.
1929: Marye, Alger and Vinour, Architects; NHL, LB

LM 15 Southern Bell Center
675 West Peachtree Street, N.E.
1982: Skidmore, Owings and Merrill (New York), and FABRAP,
Architects

The **Fox Theater** is the last surviving grand movie palace in Atlanta. It
was first designed as the Yaarab Temple, headquarters for Atlanta's Ara-
bic Order of the Nobles of the Mystic Shrine. When the initial client met
with financial difficulties, the project was rescued by cinema magnate
William Fox (whose wife took an active part in furnishing the theater).
Decorated with lancet arches, minarets, and onion domes, this imposing
structure shares a whole city block with the International Style tower
of the **Southern Bell Center,** which was redesigned to cantilever over
the subterranean MARTA system when Atlantans mounted the drive to
"Save the Fox" from the wrecking ball in the late 1970s. The Moorish
exterior neatly accommodates the fire exit on Ponce de Leon Avenue,
which is covered with the same alternate layers of buff and beige brick
as the rest of the theater. Welcomed by a bronze marquee, patrons proceed through a spacious arcade originally intended for commercial and
office use. In the four-thousand-seat "atmospheric auditorium," they are
carried away into the Arabia of a *Thousand and One Nights*. The illusion of sitting at sunrise or sunset (depending on the concealed lighting
effects) in the middle of a courtyard surrounded by castellated walls is
perfect. A mock canvas tent canopy serves as an acoustic reflector as
well as disguising a system of ventilation that was very sophisticated
for its time. The Fox Theater also includes a smaller auditorium and a
conference room, as well as a ballroom and a lounges in the Egyptian
style. Opened on Christmas Day 1929, the "Fabulous Fox" was hit hard
by the Depression and never turned a decent profit. In 1974, at the same
time it was declared a National Historic Landmark, the Fox Theater was
purchased by Southern Bell, which had plans to replace it with offices.
Fortunately, a nonprofit foundation, Atlanta Landmarks, mobilized pub-

LM 14

lic opinion in the first significant preservation campaign Atlanta had known and raised enough money to purchase the aging facility from Southern Bell. Today, this exceptional witness to the golden age of Hollywood hosts major theatrical and concert performances during the season, while in the summer, as in the good old days, enthralls families with the experience of seeing the Mohler organ rise from the orchestra pit before watching feature movies on the giant screen. Special tours can be arranged through the Atlanta Preservation Center.

LM 16

LM 16 **Georgian Terrace Apartments (Georgian Terrace Hotel)**
659 Peachtree Street, N.E.
1911: William L. Stoddart, Architect (New York); NR, LB. Adaptive
Reuse and Addition 1991: Smallwood, Reynolds, Stewart, Stewart and
Associates, Architects

LM 17 **Days Inn Hotel—Peachtree (Cox-Carlton Hotel)**
683 Peachtree Street, N.E.
1925: Pringle and Smith, Architects

At the time of its construction, the Georgian Terrace Hotel was often
referred to as the "Southern version of a Parisian hotel." Selected to
house the guests at the world premiere of *Gone with the Wind* in 1939,
it remained for many years the most luxurious tourist accommodation in
Atlanta. Although less flamboyant, the neoclassical ornamentation of this
ten-story buff structure anticipates the decor of the neighboring Ponce de
Leon Apartments (LM 13), which was built by the same New York–based
architect and contracting firm two years later. After changing ownership
in 1964 the hotel began a steady decline and eventually closed in 1981.

Plagued by fires set by vagrants, the structure was rescued by local developer Frank Howington, in a joint venture with a Japanese concern, and given new life as the **Georgian Terrace Apartments**. Their project for a residential, entertainment, and commercial complex includes the construction of an eighteen-story annex of similar architectural style. In the same block of Peachtree Street, the twelve-story structure currently known as the **Days Inn Hotel—Peachtree** was originally built as a bachelor apartment hotel and features classical stone accents on a formal facade.

LM 18

LM 18 **Saint Mark United Methodist Church**
781 Peachtree Street, N.E.
1903: Willis F. Denny, Architect; NR, LB. Chapel 1945: Lewis E. Crook Jr., Architect

LM 19 **First Baptist Church**
754 Peachtree Street, N.E.
1929: Stevens and Wilkinson, Architects

LM 20 **Evangelical Lutheran Church of the Redeemer**
731 Peachtree Street, N.E.
1952: Harold A. Wagoner, Architect (Philadelphia)

An interesting concentration of churches along this section of Peachtree Street bears witness to three different periods of church construction. The oldest, the neo-Gothic **Saint Mark United Methodist Church,** has an asymmetrical massing characteristic of the Victorian age: a gabled central section is framed by a high square bell tower and a modest polygonal-shaped turret (the portion on the right end of the Peachtree Street elevation is a more recent addition). The unusual tautness of the general proportions and of the lancet arched openings (notice the spectacular window dominating the large central bay) counterbalance the massive aspect of the coarse Stone Mountain granite ashlar walls articulated by buttresses. On the north and south facades twelve pictorial stained-glass windows of exceptional coloristic quality by the Franz Mayer Studios in Munich were installed between 1909 and 1959. The monumental neo-Georgian **First Baptist Church,** of brick with stone accents, combines a multi-storied steeple and a colossal Ionic portico in a way popularized by eighteenth-century English architect James Gibbs. On the central pediment nicely crafted motifs include a swag framing a medallion engraved with the date of the church's dedication. The church and its extensive grounds have been sold recently to a private developer. The congregation will move to the suburbs, and the future of this pleasant addition to the streetscape is uncertain. Across the street, the elegant setback facade of the **Evangelical Lutheran Church of the Redeemer** is nicely poised above Peachtree Street and framed by greenery. The 1950s church exemplifies the last "Deco" phase of the Gothic Revival (in the spirit of Bertram Grosvenor Goodhue), hence the abstracted and sparse medieval decorative elements in smooth stone contrasting with the rough-hewn, coursed stone of the massive towering walls.

LM 21

LM 21 Crum and Foster Building

771 Spring Street, N.W.
1927: Helmle, Corbett and Harrison, Architects (New York); Ivey and Crook, Associate Architects; NR

Designed by a noted New York firm (which a few years later would participate in the design of Rockefeller Center), the Crum and Foster Building housed one of the first regional headquarters for a nationwide insurance company. The building is said to be the exact duplicate of another building by the same architectural firm in Freeport, Illinois. Its simple mass, low-pitched tile-covered roof, understated upper floor, and arcaded entrance (notice that the Tuscan columns have been omitted on both sides) are reminiscent of Florentine architecture of the early Renaissance. The use of brick with limestone accents, however, is not Italianate but neo-Georgian in spirit (probably an attempt to match neighboring commercial buildings and the Georgian Terrace Apartments [LM 16]). The overall impression is that of stability, fitting with the image of an insurance company. Subsequent tenants, including a law firm and an architectural engineering firm, have benefited from this image as well.

LM 22

LM 22   **Biltmore Hotel**
817 West Peachtree Street, N.E.
1924: Shultze and Weaver, Architects (New York); Leonard Shultze, Designer; NR, LB

LM 23   **Biltmore Inn (Biltmore Apartments)**
30 Fifth Street, N.E.
1924: Shultze and Weaver, Architects (New York); NR, LB. Renovation 1985: Richard Rothman and Associates, Architects

At a time when the travel industry was booming, Asa Candler's son William hired Leonard Shultze—the architect who had designed the Los Angeles Biltmore—to design Atlanta's **Biltmore Hotel** in a prestigious residential district. The narrow, elongated eleven-story structure and its independent luxury apartment tower, the **Biltmore Inn,** framed a southern-style garden and a terrace capable of accommodating six hundred guests for dinner or tea. Later additions greatly reduced the size and charm of this space. The reinforced concrete structure exhibits a facing in red tapestry brick with stone accents in the neo-Georgian style ("a type of architecture characteristic of the feelings and traditions of the

South," according to *American Architect* of August 27, 1924). Of special interest are the pedimented arched windows framed by paired pilasters on the top floor, the corner pilasters, the broken scroll pediments surmounting the windows, and the two-story porticoes supported by paired Corinthian columns at the front and rear entrances. The Biltmore Hotel was renovated in 1969 by the Sheraton chain, but closed its doors again in 1982. As of this writing, the renovated apartment wing, to which a two-story penthouse has been added, is back in operation, and the hotel has been purchased by Swedish developer G. Lars Gullstedt. His recently published proposal, for what will be called GLG Park Plaza, will entail the complete renovation of the building into a five-hundred-room luxury hotel with all grand interior spaces faithfully restored to their original condition. A new wing will be added to complete the symmetry suggested by the present Biltmore Inn and all structures between the hotel and Peachtree Street will be demolished to create a grand park as a formal gateway. The architectural firm of Rabun Hatch and Associates is scheduled to design the multi-use project.

LM 24

LM 24 **Hotel Peachtree Manor (696 Peachtree Apartments)**
826 Peachtree Street, N.E.
1922: Hentz, Reid and Adler, Architects; Philip Shutze, Designer.
Restoration 1986: Richard Rothman and Associates, Architects

Designed as a fifty-unit apartment building (its original name dates from before the renumbering of Peachtree Street), the five-story Hotel Peachtree Manor was converted from apartments in 1947. On the Peachtree Street facade, limestone ornaments focus on the slightly projecting central portion: a two-story arched entrance surrounded by heavy rustication incorporates a pedimented opening at its top; swags of fruit and flowers decorate the upper stairway window. The vertical thrust of this pedimented portion is counterbalanced by the stringcourse between the second and third floors and dentiled band at the top. The 1986 restoration was never completely finished and the building remains vacant as of this writing.

LM 25

LM 25 **Shellmont Bed and Breakfast Lodge (William P. Nicolson House)**
821 Piedmont Avenue, N.E.
1892: Walter T. Downing, Architect; NR, LB. Adaptive Reuse 1984:
Vintage House Restorations; Edward and Debra McCord, Designers;
UDC Award

LM 26 **Howard Johnson Hotel—Atlanta/Midtown (Atlanta Cabana Hotel)**
870 Peachtree Street, N.E.
Circa 1960: Architect Unknown

The **Shellmont Bed and Breakfast Lodge** is one of the few remaining examples of Walter Downing's eclectic residential practice. The asymmetrical front facade, clad in clapboard as well as board-and-batten siding, and the presence of many different types of openings are typically Victorian and reflect the complexity of the interior layout. Inspired by Renaissance and classical motifs, the delicate ornamentation (notice the coupled Corinthian columns that support the porch, the thin banisters, as well as the swag and shell motif on the second floor of the projecting wing) deviates dramatically from the heavy-handed Queen Anne decor that was fashionable in the previous decade. The **Howard John-**

son Hotel—Atlanta/Midtown, with a zigzag carport and glazed street facade, brings a little of the glitzy kitsch of Las Vegas and Miami to Atlanta. Nothing to complain about, the diversity in use and style among structures lining Peachtree Street in Lower Midtown contributes to some of the charm of this artery, a characteristic worth preserving in itself.

LM 27 **Academy of Medicine**
875 West Peachtree Street, N.E.
1940: Shutze and Armistead, Architects; Philip Shutze, Designer; R. Kennon Perry, Project Architect; NR, LB. Restoration and Interior Remodeling 1983: Surber, Barber and Mooney, Architects; Main Floor Interiors, Jova/Daniels/Busby, Architects; UDC, GAAIA Awards

The commission for a meeting place, library, and training center for Atlanta-area physicians was first entrusted to Atlanta-based architect R. Kennon Perry. After Philip Shutze was hired as designer, Perry remained responsible for the working drawings and field inspection. Shutze claimed he was inspired by the Medical College of Georgia in Augusta (circa 1835) for the proportions of the central pedimented portico. However, the overall design of the Academy of Medicine, with its unfluted Doric columns and engaged pilasters, smooth light-colored stucco surfaces, slightly recessed arched windows, and beautiful details including the wrought-iron balcony on the Seventh Street entrance, seems closer in spirit to the work of the English architect John Soane (1753–1837) and of his disciple, Philadelphia-based Benjamin Latrobe. The motif of the colonnade topped by the low square tower with large

LM 27

coffered lunette windows can also be found in Russian neoclassical buildings. The tower mantles a formal entrance sheltering a chandelier used in the movie *Gone with the Wind*; serpent-entwined caducei ornament the pendentives of its interior cupola. On axis is an oval-shaped auditorium decorated in the same severe but elegant Grecian manner. In 1979 the Academy of Medicine was added to the National Register. This recognition, which came well before the minimum fifty years, allowed for the much-needed restoration of this fascinating structure. The Medical Association of Atlanta now holds office space on the lower floor, while the restored reception rooms and auditorium, in hues much brighter than the original paint, are made available for community use.

LM 28

LM 28 **Palmer House**
81 Peachtree Place, N.E.
1912: Architect Unknown

LM 29 **Phelan Apartments**
93 Peachtree Place, N.E.
1915: Hentz and Reid, Architects

Featuring spacious apartment units, these two structures recall an upper-class clientele living in turn-of-the-century Midtown. The **Palmer House** has a composite street facade in rough-hewn brick, embellished by stone accents on the upper floors. The archway, gables, and high chimney stacks are reminiscent of the "Jacobethan Revival" style, while the Ionic frieze and columns of the recessed doorway demonstrate classical details. The ornamentation of the adjacent **Phelan Apartments,** more restrained and unified, focuses on the doorways. Philip Shutze, an instructor at Georgia Tech and a part-time employee in Reid's office at the time, designed the ornate pediments broken by a cascading garland on the Peachtree Place entrance.

Area 7

Upper Midtown (UM)

Any visitor to the High Museum of Art (UM 20) should take the time to view firsthand this fast-developing district, which until the 1960s was often referred to as "uptown." Highly visible from Piedmont Park (AP 13), the dense skyline continues that of Downtown. New construction stemmed from the intersection of Peachtree and Fifteenth streets with the erection of the Robert W. Woodruff Arts Center (UM 19) in the late 1960s and Colony Square (UM 9) in the late 1970s, and expanded to the northern and later southern portions of Peachtree Street. In the 1980s, landmarks by renowned designers Richard Meier and Philip Johnson set the tone. Since then the overall architectural quality of buildings in this area has exceeded the average for Atlanta. Upper Midtown is remarkable for its mix of activities, something almost unheard of in Atlanta. The area hosts cultural institutions and corporations, as well as residential units—old and new, single-family homes and apartment buildings. Still, with the exception of the portion of Peachtree Street between Fourteenth Street and Pershing Point, a real feeling of "urbanity" has not yet been achieved. One witnesses a strange cross-section of urban and suburban cultures: for instance, each new office tower tends to be an isolated and heroic statement with its own piazza, sidewalk treatment, and street lamps rather than a contribution to some cohesive whole.

Area 7

Upper Midtown (UM)

1 Spring Hill Mortuary
2 Ten Peachtree Place
3 First Union Plaza
4 New Visions Gallery
5 Windsor House Apartments
6 Atlanta Woman's Club
7 Campanile
8 Eleven Hundred Peachtree Street Building
9 Colony Square
10 Mayfair
11 GLG Grand
12 One Atlantic Center
13 The Granada All Suite Hotel
14 The Castle
15 Promenade Two
16 Promenade One
17 First Church of Christ, Scientist
18 1275 Peachtree at the Circle
19 Robert W. Woodruff Arts Center
20 High Museum of Art
21 First Presbyterian Church
22 1315 Peachtree Building
23 Reid House
24 The Peachtree
25 Nix, Mann and Associates Office
26 NSI Center
27 Federal Home Loan Bank of Atlanta Building
28 Rhodes Hall
29 The Temple
30 Peachtree Christian Church
31 Brookwood Station

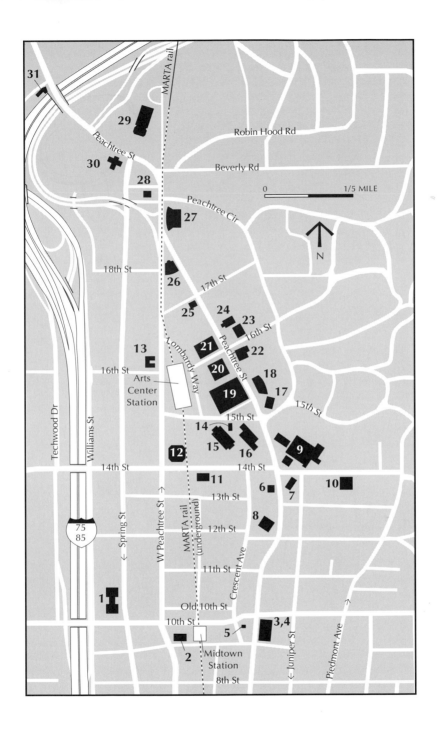

MARTA rail

31

29

Peachtree St

Robin Hood Rd

30

Beverly Rd

28

0   1/5 MILE

Peachtree Cir

27

N

18th St

26

17th St

25   24   23

16th St

21   22

13

Lombardy Way

Peachtree St

16th St

Arts
Center
Station

20

18

19   17

Techwood Dr

Williams St

15th St

15th St

14   15th St

12   15   16   9

14th St

14th St

Spring St

W Peachtree St →

MARTA rail (underground)

11   13th St

6   7   10

12th St

8

11th St

75
85

Crescent Ave

1

Old 10th St

10th St

5   3,4

2   Midtown
Station

Juniper St

Piedmont Ave

8th St

113   **Upper Midtown**

UM 1 **Spring Hill Mortuary**
1020 Spring Street, N.W.
1928: Hentz, Adler and Shutze, Architects; Philip Shutze, Designer

Spring Hill Mortuary, with its bow windows, gables, and high chimney
stacks, looks like one of the English manor houses typically perched
above a Buckhead residential road. According to architectural historian
Elizabeth Dowling, "Shutze specified an inexpensive grade of paint to
provide a thin white wash of white over the brick walls with the desire it
would rapidly disappear and produce an impression of age by its subtle
patina" (*American Classicist*, p. 143). The all-white principal chapel is
notable for its delicate Adamesque stucco work.

UM 2 **Ten Peachtree Place**
10 Peachtree Place, N.E.
1990: Michael Graves, Architect (Princeton, New Jersey)

Designed as part of L. J. Hooker's defunct Gateway Atlanta development,
Michael Graves's Ten Peachtree Place is less spectacular and more
severe than his well-known skyscrapers of Portland and Louisville. Still

the twenty-story speculative office building has a kind of awe-inspiring Egyptian look that is unmistakably Gravesian. Although he adopted a flat roofline, the architect emphasized the tripartite composition. The multi-story base is crowned on the street elevations with a deep arch. On the shaft, the horizontals of uniform dark glass and the red granite facade are enlivened by vertical projections. A thick overhanging cornice terminates the design. Preceded by a covered arcade, the lobby features a marble-clad rotunda leading to a grand staircase.

UM 2

UM 3 **First Union Plaza (999 Peachtree Building)**
999 Peachtree Street, N.E.
1987: Heery Architects and Engineers; John Cheek, Project Architect;
UDC Award

UM 4 **New Visions Gallery**
999 Peachtree Street, N.E., Ground Floor
1987: Scogin, Elam and Bray, Architects; GAAIA Award

UM 5 **Windsor House Apartments**
979 Crescent Avenue, N.E.
Circa 1900: Architect Unknown; LB

First Union Plaza is the major element of the planned five-block Peachtree Place development. This twenty-eight-story office tower, with its
arcaded commercial space directly connected to a repaved sidewalk on

Peachtree Street and landscaped plaza at the corner of Peachtree and Tenth streets, restores a feeling of urbanity to this part of Midtown. It attempts also to recreate the glamour of Art Deco skyscrapers, with its travertine marble veneer, setback silhouette reminiscent of the Empire State Building, and flattened top adorned with stone globes, as well as its monumental lobby (notice the light fixtures and elevator cabins). Do not miss the canopied deconstructionist entry to **New Visions Gallery** on the ground floor. Across Peachtree Street stands the **Windsor House Apartments**. Had this not been the place where *Gone with the Wind* was written, it would have been demolished long ago. Referred to by Margaret Mitchell herself as "the dump," the structure is deteriorating fast, but because of its assumed significance as a cultural artifact it remains the object of a preservation battle.

UM 6

UM 6 Atlanta Woman's Club (Wimbish House)
1150 Peachtree Street, N.E.
1898: Walter T. Downing, Architect; NR. Banquet Hall 1921, Peachtree Playhouse 1922: Marye and Alger, Architects. Remodeling (Petrus Restaurant) 1989: Peter Leonard, Architect

Damaged by fire in 1990 and now in need of renovation, the Atlanta Woman's Club is nevertheless one of the very few mansions still standing on Peachtree Street. Since 1919 it has served as the headquarters of the Atlanta Woman's Club, a group founded in 1895. For a residence of the Victorian era, the facade on Peachtree Street is unusually symmetrical. Its uniform and smooth stone veneer, picturesque high-pitched roofs and turret, and mullioned dormers recall images of Loire Valley chateaux, in particular Azay-le-Rideau (1518–27). In 1921 on the west side of the property P. Thornton Marye and Barrett Alger added a nonintruding banquet hall, with exterior detailing inspired by the Petit Trianon in Versailles (1761–68). An auditorium, the Peachtree Playhouse, was opened the following year. These two additions are currently occupied by Petrus, a posh restaurant and nightclub.

UM 8, *left;* UM 9, *center;* UM 7, *right*

UM 7 **Campanile**
1155 Peachtree Street, N.E.
1987: Thompson, Ventulett, Stainback and Associates, Architects

UM 8 **Eleven Hundred Peachtree Street Building**
1100 Peachtree Street, N.E.
1990: Smallwood, Reynolds, Stewart, Stewart and Associates, Architects; UDC Award

The nearby Atlanta Woman's Club (UM 6) is dwarfed by two recently completed office towers in the postmodern idiom. The forty-five degree rotation of the ground-floor plan aligns the twenty-story **Campanile** with its neighbors at the intersection of Peachtree and Fourteenth streets, allowing for the creation of an elaborate two-sided plaza. The **Eleven Hundred Peachtree Street Building** also rotates its shaft but keeps grade level construction oriented to the street grid.

UM 9   **Colony Square**
1175 and 1201 Peachtree Street, N.E.
1969, 1975: Jova/Daniel/Busby, Architects; SARC, GAAIA Awards.
Interior Remodeling 1978, 1986: Thompson, Ventulett, Stainback and
Associates, Architects

UM 10   **Mayfair**
199 Fourteenth Street, N.E.
1990: Smallwood, Reynolds, Stewart, Stewart and Associates, Architects

Colony Square was the first multi-use development in the South. A five-hundred-room hotel and two office towers are directly connected to a skylit atrium. At the rear are three midrise residential buildings of compatible design; they take their slab-like configuration, concrete facade treatment, and (for a number of units) two-story layouts from Le Corbusier's Unités d'Habitation in Europe. Several floors have no central corridors, allowing multi-level units to have both east and west exterior exposures. While the same basic materials and colors have been used for the exterior of all buildings, the width of openings differentiates their functions. Provisions for underground parking create an automobile-free environment with carefully landscaped pedestrian terraces. The entertainment component of Colony Square is the only element of the original conception that failed. In 1978 the ice rink in the atrium was replaced by a food court surrounded by shops (including the AIA's Architectural Book Center). The lobbies of both office buildings were remodeled with neo–Art Deco marble square columns and torchères to offset the severity of the original design, which met the design expectations for office buildings of the early 1970s but was too austere for corporate tastes of the late 1980s. Across Fourteenth Street, the prominent **Mayfair** residential tower, with its four high-pitched turrets, stands in marked contrast to its antecedent of twenty years. A second tower of the same eclectic type is planned for this site.

UM 11   **GLG Grand**
75 Fourteenth Street, N.E.
1992: Rabun Hatch and Associates, Architects

Developed by G. Lars Gullstedt, the multi-use GLG Grand is a dramatic
presence in the midtown skyline. The stately skyscraper rises fifty stories
in a traditional tripartite composition, its vertical shaft interrupted by
horizontal banding and terraces at various levels, reminiscent of New
York's Chrysler and Empire State buildings. Unlike those office buildings,
the GLG Grand will house a hotel on its first nineteen floors, offices on
the next five, and apartments on the top twenty-six. Clad in red granite
and precast panels highlighted with bronze accents, the project main-
tains Midtown's reputation for attracting premier development.

UM 12, *foreground;* UM 3, *background*

UM 12 One Atlantic Center (IBM Tower)

1201 West Peachtree Street, N.E.
1987: John Burgee Architects with Philip Johnson, Architects; Heery
Architects and Engineers, Associated Architects; Zion and Breen,
Landscape Architects; UDC Award

One Atlantic Center, a slender fifty-story skyscraper known to Atlantans as the IBM Tower because of its prime tenant, serves as an anchor
to the fast-changing Upper Midtown skyline, as well as a campanile
visible from many parts of the city. Undoubtedly, it is the handsomest
of all revivalist skyscrapers devised by Philip Johnson and John Burgee. These architects, well known for their precedent-setting AT&T
Building in Manhattan, have superimposed a copper pyramid roof—
inspired by the steeple of H. H. Richardson's Trinity Church in Boston
(1877)—on a square shaft in pink granite, the proportions of which have
been borrowed from Raymond Hood and John Mead Howells's Chicago Tribune Tower (1922). Simplified and magnified gothic ornaments
(which are also used in the parking lot across West Peachtree Street) are
concentrated on the entrance level and the roof and echo those of the

Healey Building (FP 8) and Atlanta City Hall (DS 10) downtown. The same yearning for restrained monumentality has dictated the systematic grouping of three floors under what appears to be the same stone window frame and the interior design of the lobby. At night, the finials that terminate the shaft, the pyramid top with its gilded crockets and neo-colonial lantern are transfigured by glamorous lighting, and the romance of early twentieth century Manhattan is resurrected in the Atlanta sky-line. Breaking the tradition of sleek modernist skyscrapers, One Atlantic Center has been well received by the general public and architectural critics as well. According to Paul Goldberger, the tower "strikes an ideal balance between delicacy and strength. . . . If it teaches us anything, it is that proportion and scale are more important than style" (*New York Times*, May 8, 1988).

UM 13

UM 13   The Granada All Suite Hotel (Granada Apartments)
1302 West Peachtree Street, N.W.
1924: Barney Havis, Augustus Constantine, Architects. Renovation
1986: Stang and Newdow, Architects; UDC Award

This beautifully restored three-story Spanish Colonial "garden apart-ment," now functioning as the Granada All Suite Hotel, conveys a Mediterranean feeling with its arched entry porch, walls of pink swirled stucco, roofs topped by red tiles with elaborate parapets, and planted courtyard featuring a "bird bath" fountain.

UM 14, *foreground;* UM 16, *background*

UM 14 **The Castle**
87 Fifteenth Street, N.E.
1910: Ferdinand McMillan, Builder; HB. Renovation and Addition
1990: Surber and Barber, Architects; UDC Award

Dwarfed by its neighbors and perched on a forbidding base of Stone
Mountain granite, the Castle is an odd survivor of a bygone era. Considered by some to be a "hunk of junk," it remained vacant and dilapidated
for many years. Because of the efforts of preservationists, it was miraculously saved from demolition. This picturesque and eclectic home was
the creation of its eccentric owner-builder, Ferdinand McMillan. His
whimsical and eccentric personality is reflected in the assemblage of
mismatched features, such as the slender Corinthian columns and brick
pillars supporting the porch, the fish-scale shingles and carved joists
gracing the front and side gables, and the Chinese-looking turret. The
interior features paintings of fairy-tale characters and large fireplaces.

Promenade Two

1230 Peachtree Street, N.E.

1990: Thompson, Ventulett, Stainback and Associates, Architects; Ray
Hoover, Partner-in-Charge; SWA Group, Landscape Architects;
UDC Award

The thirty-eight-story, 900,000-square-foot Promenade Two is the first
element of a mixed-use development on twelve acres, set between
Fourteenth and Fifteenth streets and incorporating in its master plan the
earlier AT&T Southern Region Headquarters, now Promenade One (UM
16). To achieve a successful interaction with its neighbor, the popular One Atlantic Center (UM 12), the Art Deco inspired Promenade
Two tower has an Adoni granite base and is sheathed in rose-colored
glass. The scheme originally proposed, which called for a much smaller
amount of stone and a green glass curtain wall, was recalled by the
client along with the original design for the top, which now features a
spectacular setback pyramid crowned by an elaborate grey steel spire.

Notice the Mayan inspiration for the tall gallery leading to the upper entrance across Fifteenth Street from the Woodruff Arts Center (UM 19). Two other towers—of forty-eight and fifty-eight stories—based on the same model as Promenade Two, a hotel, a conference center, and a performing arts theater are planned for the site and will be organized around a water garden.

UM 16

UM 16 **Promenade One (AT&T Communications, Southern Regional Headquarters)**
1200 Peachtree Street, N.E.
1981: Thompson, Ventulett, Stainback and Associates, Architects; UDC, GAAIA Awards

The midrise Promenade One consolidates multiple corporate functions into a single building and provides offices and open-plan work areas for approximately fourteen hundred persons. The long slab is divided into halves, offset from one another in order to maximize the available natural light. Walls are in cast-in-place textured concrete, with large expanses of glass sheltering the hallway and collective areas that face Peachtree Street. The marked horizontals of the ribbon windows are stabilized by the vertical thrust of taut circular columns at the three-story base. On the southern and western facades, energy conservation measures include windows recessed behind sun shades and reduced glass surfaces.

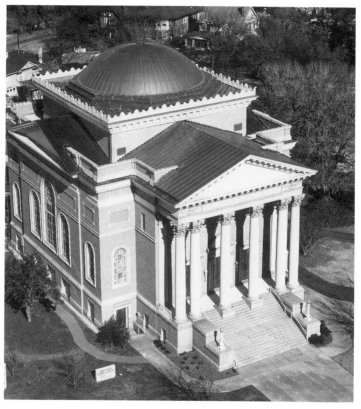

UM 17

UM 17 **First Church of Christ, Scientist**
1235 Peachtree Street, N.E.
1914: Edward Dougherty and Arthur Neal Robinson, Architects (Nashville); NR. Restoration 1985: Henry Howard Smith, Architect

UM 18 **1275 Peachtree at the Circle**
1275 Peachtree Street, N.E.
1984: Thompson, Ventulett, Stainback and Associates, Architects; UDC Award

Designed by Edward Dougherty, a former student of the Paris Ecole des Beaux-Arts, the **First Church of Christ, Scientist** serves now as a transition between the monumental scale of the Robert W. Woodruff Arts

126   **Upper Midtown**

Center (UM 19), the Promenade complex (UM 15 and 16), and Colony Square (UM 9) and the residential scale of Ansley Park. In such a conspicuous location, its elegantly proportioned square mass and the striking contrast between the copper dome and the walls of cream-colored textured brick and terra-cotta make this centrally planned structure a perfectly suited urban marker. Set on a high base, the entrance facade is angled rather than "squared" on either Peachtree or Fifteenth street (setting the precedent for this entire area), and the pedimented Corinthian portico masterfully addresses the intersection. In addition to the traditional classical motifs, treated here in high relief, the visitor will notice the elegant detailing of the brickwork and the delicate wave pattern gracing the band running two-thirds of the height. For a view of the classically designed interior, visitors should inquire at the reading room next door. The thoughtful entrance portico of **1275 Peachtree at the Circle,** a seven-story office building of concrete and reflective glass, is angled in such a way that it both echoes the church entrance and respects the urban continuum on Peachtree Street.

UM 19

UM 19   **Robert W. Woodruff Arts Center (Atlanta Memorial Arts Building)**
1280 Peachtree Street, N.E.
1968: Toombs, Amisiano and Wells, Architects; Stevens and Wilkinson, Associated Architects. Interior Renovation 1984: Stevens and Wilkinson, Architects

Dedicated to the memory of local art patrons who died in a 1962 plane crash in Paris, the Robert W. Woodruff Arts Center is a cultural megastructure of 230 by 300 feet. The Center includes an art school, a 1700-seat concert hall, a smaller repertory theater, a three-story transverse foyer, and an experimental theater located at the same level as the underground parking deck. The structure incorporates space that once housed the collection of the High Museum of Art (UM 20). This somewhat forbidding white concrete block is surrounded by a nonstructural peristyle of precast members which defines an uncovered promenade. The design of the building is more successful as a monument to civic pride than as an expression of the building's functional requirements. In order to provide a more recognizable image for the Woodruff Arts Center, a marquee was subsequently added to the Peachtree Street entrance.

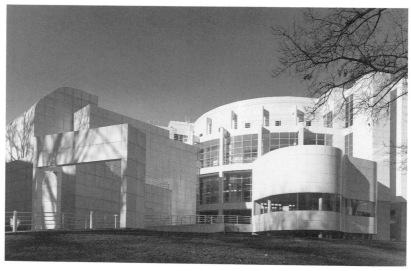

UM 20

UM 20　**High Museum of Art**
1280 Peachtree Street, N.E.
1983: Richard Meier, Architect (New York); UDC, AIA Awards

UM 21　**First Presbyterian Church**
1328 Peachtree Street, N.E.
1919: Walter T. Downing, Architect

UM 22　**1315 Peachtree Building**
1315 Peachtree Street, N.E.
1988: Thompson, Ventulett, Stainback and Associates, Architects; GAAIA Award

Established in 1926, the **High Museum of Art** owes its name to the donor of the house in which it originated, Harriett High. A major challenge grant from Robert W. Woodruff initiated a new building campaign, which resulted in one of Richard Meier's most discussed works and Atlanta's best-known landmark of the 1980s. Beautifully located at the corner of Sixteenth and Peachtree streets, the High Museum of Art is very successful as an urban artifact, which wisely keeps its distance from the overpowering mass of the Woodruff Arts Center (UM 19). With its distinctive cladding of square white panels in porcelain-enameled steel and its neo-Corbusian detailing, it is a pristine and quite surreal object, following Meier's characteristic manner of combining abstract forms. Visitors experience a carefully orchestrated "architectural promenade." From Peachtree Street they climb an oblique ramp, enter a piano-curved reception area where they can enjoy beautiful outside views from its ribbon window, penetrate into the brightly lit atrium (a spectacular setting for parties), and proceed through the upstairs exhibition spaces by way of a narrow curvilinear ramp. Meier's parti is not without problems: it feels uneasy to land on alternate sides of the L-shaped exhibition spaces; after a while, the empty atrium and stark ramps, which offer relatively few views of the collections, become obsessive; though straightforward and practical, the museography remains traditional. Like its most famous precedent, Frank Lloyd Wright's Guggenheim Museum in New York, and in fact like many contemporary museum designs, the High Museum of Art places more emphasis on the circulation of visitors than on their experiencing the works of art. With this building, Atlanta may not have found an ideal showcase for art, but certainly an impressive monument for its emerging visual culture. Across Sixteenth Street, the **First Presbyterian Church** is a fine neo-Gothic structure, which features stained-glass windows by the Tiffany Studio of New York and the D'Ascenzo Studios of Philadelphia. Across Peachtree Street, the **1315 Peachtree Building** integrates a branch of the Atlanta–Fulton County Library System with a speculative office building using an exposed concrete structural system.

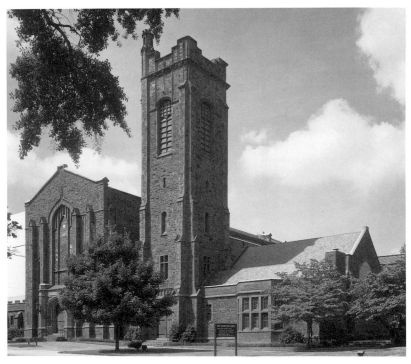

UM 21

UM 23   Reid House (Garrison Apartments)

1325 and 1327 Peachtree Street, N.E.
1924: Hentz, Adler and Shutze, Architects; Hal Hentz and Philip
Shutze, Designers. Remodeling 1975: Eugene E. Lowry, Architect;
UDC Award

According to architectural historian Elizabeth Dowling, Reid House, a
luxury apartment building in the neo-Georgian style, was designed by
Hal Hentz and Philip Shutze, who were responsible for the plan and
the facade respectively (*American Classicist*, p. 78). Shutze brilliantly
met the challenge of minimizing the height and bulk of the building and
alleviating the monotony created by evenly spaced sash windows and
large expanses of red brick. Stone quoins divide the Peachtree Street
facade into five vertical parts, the larger central bay crowned by a raised
pediment. Stringcourses and a dentiled beltcourse generate horizontal
rhythms. On the third and fourth floors, bow windows provide the illusion of a stone base. Notice the delicacy of the Roman-inspired medallion and bull's-skull motifs on the pediment, the wrought-iron arches,
and the lanterns framing the doorways. Reid House was converted into
condominiums in the mid-1970s. Apartments were modernized and
enlarged by adding garden rooms and solaria to the unadorned back of
the building.

UM 24 **The Peachtree**
1355 Peachtree Street, N.E.
1989: Smallwood, Reynolds, Stewart, Stewart and Associates, Architects

UM 25 **Nix, Mann and Associates Office (Mitchell King House)**
1382 Peachtree Street, N.E.
1912: Architect Unknown. Renovation 1982: Nix, Mann and
Associates, Architects; UDC Award

UM 26 **NSI Center (National Service Industries Headquarters Building)**
1420 Peachtree Street, N.E.
1989: Cooper Carry and Associates, Architects; Roger Miller, Lead
Designer

UM 27 **Federal Home Loan Bank of Atlanta Building (Lincoln Pershing Building)**
1475 Peachtree Street, N.E.
1984–1986: Smallwood, Reynolds, Stewart, Stewart and Associates,
Architects

UM 25

The brick and concrete **Peachtree,** an office condominium, was designed in the Georgian style in an attempt to be contextual with the
nearby Reid House (UM 23). The **Mitchell King House,** now the offices
of the architectural firm Nix, Mann and Associates, is the only single-
family structure remaining in this corporate portion of Peachtree Street.

Farther north, where West Peachtree and Peachtree streets meet, Pershing Point has been a focus for office development in recent years. A thirty-five-story tower is planned at the back of triangular-shaped **NSI Center,** a building restrained in size and design in order to avoid overpowering the tiny park it overlooks. Across Peachtree Street, the **Federal Home Loan Bank of Atlanta Building** conceals its bulk behind a gently curving facade that addresses the curvature of the street.

UM 28

UM 28 **Rhodes Hall**
1516 Peachtree Street, N.W.
1904: Willis F. Denny, Architect; NR, LB

Amos Giles Rhodes (1850–1928), a wealthy furniture dealer who successfully ventured in real estate, spared no expense to build his dream house on what was then a 150-acre site. Built entirely of rough-hewn Stone Mountain granite, Rhodes Hall is often said to be modeled after the romantic castles of the Rhineland. The picturesque assemblage of an arcaded portico, castellated porte cochere, four-story square tower, and turret with a high-pitched roof characterizes the irregular massing of Victorian mansions. The most prominent feature, the curving staircase, which had been removed to the Georgia Department of Archives and History Building (SE 11), has been returned to the house. Rhodes Hall was deeded to the State of Georgia in 1929 and now serves as headquarters for the Georgia Trust for Historic Preservation.

UM 29 **The Temple**
1589 Peachtree Street, N.E.
1920: Hentz, Reid and Adler, Architects; Philip Shutze, Designer;
NR, LB

UM 30 **Peachtree Christian Church**
1580 Peachtree Street, N.W.
1925: Charles H. Hopson, Architect; LB

Dominating a curve in Peachtree Street, the **Temple** is a severe, square building, crowned by a dome resting on a drum, in red brick with classical stone accents. By adopting for its synagogue an American neo-Georgian style (a mainstream idiom for Atlanta churches in the 1920s), the Hebrew Benevolent Congregation chose to blend in rather than reflect its own historical precedents. The templelike front has four engaged Ionic columns supporting an unadorned pediment. The central projecting semicircular porch, adapted from Bernini's Sant'Andrea al Quirinale in Rome (1658–70), is the only reminder of Shutze's first design for the Temple, which was thoroughly Italian Baroque. In a fashion typical of Shutze, ornamentation is concentrated on the central bay, with an entablature carved with Jewish emblems and topped by an elaborate cartouche framing the Tablets of the Law. Notice how, in order to prevent this ornate porch, whose slender Tuscan columns duplicate those supporting the dome, from overpowering the facade, Shutze carved out behind it a lunette of the same diameter. According to architectural historian Elizabeth Dowling, "the original design called for a staircase of increasing width as one approached from the street," which would have made the Temple's presence on Peachtree even more predominant (*American Classicist*, p. 127). The pristine white interior follows the description of the plan of Solomon's temple in Jerusalem, with delicate plaster ornamentation of both Hebraic and classical origin applied to the vaults. At the back are a school and offices, also by Shutze. Across Peachtree Street, the taut brick and stone Gothic Revival **Peachtree Christian Church** is said to have been modeled after sixteenth-century Melrose Abbey in England.

UM 31

UM 31 **Brookwood Station (Peachtree Southern Railway Station)**
1688 Peachtree Street, N.W.
1917: Hentz, Reid and Adler, Architects; Neel Reid, Designer; NR

Brookwood Station's well-balanced elevation on Peachtree Street is
characteristic of Neel Reid's classicism. It perfectly matched the stately
atmosphere that reigned in the upper Peachtree residential district at
the time of its construction. With its low-pitched roof and limestone
entablature, this brick building looks like a small Italian casino. Three
elegantly proportioned Palladian openings, framed in limestone, lead to
two waiting rooms, with marble floors and wainscot trim. The benches
and column lamps are original. In 1925, each day 142 passenger trains
passed through what was then a suburban station. Today, only two trains
make that stop, and Brookwood Station is the only remaining railway
station in Atlanta. Originally designed for the downtown Terminal Station, a seated figure of Samuel Spencer (1867–1906), the first president
of the Southern Railway, by the noted sculptor Daniel Chester French,
has been placed in a small garden, where ironically it faces the Interstate
highway.

Area 8

Ansley Park (AP)

Ansley Park, the first automobile-oriented suburb in Atlanta, was developed by Edwin P. Ansley, who entrusted its layout to Solon Z. Ruff, a civil engineer who had worked on the first plans for Druid Hills with Frederick Law Olmsted. The 350-acre site, formerly the George Washington Collier Estate, was developed in four phases between 1904 and 1913. The natural rolling terrain, the presence of mature trees, and the small irregularly shaped parks nestled in the steep unbuildable slopes invite visitors and residents alike on long walking tours. Because of its proximity to Piedmont Park (AP 13) and to Downtown, Ansley Park has remained a desirable residential neighborhood. The Governor's Mansion once stood at 205 The Prado (1924–1967), and single-family homes of different sizes and styles still coexist harmoniously in this National Register neighborhood of some six hundred structures that has brooked very few intrusions.

Area 8

Ansley Park (AP)

1 Frank S. Ellis House
2 David Black House
3 Robert Crumley House
4 174 The Prado
5 Stephen S. Lynch House
6 Frank W. Hulse IV House and Pool Pavilion
7 George Washington Collier House
8 The Villa
9 Garden House, Atlanta Botanical Garden
10 Dorothy Chapman Fuqua Conservatory, Atlanta Botanical Garden
11 Piedmont Driving Club
12 Habersham Memorial Hall
13 Piedmont Park
14 Play Scapes
15 Piedmont Arbors

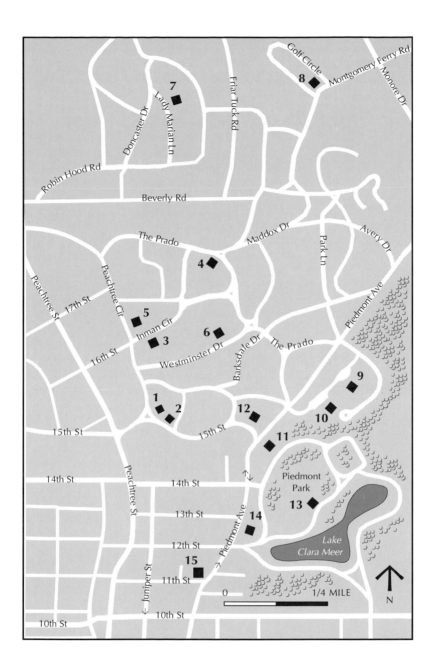

AP 1

AP 1   **Frank S. Ellis House**
       1 Peachtree Circle, N.E.
       Circa 1911: Walter T. Downing, Architect

AP 2   **David Black House**
       186 Fifteenth Street, N.E.
       1921: Hentz, Reid and Adler, Architects; Neel Reid, Designer

AP 3   **Robert Crumley House**
       17 Inman Circle, N.E.
       1917: Hentz, Reid and Adler, Architects; Neel Reid, Designer

AP 4   **174 The Prado**
       174 The Prado, N.E.
       1920: Charles Mion, Builder

AP 5   **Stephen S. Lynch House**
       109 Peachtree Circle, N.E.
       1921: Hentz, Reid and Adler, Architects; Neel Reid, Designer

The **Frank S. Ellis House,** an Italianate villa, serves as the focal point of
the major entrance to Ansley Park at Fifteenth Street. Neo-Georgian and
neo-Tudor homes (see in particular Neel Reid's **David Black House** and
Robert Crumley House); and more modest Craftsman or even Prairie
School bungalows (see **174 The Prado**) are excellent examples of the

diversity in this neighborhood. The most original design is Neel Reid's **Stephen S. Lynch House,** a small yet stately house flanked by flat-roofed pavilions with asymmetrical openings (the white paint on the exterior brick walls is not original).

AP 6 **Frank W. Hulse IV House and Pool Pavilion**
96 Westminster Drive, N.E.
Pool Pavilion 1976, House 1986: Anthony Ames, Architect; Douglas C. Allen, Landscape Architect; UDC, GAAIA Awards

On this prime but relatively narrow property facing intimate Winn Park, Anthony Ames was first asked to design a one-bedroom bachelor home behind an existing 1920s residence. Inspired by the residential works of Le Corbusier and Richard Meier, the pristine structure he designed now serves as a pool pavilion and guest house, which is no longer visible from the street. At the time of the client's marriage, Ames was called upon to design a home on a grand scale, suitable for large parties and a family. This new structure would replace the existing 1920s residence and relate thematically to the pool pavilion, which was to remain. In order to look less obtrusive, the taut street elevation of the Hulse House is painted grey and surmounted by a small gable. The double-story living room is expressed by a large square-mullioned window; on the mezzanine level, a lateral piano-shaped projection houses, appropriately enough, a piano. The master bedroom opens onto a small balcony on

AP 6

the upper floor. Two screens in brick painted white extend to the property limits. Parallel to the street, a wall provides a framed view of the park from the tiled patio. The entrance stair wall becomes, according to architect and critic Thomas Schumacher, "the ghosted party-wall of the semi-detached house, complete with empty window-holes, as if the house had been cleaved from its neighbor and is now awaiting its glazing" (*Five Houses*, p. 13). Both the patio and staircase screens are set at slightly different angles from the street elevation. Inspired by the cubist paintings of Juan Gris, this rotation of axis, one of Ames's favorite devices, is also to be found in the interior planning. The Hulse House is proof that, in the field of residential architecture, a resolutely contemporary style is a viable alternative to the revivalist pastiches that have blossomed in Atlanta.

AP 7

AP 7   **George Washington Collier House**
1649 Lady Marian Lane, N.E.
Begun 1823: Builder Unknown

AP 8   **The Villa (Villa Apartments)**
200 Montgomery Ferry Road, N.E.
1920: Hentz, Reid and Adler, Architects; Philip Shutze, Designer

It is necessary to disregard the nearby ranch houses, with their neatly combed lawns and trimmed hedges, in order to appreciate the simple grandeur of the **George Washington Collier House,** Atlanta's oldest extant residential structure, which was restored and beautified in the 1950s (the shutters and porch balustrade are among added decorative elements). Set high above this suburban-looking street (once an Indian trail), this white clapboard house with end chimneys in masonry and an expansive front porch has for its nucleus the four-room squarish farmhouse (with a detached kitchen) of George Washington Collier, whose estate later became Ansley Park. **The Villa,** Philip Shutze's apartment building now converted to condominiums, first served as guest quarters for visitors to the Ansley Park Golf Club. The Italian villa flavor is enhanced by the plain ocher-colored stucco walls and tall windows with shutters. The ornamentation, unmistakably Shutze's, focuses on the overscaled entrance doorway with its four detached Tuscan columns, its broken pediment framing a large window, and its oculus surrounded by swags enriched by floral motifs.

AP 9 **Garden House, Atlanta Botanical Garden**
1345 Piedmont Avenue, N.E.
1987: Anthony Ames, Architect; Edward L. Daugherty, Landscape Architect

Adjacent to Piedmont Park (AP 13), the Atlanta Botanical Garden was founded in 1976 on land leased from the City of Atlanta. The two-story, 23,000-square-foot Garden House includes a visitor's center, administrative offices, and, at the back, a ballroom/exhibition hall for private parties and horticultural shows. Anthony Ames likes to combine what he calls "pre-Modern paradigms" (in this case the Villa Giulia in Rome, 1555) with the architectonic imagery of the Machine Age (the Garden House detailing is uncompromisingly modern). The interior courtyard features a one-story colonnade, as well as an Italian-inspired fountain

AP 9

with shrubbery on the blind end wall. A slight rotation of the vertical circulation, emphasized by the paving strip originating at the main entrance, acts as a dynamic counterpoint to the symmetrical layout. The Garden House was originally designed in glazed white brick, but the client regarded the earth tones of unglazed clay brick to be more suitably "southern." Ames's plan for an accompanying formal garden was not executed, but the grounds feature numerous walking paths through the informal gardens and a hardwood forest. Call the Atlanta Botanical Garden for information on hours, admission fees, and special seasonal events.

AP 10

AP 10   **Dorothy Chapman Fuqua Conservatory, Atlanta Botanical Garden**
1345 Piedmont Avenue, N.E.
1989: Heery Architects and Engineers, Architects

Dominated by a cylindrical greenhouse, the unusual design of the Dorothy Chapman Fuqua Conservatory was conceived as a showcase for tropical, desert, and endangered plants from around the world. The 16,000-square-foot facility looks truly monumental. Its architects were inspired by two precedents: the classical garden pavilion and the Victorian greenhouse. The materials—pink precast concrete and large glass planes with aluminum mullions—are uncommon for this type of facility and convey a greater sense of permanence. The offset entrance portico surmounted by a lunette and the coupled vertical supports topped by roundels allude to neoclassical examples. From its commanding position above Piedmont Park (AP 13), the Fuqua Conservatory's overlook area above the rotunda provides a magnificent view of the downtown skyline.

AP 11 **Piedmont Driving Club**
1215 Piedmont Avenue, N.E.
Begun 1887: Architect Unknown

AP 12 **Habersham Memorial Hall**
270 Fifteenth Street, N.E.
1923: Henry Hornbostel, Architect (New York); NR

AP 13 **Piedmont Park**
Piedmont Avenue at Fourteenth Street, N.E.
Present Landscaping Begun in 1912: Olmsted Brothers, Landscape
Architects (Brookline, Massachusetts); NR

AP 14 **Play Scapes**
Piedmont Avenue at Twelfth Street, N.E.
1976: Isamu Noguchi, Sculptor

AP 15 **Piedmont Arbors**
1050 Piedmont Avenue, N.E.
1984: Taylor and Williams, Architects; David Marlatt, Project Architect;
UDC, GAAIA Awards

Opposite the intersection of Fifteenth Street and Piedmont Avenue
are the posh facilities of the **Piedmont Driving Club**. In the homelike
and rambling mass of the clubhouse, a millstone from an 1868 farmhouse that originally stood on the site has been embedded in the front

AP 13

gable and is visible from the Fifteenth Street entrance. Interiors were remodeled in the neoclassical style by Philip Shutze. Across Piedmont Avenue is the only nonresidential structure in Ansley Park, **Habersham Memorial Hall,** which was erected by the Georgia Chapter of the Daughters of the American Revolution and modeled after the Bulloch-Habersham House in Savannah. At Fourteenth Street is the entrance to **Piedmont Park,** Atlanta's largest municipal park (185 acres). The grounds, once used as the racetrack of the Gentlemen's Driving Club (organized in 1887), were originally laid out for the Cotton States and International Exposition of 1895. The fair's organizers first consulted Frederick Law Olmsted, but in the end entrusted the master plan to Grant Wilkins, a local (and far less skilled) engineer and contractor, who fortunately incorporated a number of Olmsted's ideas. When the city of Atlanta purchased the fairgrounds in 1904, its buildings were already deteriorating. In 1910 the Olmsted Brothers completed a comprehensive improvement plan, implementing their late father's ideal of a picturesque landscape as a moral and physical haven for city dwellers. The major surviving mark from the 1895 Exposition is the stone stairway, with its tall circular stone urns, that leads to the site of the original fair building. Among the elements to survive from the partially implemented 1912 plan are the winding driveway, which focuses on a series of changing views of the existing lake and landscape, a wooded area with trails (which today adjoins the Atlanta Botanical Garden), and open recreational space (the Exposition's racetrack became an athletic ground). In the 1970s a much-needed children's **Play Scape** (near the Twelfth Street entrance to the park) was commissioned to renowned sculptor Isamu Noguchi, whose abstract forms are highlighted against the trees in bright primary colors. Until recently, the section of Piedmont Avenue adjacent to the park was mostly lined by modest garden apartments built in the 1920s and 1930s. The new residential influx to Midtown has generated the construction of midrise and highrise buildings of greater density. One of the most successful of these is **Piedmont Arbors,** with wood frame facades and Victorian detailing. The provision for covered parking and the preservation of mature trees creates a villagelike atmosphere.

AP 15

Area 9

Georgia Tech (GT)

Founded in 1885, the Georgia Institute of Technology is a nationally renowned scientific institution with eleven thousand students. The original nine-acre campus, with its informal layout and its eclectic structures in red brick with stone accents is well preserved and included on the National Register. In recent buildings, which have for the most part been entrusted to local firms, the uniformity of materials proves a central concern and the bulk of parking decks and laboratories is significantly minimized. The Georgia Tech district includes a large industrial zone where the Coca-Cola Company placed its headquarters adjacent to its syrup-manufacturing facility. Plans at this time call for the Olympic Village for the 1996 Summer Games to be built in this area.

Area 9

Georgia Tech (GT)

1 The Coca-Cola Company Corporate Headquarters, Central Reception Building
2 Coca-Cola USA Building
3 Coca-Cola North Avenue Tower
4 Coca-Cola Enterprises Building
5 Coca-Cola Technical Center
6 Techwood Homes
7 Clark Howell Homes
8 William C. Wardlaw Jr. Center, Georgia Tech
9 L. W. "Chip" Robert Alumni and Faculty House, Georgia Tech
10 Administration Building, Georgia Tech
11 Carnegie Building, Georgia Tech
12 Catholic Center, Georgia Tech
13 Hightower Textile Engineering Building, Georgia Tech
14 Architecture Building, Georgia Tech
15 Price Gilbert Memorial Library, Georgia Tech
16 William Vernon Skiles Classroom Building, Georgia Tech
17 Wesley Foundation, Georgia Tech
18 Manufacturing Research Center, Georgia Tech
19 Atlanta Water Works, Hemphill Pumping Station

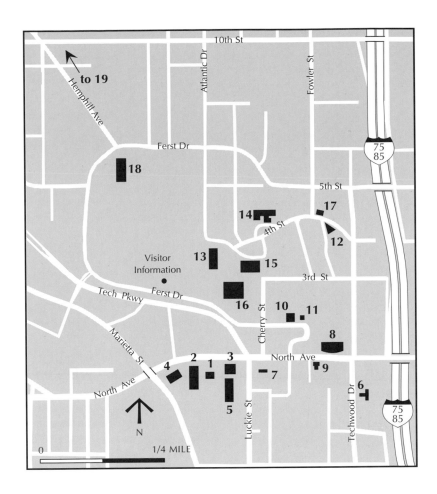

10th St

Atlantic Dr

Fowler St

to 19

Hemphill Ave

75
85

Ferst Dr

18

5th St

17

14

4th St

12

Visitor
Information

13

15

3rd St

Ferst Dr

Tech Pkwy

16

Cherry St

10

11

Marietta St

8

North Ave

2

1

3

North Ave

4

7

9

Techwood Dr

6

5

Luckie St

75
85

0

1/4 MILE

N

GT 1, *left;* GT 3, *right*

GT 1 **The Coca-Cola Company Corporate Headquarters, Central Reception Building**
310 North Avenue, N.W.
1986: Heery Architects and Engineers, Architects; Heery Interiors, Interior Designers; Sheila A. Hunt, Project Architect; Turner Associates, Associate Architects; UDC, GAAIA Awards

GT 2 **Coca-Cola USA Building**
310 North Avenue, N.W.
1987: Heery Architects and Engineers, Architects; Turner Associates, Associate Architects

In contrast to the playfully designed World of Coca-Cola Pavilion (DS 5) near Underground Atlanta (DS 1), the **Central Reception Building** across from the Georgia Tech campus conveys a more formal image for the **Coca-Cola Company Corporate Headquarters** (and the company's products in general). Visitors proceed through the monumental gatehouse on North Avenue and around a shallow reflecting pool that serves as a showcase for George Rickey's sculpture "Triple L Excentric Gyratory Gyratory II." The highly articulated facade is composed of planes of white marble and expanses of glass divided by aluminum mullions. The plan is centered on the three-story neoclassical Robert W. Woodruff Rotunda. This marble-clad oval space, paved with polished granite, leads to VIP lounges and a landscaped courtyard in the back. The granite-clad base and top of the adjoining twenty-story **Coca-Cola USA Building** utilize the same square motif as the large aluminum grid that enlivens its curtain wall. Heery also designed the elaborate fence surrounding the compound.

GT 2, *left;* GT 1, *center;* GT 5, GT 3, *right*

GT 3 **Coca-Cola North Avenue Tower**
310 North Avenue, N.W.
1980: FABRAP, Architects; Tom Pardue, Designer

GT 4 **Coca-Cola Enterprises Building (One Coca-Cola Plaza)**
310 North Avenue, N.W.
1970: FABRAP, Architects

GT 5 **Coca-Cola Technical Center**
310 North Avenue, N.W.
1981: FABRAP, Architects; Jack Dobson, Designer

On opposite corners of the granite-clad twenty-six-story **Coca-Cola North Avenue Tower,** unbroken shafts express the interior division into triangular open office spaces divided by a diagonal service core. Its top two floors feature skylit atriums. The ten-story **Coca-Cola Enterprises Building** was the first corporate structure on this site, but its location on the western edge of the property and its orientation at an angle to the other main structures make it less a part of the composition than the nine-story **Coca-Cola Technical Center** on the eastern side, which balances the collection of high-, medium-, and low-rise structures in this corporate compound.

GT 6

GT 6   **Techwood Homes**
Techwood Drive at North Avenue, N.W.
1935: Burge and Stevens, Architects; Edith Henderson, Landscape Architect

GT 7   **Clark Howell Homes**
Clark Howell Place at Luckie Street, N.W.
1941: Hentz, Adler and Shutze, with J. Warren Armistead, A. Ten Eyck Brown, Ivey and Crook, and F. P. Smith, Architects

Techwood Homes was the first federal slum-clearance project in the United States to reach the construction stage. (Atlanta, thanks to the city's connections with the Roosevelt family, received a large share of New Deal money in the 1930s). Sponsored by the Housing Division of the Public Works Administration, Techwood Homes was the brainchild of Charles F. Palmer, who convinced a group of local businessmen and civic leaders that the spread of slums would lower real-estate values in downtown Atlanta. Set on twenty-five acres and anchored to Georgia Tech, the low-density project provides a large expanse of public open space. It includes three-story apartments and two-story row houses for 604 families, and dormitories for 307 Tech students. At the time they were built the units included such modern amenities as bathtubs, electric stoves, and laundry facilities in the basement of each building, as well as garages for 189 units, a library, and a kindergarten. Despite large casement windows and flat roofs constructed of concrete, the style of the units, sheathed in red brick with stone accents, is less straightforwardly modern than stripped-down Georgian. Techwood Homes was dedicated with great pomp by President Franklin Delano Roosevelt on November 29, 1935. In 1941 **Clark Howell Homes** was built as a westward extension. Until 1968 these homes were reserved for whites only, the all-black counterpart being the P.W.A. sponsored University Homes (Edwards and Sayward, Architects; William C. Pauley, Landscape Architect), a nineteen-acre project close to Atlanta University Center. In the 1970s Techwood Homes began to deteriorate. Despite its designation as a National Register Historic District in 1976, and its renovation in 1983, this crime-stricken area, so close to prime downtown properties, is periodically the object of controversial redevelopment plans.

GT 8

GT 8 **William C. Wardlaw Jr. Center, Georgia Tech**
177 North Avenue, N.W.
1988: Jova/Daniels/Busby, Architects; UDC Award

GT 9 **L. W. "Chip" Robert Alumni and Faculty House (John D. Rockefeller YMCA Building), Georgia Tech**
190 North Avenue, N.W.
1910: Morgan and Dillon, Architects. Renovation 1979: Jova/Daniels/ Busby, Architects; UDC Award

The **William C. Wardlaw Jr. Center** is a mixed-use facility that replaced the south stands of Grant Field, the Tech football field named after the benefactor who funded the original west stands in 1913. The stadium itself is now named for Tech's longtime coach and athletic director, Bobby Dodd. Three levels of parking space are placed underneath a plaza leading to a reception area for major alumni functions. The upper floor has offices, and private patron boxes are placed at the back. Capitalizing on its location on North Avenue, the architects envisioned the Wardlaw Center as a gateway to Georgia Tech and designed a stylized representation of the Administration Building (GT 10) tower as the entrance motif. The use of Tech's traditional materials (the horizontal bands of brick and stone) and the unpretentious low curved facade contribute to a successful integration with the old campus. Across North

Avenue stands the Italianate **L. W. "Chip" Robert Alumni and Faculty House,** formerly a YMCA building. Adaptive reuse has converted it to a social hall and public meeting facility that also houses alumni association offices. Interior detailing, including pilasters, coffered ceilings, and raised panel doors, is executed in a contemporary manner that is nevertheless reminiscent of the character of the original space.

GT 10

GT 10 **Administration Building, Georgia Tech**
225 North Avenue, N.W.
1888: Bruce and Morgan, Architects; NR

GT 11 **Carnegie Building, Georgia Tech**
223 Uncle Heinie Way, N.W.
1907: Architect Unknown, NR

The **Administration Building,** which originally housed offices, classrooms, and a library, is the focal point of Georgia Tech's historic district and its oldest building. With its red brick walls, high-pitched slate roofs, arched openings, and white accents, it epitomizes the no-nonsense Victorian approach to the design of academic facilities, and sets the tone and color scheme for the campus as a whole. Located on the crest of the "Hill," the North Avenue elevation of this four-story structure features a slightly projecting central block crowned by a highly visible, square landmark-tower. The picturesque assemblage of gables and turrets, and the nicely detailed high relief brick work, are in part concealed by the neon letters spelling out "TECH." A major interior remodeling took place in 1963. Adjacent to the Administration Building stands the **Carnegie Building,** a small structure dignified by a classical portico (such Beaux-Arts inspired decor is to be found in other library facilities funded by the Carnegie Foundation). Interiors were modernized in 1954 and 1982 for office use.

GT 12

GT 12 Catholic Center, Georgia Tech
172 Fourth Street, N.W.
1986: Durfee and Hughes, Architects; UDC Award

A freestanding portico provides a stately entry to the dynamic facade of the Georgia Tech Catholic Center. Treated in simple cantilevered masses, this mixed-use facility is well adapted to its small and sloped triangular site. In keeping with the prevailing campus context the architects enlist red brick with clearer accents in concrete. Furnishings and liturgical pieces were also designed by the architects.

GT 13 **Hightower Textile Engineering Building, Georgia Tech**
725 Atlantic Drive, N.W.
1949: Bush-Brown, Gailey and Heffernan, Architects; Paul M.
Heffernan, Designer

GT 14 **Architecture Building, Georgia Tech**
245 Fourth Street, N.W.
1952: Bush-Brown, Gailey and Heffernan, Architects; Paul M.
Heffernan, Designer. Addition 1976: Cooper Carry and Associates,
Architects

GT 15 **Price Gilbert Memorial Library, Georgia Tech**
704 Cherry Street, N.W.
1953: Bush-Brown, Gailey and Heffernan, Architects; Paul M.
Heffernan, Designer. East Wing and Entry Rotunda Additions 1967:
Robert and Company, Architects

GT 16 **William Vernon Skiles Classroom Building, Georgia Tech**
686 Cherry Street, N.W.
1959: Bush-Brown, Gailey and Heffernan, Architects; Paul M.
Heffernan, Designer

GT 17 **Wesley Foundation, Georgia Tech**
189 Fourth Street, N.W.
1961: Sam T. Hurst and Paul M. Heffernan, Architects

After World War II the International Style debuted on the Georgia Tech
campus in a series of new buildings. Designed by a "home-based" team
that included Harold Bush-Brown, then director of Tech's School of

Architecture, and his successor to that position, Paul M. Heffernan, modern architecture materialized as a series of low concrete-frame buildings sheathed in brick. Paradoxically, Heffernan's first-rate Beaux-Arts educational background in the United States and in France (where he studied as a recipient of the Paris Prize) explains in great part the rationalism and clarity of both plan and elevation in these Bauhaus-inspired compositions, starting with the **Hightower Textile Engineering Building** of 1949. On its completion in 1952, the **Architecture Building** received national attention in the architectural press as one of the most modern and well-equipped facilities of its kind. The two-story south wing houses an auditorium seating three hundred people, administrative offices, and what was originally an exhibition and jury room. The four-and-a-half-story north wing contains classrooms, studios, and workshops. Its

facades alternate ribbon windows protected by cantilevered canopies with spandrels faced in glazed tile (the original delicate steel window frames have recently been replaced by much larger aluminum members). The connecting structure, raised above ground, originally housed the library and a gallery. As enrollment in the College of Architecture expanded, so did the need for additional space to house the program. In 1976 Cooper Carry and Associates undertook the task of designing an addition to the Architecture Building. Their plan, in conjunction with the original edifice, forms a pleasant landscaped courtyard. It is unfortunate, however, that its concrete facing breaks with the traditional use of brick on campus as well as on the original building. Other campus structures, including the **Price Gilbert Memorial Library,** the **Skiles Classroom Building,** and the **Wesley Foundation,** bear the unmistakable design signature of "P. M." Heffernan.

GT 18

GT 18   **Manufacturing Research Center, Georgia Tech**
813 Ferst Drive, N.W.
1990: Lord, Aeck, Sargent, Architects; Terry Sargent, Designer

In the 120,000-square-foot Manufacturing Research Center, Georgia Tech wanted to display its capabilities in pure and applied research for a range of manufacturing-related disciplines. Sources for the refined "manufactured object" imagery are to be found, according to the architects, in Albert Kahn's rational daylight factories for the automobile industry, specifically his streamlined Ohio Steel Foundry Roll Shop in Lima, Ohio (1939). Without entirely discarding Tech's traditional red-brick veneer, the exterior of the Manufacturing Research Center expresses an original and successful response to the "low tech" requirements of a flexible program. The rectangular block is entered by way of bridges and defined at the corners by rounded staircase towers. On the north and south sides, glass planes indicate the presence of an atrium lined by laboratories; on the east and west sides, ribbon windows with prominent sunshades provide light to the outlying offices. The entrance motif, with its portico supported by magnified bolts and conspicuous lettering, wittily combines classical references with allusions to the gear mechanism that trapped Charlie Chaplin in the movie *Modern Times*. A second building by the same architects is planned to meet additional space requirements.

GT 19

GT 19 Atlanta Water Works, Hemphill Pumping Station
1210 Hemphill Avenue, N.W.
1892, 1908: Robert M. Clayton, City Engineer; NR

In a landscaped setting, the Hemphill Pumping Station draws and treats water from the Chattahoochee River (some of its original nineteenth-century equipment is still in use). Its two main block buildings—the most recent one located closest to Hemphill Avenue—are connected by a lower entrance pavilion structure crowned by a classical balus-trade. This utilitarian assemblage of buildings attains a Roman grandeur through its elegant proportions and fine brick work. Notice in particular the templelike gable end of the plant building, with its low "pediment" and recessed arches, niches, and oculus.

Area 10

West End (WE)

Formed around the White Hall Tavern, which was built in 1835 at the southeast corner of Lee Street and Gordon Street (now Ralph David Abernathy Boulevard), West End is Atlanta's oldest residential neighborhood. Its growth is explained in part by good transportation to Downtown, first by rail lines and then by streetcars. It was most fashionable in the later part of the nineteenth century and was incorporated into the city limits in 1894. West End is slowly recovering from a decline that started during World War II and accelerated when Interstate 20 bisected it. This tour begins with a visit to Atlanta University Center, the world's largest predominantly black higher education complex. Established in 1865 and chartered in 1867, the first of its five independent schools, Morris Brown College, is also Atlanta's oldest institution of higher learning. Buildings of major architectural significance have been placed on the National Register of Historic Places. Tours are available through the Atlanta Preservation Center.

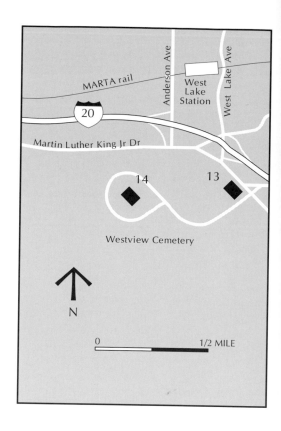

Area 10

West End (WE)

1 Fountain Hall, Morris Brown College
2 Gaines Hall, Morris Brown College
3 Furber Cottage, Morris Brown College
4 Alonzo F. Herndon Home
5 Robert W. Woodruff Library
6 Graves Hall, Morehouse College
7 The Sisters Chapel, Spelman College
8 Tapley Hall, Spelman College
9 Giles Hall, Spelman College
10 Rockefeller Hall, Spelman College
11 Wren's Nest, Joel Chandler Harris House
12 Otis Thrash Hammonds House
13 Main Gate, Westview Cemetery
14 Abbey Mausoleum, Westview Cemetery
15 Booker T. Washington High School

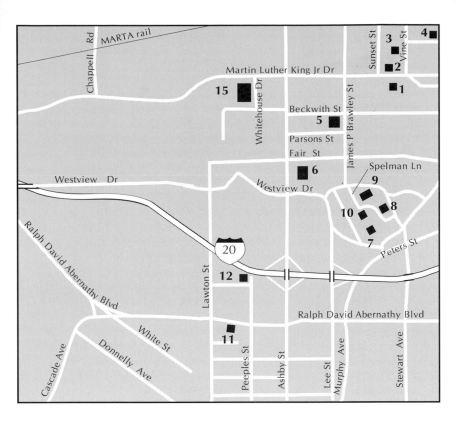

WE 1   **Fountain Hall (Stone Hall), Morris Brown College**
643 Martin Luther King Jr. Drive
1882: Gottfried L. Norrman, Architect; NHL, LB

WE 2   **Gaines Hall (North Hall), Morris Brown College**
643 Martin Luther King Jr. Drive
1869: William H. Parkins, Architect

WE 3   **Furber Cottage, Morris Brown College**
643 Martin Luther King Jr. Drive
1899: Architect Unknown

Atlanta University Center's oldest individual campus stands at the north-
ernmost end of the grouping of campuses on one of Atlanta's highest elevations. First occupied by Atlanta University, since 1932 it has housed
Morris Brown College, an institution chartered in 1867 and named after
a bishop of the African Methodist Episcopal Church. Completed in 1882
Fountain Hall is the three-and-a-half-story structure that dominates the
campus. Its Romanesque Revival openings in a red brick facade with
decorative stone and brick accents (notice the crenellated corbelling
below the eaves) and its hipped roof pierced by a taut centrally located
clocktower became standard features for administrative buildings on
Atlanta campuses of the late Victorian era. Fountain Hall was preceded
by **Gaines Hall,** the oldest university building in Atlanta. It is reached by
way of an iron bridge over Martin Luther King Jr. Drive (formerly Hunter
Street). On this three-story structure of red brick resting on a granite base,

notice the Italianate detailing of the bracketed eaves which continue along the pediment on the left side of the entrance facade. The neo-Georgian two-story brick **Furber Cottage** was built as a model home for home economics classes.

WE 4 **Alonzo F. Herndon Home**
587 University Place, N.W.
1910: William Campbell, Builder; NR, LB. Restoration 1982: Norman D. Askins, Architect; UDC Award

Set well back from this residential street, which was part of the original land holdings of Atlanta University, the Alonzo F. Herndon Home, a two-story, fifteen-room structure in varicolored brick with classical accents flanked by two detached porches, stands out among its neighbors, which were initially built as faculty houses. Its colossal portico reflects the social position of its original owner, Atlanta Life Insurance Company founder Alonzo F. Herndon (see SA 3). An elliptical fanlight over the entrance and the balustrade above the full entablature of the building's cornice add a distinctly Georgian Revival flavor to this imposing structure. The refined interior decor reflects the personal imprint of Herndon's first wife, Adrienne. Norris Herndon's collection of antique furniture and decorative arts complements his parents' interior design and original furnishings. Since 1977 the house has been maintained by the Herndon Foundation as a museum.

WE 4

Robert W. Woodruff Library
111 James P. Brawley Drive, S.W.
1982: Toombs, Amisano and Wells with J. W. Robinson and Associates,
Joint Venture Architects; Joseph Amisano, Designer

The Robert W. Woodruff Library serves six colleges and contains one of
the largest archival collections of black literature in the world. The design architect, Joseph Amisano, respected the low height of neighboring
residential and commercial structures, but created an uncompromisingly
modern building with large masonry masses (articulated by horizontal
brick stripes in brown and white) broken up by great expanses of glass
(articulated by vertical Vierendeel-trussed window mullions in a bright
red hue). The rectilinearity of the scheme is interrupted by the slanted
semicircular skylight above the outer lobby. A three-story layout with

WE 5

the main entrance on the second floor minimizes the need for elevators,
allowing for a monumental central stairwell that gives a focus to the
interior plan and provides natural light to all floors. Inside, the structural
system of cast-in-place concrete is left exposed.

WE 6 **Graves Hall, Morehouse College**
830 Westview Drive, S.W.
1889: Architect Unknown. Restoration 1982: Leon Allain and
Associates, Architects; UDC Award

Morehouse College was founded in Augusta, Georgia, in 1867 as
Augusta Institute. The school moved to Atlanta in 1879, when it became
Atlanta Baptist Seminary, and was given its present name in 1913. The
campus is dominated at the western end by the open tower topped by a
pyramidal roof of Graves Hall (the building was named for the president
of the college at the time of its construction). The four-story brick structure follows the model of Fountain Hall (WE 1) with slight variations,

such as the Richardsonian Romanesque central archway in rough-hewn stone supported by squat columns and the charming wooden porch with spool-work.

WE 7 **The Sisters Chapel, Spelman College**
350 Spelman Lane, S.W.
1923–1927: Hentz, Reid and Adler, Architects; Neel Reid, Designer

First named Atlanta Baptist Female Seminary, Spelman College was founded in 1881 by two New Englanders, Sophia B. Packard and Harriet Giles, and was renamed in honor of Lucy Henry Spelman, the mother-

in-law of John D. Rockefeller, an important benefactor. The first buildings of the oldest college for black women in the United States were
erected in 1883 on the thirty-two-acre walled-in campus, around a
quadrangle planted with mature trees. Located at the southern end of
this quadrangle, the templelike Sisters Chapel was named in honor of
Lucy Spelman's daughters, Laura Spelman Rockefeller and Lucy Maria
Spelman. The white Doric ornaments on the red brick exterior and
the neo-Georgian accents of the 1,040-seat auditorium, used for daily
chapel services, concerts, and commencement exercises, were both
treated with elegant restraint by Neel Reid.

WE 8 **Tapley Hall, Spelman College**
350 Spelman Lane, S.W.
1923: Hentz, Reid and Adler, Architects; Neel Reid, Designer

WE 9 **Giles Hall, Spelman College**
350 Spelman Lane, S.W.
1893: Architect Unknown

WE 10 **Rockefeller Hall, Spelman College**
350 Spelman Lane, S.W.
1885: Architect Unknown

WE 10

Across the quadrangle from the Sisters Chapel (WE 7) stands the neo-
Georgian **Tapley Hall,** also designed by Neel Reid. Among Victorian
structures of architectural interest is **Giles Hall,** at the north end of the
quadrangle, a large three-and-a-half-story structure named after one of
Spelman's founders. Originally used for classrooms and dormitories,
it features gables and pavilions on each end that echo the larger pedimented central portion. **Rockefeller Hall,** the first permanent building
erected from funds donated to the school by John D. Rockefeller was

initially a chapel and dormitory. The assembly room was later converted into a theater. Notice the pattern bricks, the cupola atop the crowning aedicula, and the semicircular dormer windows, echoing the arched entrances, on the narrow sides.

WE 11

WE 11   **Wren's Nest, Joel Chandler Harris House**
1050 Ralph David Abernathy Boulevard, S.W.
Circa 1885: Builder Unknown; NHL, LB. Restoration 1992: W. Lane Greene, Architect

WE 12   **Otis Thrash Hammonds House (Madge Bingham House)**
503 Peeples Street, S.W.
Circa 1857: Builder Unknown; UDC Award

The family of newspaper editor, author, and humorist Joel Chandler Harris (1848–1908), who is best known for *Uncle Remus: His Songs and Sayings*, lived in **Wren's Nest** from 1881 to 1913. The house was given its picturesque name by Harris after a wren had built a nest in the mailbox. Built around 1867, the nucleus of the house consisted of only two rooms; it was first enlarged approximately five years later. In 1884 Harris turned this simple clapboard cottage into a stylish residence by adding six more rooms and redesigning the street facade in the then fashionable Queen Anne style. Notice the unusual banister and entrance motifs on the expansive porch and the fish-scale shingles on the upper floor walls. In 1913 Wren's Nest was bought with its original furnishings by the Joel Chandler Harris Memorial Association and turned into a museum. West End's most interesting old restored houses are to be found within walking distance of Wren's Nest on Oglethorpe Avenue, Peeples and Atwood streets. The **Otis Thrash Hammonds House,** built in the Eastlake style, was purchased by Fulton County and houses a collection of African art.

WE 13

WE 13 **Main Gate, Westview Cemetery**
1680 Ralph David Abernathy Boulevard, S.W.
1884: Architect Unknown; NR

WE 14 **Abbey Mausoleum, Westview Cemetery**
1680 Ralph David Abernathy Boulevard, S.W.
1943: Harvey, Hellington and Day, Architects (Detroit); Cecil E. Bryan,
Designer

Privately owned, the 577-acre Westview Cemetery was opened in 1884
as an alternative to the overcrowded Oakland Cemetery (SE 1). Joel
Chandler Harris, Henry Grady, and William B. Hartsfield are buried
here. Built in cyclopean blocks of grey granite, the Richardsonian

WE 14

Romanesque **Main Gate** looks almost like an overscaled European farm building and complements the unassuming pastoral character of the cemetery's landscaping. Notice the fine treatment of the arched openings and the delicate balance between the elongated mass and the bell tower, which once announced processions. Commissioned by Coca-Cola entrepreneur Asa Candler, the **Abbey Mausoleum** illustrates a building type that is fascinating, if not very well known because of its association with death. Rising above the grass, the awe-inspiring severity of the three-story elongated mass constructed of rough-hewn granite in variegated tones of pink and ocher, recalls an Italian monastery of the Middle Ages. Notice the small picturesque octagonal tower and the smooth ornate Spanish Revival decor applied to the eastern loggia. The lofty and rich interior, with space for twelve-thousand entombments, is almost surrealistic. It includes two galleries (running parallel and entered at midpoint, featuring no fewer than thirty-five varieties of marble), a Memorial Hall, and the Florence Candler Chapel in the late English Gothic style.

WE 15

WE 15 **Booker T. Washington High School**
45 Whitehouse Drive, S.W.
1924, Additions 1937: Eugene C. Wachendorff, Architect; NR.
Renovation 1987: W. S. McDuffie and Associates, Architects;
UDC Award.

As the first public high school for blacks built by the city of Atlanta, this impressive and well-maintained four-story structure was named after reformer and Tuskegee Institute founder Booker T. Washington (1856–

1915). A statue of Washington, by noted sculptor Charles Keck, is placed on axis with the raised main entrance and framed by an alley of mature trees. The red brick veneer, sheathing a reinforced concrete frame, and the eclectic decor of the Booker T. Washington High School are characteristic of Atlanta's school buildings of the 1920s. The brick corbelling, in high relief, contributes to the definition of the cornice line. Touches of color on the two-tiered central arcade reinforce the contrast between the entrance block, with its stone and terra-cotta accents and elaborate brick patterns, and the classroom wings, with rows of unadorned windows. The interior features interesting 1920s murals by student Wilmer Jennings. When it was constructed the new school became an immediate asset to black entrepreneur Heman Perry's nearby Washington Park suburban community.

Area 11

South East (SE)

Though not a coherent district in itself, the South East quadrant of Atlanta contains three National Register Districts that contribute to this area's historic significance: Oakland Cemetery, Cabbage Town, and Grant Park. Less developed than areas north of Interstate 20, the South East is largely a light industrial zone with scattered pockets of residential neighborhoods. In the recent past this area has contained, within a two-mile radius, such diverse structures as a theological seminary, a federal penitentiary, a sports stadium, a zoo, a debtor's prison, and an antebellum house. With this assortment, it is not surprising that it also contains a rich assortment of architectural styles from a number of historical periods.

Area 11

South East (SE)

1 Oakland Cemetery
2 Fulton Bag and Cotton Mills
3 Cabbage Town
4 GlenCastle
5 The Roosevelt
6 Cyclorama
7 Julius Fisher House
8 Lemuel P. Grant House
9 Martin Luther King Jr. Middle School
10 Atlanta–Fulton County Stadium
11 Georgia Department of Archives and History Building
12 George Washington Carver High School
13 Atlanta Federal Penitentiary

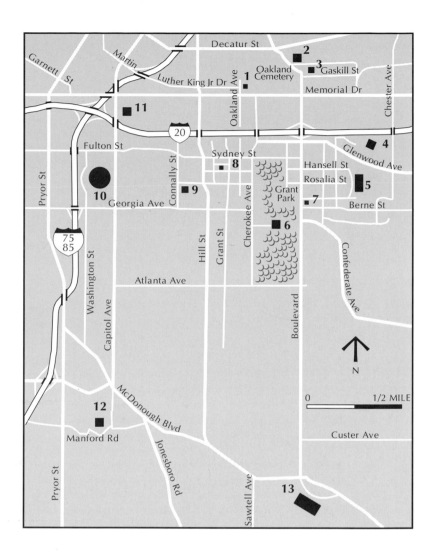

SE 1 Oakland Cemetery
248 Oakland Avenue, S.E.
Begun 1850, NR

Oakland Cemetery is the oldest city-owned cemetery still in existence in Atlanta. In 1850, when the first cemetery at the corner of Peachtree and Baker streets became too small, the city purchased six acres in what is now the southwest corner of the present eighty-eight-acre cemetery. The original gridiron layout is now softened by the presence of old magnolias and oaks. In 1896 a brick wall was erected around the site and gates were built at the Oakland Avenue and Memorial Drive entrances. Oakland Cemetery, with its ethnic divisions and endless variety, resembles a city in miniature. Its Jewish section, for instance, features closely spaced monuments, while other areas exhibit an extraordinary assemblage of mausoleums, urns, and columns of different styles and sizes. There are chapels, complete with spires and stained-glass windows (such as the one visible in the photograph above, which was constructed in 1882 for the Austell family), alongside Egyptian mastabas. Notice also the fine nineteenth-century cast-iron furniture and funerary carvings with fascinating iconic representations. An excellent brochure, available at the cemetery, maps out a tour of the resting places of such prominent Atlantans as retailer Morris Rich, author Margaret Mitchell, and golfer Bobby Jones. Guided tours of the cemetery can be arranged through the Atlanta Preservation Center.

SE 2 Fulton Bag and Cotton Mills
170 Boulevard, S.E.
Begun 1881: Architect Unknown

SE 3 Cabbage Town
Boulevard at Memorial Drive
Begun 1880s, NR

SE 2

Because Atlanta's economy has always relied more on transportation
and services than on manufacturing, the **Fulton Bag and Cotton Mills**
are among the few examples of early industrial architecture in the city.
Built between 1881 and 1921 with brick bearing walls and timber interior framing, buildings of historical interest in this factory complex
have been enlarged many times over the years and now occupy no
fewer than 650,000 square feet of usable space. On Boulevard, notice
the elegant facade of the office structure erected in 1902, with its seven
arcaded bays divided by pilasters and topped by terra-cotta consoles
used as keystones. The self-contained textile mill had 2,600 employees and produced its own energy supply. It began to decline in the late

SE 3

1950s and was finally closed in 1977. As of this writing, architect John Reagan is planning an ambitious adaptive reuse project including 350 to 500 moderately priced loft style residential units, performing and visual arts facilities, and tourism-related spaces. Linked to downtown Atlanta by streetcar as early as 1884, the National Register district of **Cabbage Town** remains a working-class community deeply concerned about its survival. It includes mill-owned homes built immediately south of the factory complex and best represented by the dignified two-story duplexes (with added porches) lining Caroll Street. Cabbage Town's tight and truly urban fabric is graced by one-story shotgun houses and small cottages. The most picturesque and well maintained of these are to be found on Berean Street, Kirkwood Avenue, and Savannah Street.

SE 4

SE 4 GlenCastle (Atlanta Stockade)
750 Glenwood Avenue, S.E.
1887–1915: Architect Unknown; HB. Adaptive Reuse 1990: Bradfield Associates, Architects

On a site purchased by the city in 1863, the Atlanta Stockade, initially built in 1887 as a small prison and work farm, was gradually enlarged over the next three decades. The result is a picturesque structure that is highly visible from Glenwood Avenue and Interstate 20. Its eclectic design mixes rustications in smooth and rough-hewn stone and features a colonnaded Doric porch, a medieval crenellated tower, and an Italianate belvedere. In 1925 the Stockade became a warehouse for Atlanta's Board of Education and was abandoned a few years later when the Grant Park Elementary School was built on the site. However, its domestic rather than institutional character allowed for its adaptive reuse as a much needed low-cost housing project. The once empty shell features a new front porch and is now occupied by sixty-seven efficiency apartments. The project was made possible by donations of time and materials from twenty-six different groups of professionals and skilled workers. The old blacksmith shop is scheduled to be renovated into a chapel and community center.

SE 5

SE 5 **The Roosevelt (Franklin D. Roosevelt High School)**
745 Rosalia Street, S.E.
1924: Edwards and Sayward, Architects; A. Ten Eyck Brown, Supervising Architect. Adaptive Reuse 1989: Surber and Barber, Architects; UDC Award

Originally a girls' high school, the Roosevelt follows the same pattern as a number of monumental public school buildings erected in Atlanta during the 1920s in its recent conversion to a residential complex. Otherwise punctured by highly functional openings, its elongated main facade (visible from the dead end of Rosalia Street but accessed from Muse and Hansell streets) is enlivened at the center and ends by Romano-Byzantine ornamentation in terra-cotta and tile. With its rose window and entrance canopy, modeled after an early Christian ciborium, the gabled portion of the main entrance wing further enhances the churchlike image. Notice behind it the huge copper dome set on a drum of alternating bands of brick and stone, not unlike the Byzantine churches of Constantinople. Roosevelt High School was closed in 1985 and renovated into ninety apartments with the addition of townhouses in the back. The adaptive reuse did not involve major interior changes, and the spectacular domed rotunda on the third floor remains intact.

SE 6

SE 6 **Cyclorama**
800 Cherokee Avenue, S.E.
1921: John Francis Downing, Architect. Renovation and Additions
1981: FABRAP with Thompson Hancock Witte, Joint Venture
Architects; James Chow, Designer

SE 7 **Julius Fisher House**
620 Boulevard, S.E.
1886: Architect Unknown

SE 8 **Lemuel P. Grant House**
327 St. Paul Avenue, S.E.
1858: Architect Unknown

The **Cyclorama** is located at the center of Grant Park, which was named for Colonel Lemuel P. Grant, a northerner who planned Atlanta's fortifications in 1863. In 1883 this engineer turned entrepreneur, whose business activities ranged from railroading to real estate, donated eighty-five acres of land to the city for use as a public park with no racial restrictions attached to his gift. Forty-four additional acres were purchased seven years later, and the initial landscaping of the hilly terrain, which includes Civil War battery Fort Walker and gentle walking paths and carriage roads through the wooded land, was improved by the Olmsted Brothers in 1909. A nicely detailed neoclassical structure, deceivingly clad in terra-cotta, the Cyclorama was built in 1921 to house a panoramic painting of the Battle of Atlanta, measuring fifty feet in height and four hundred feet in circumference, which the city had acquired in 1898. By the late 1970s the building and the painting were in such disrepair that it was feared both would be lost. In 1981 the city decided to rescue this unique relic and renovate the building so that the public could again enjoy this tourist attraction. Because the painting was too fragile to be moved, renovation of the existing structure had to take place around and within the hanging artwork. The existing walkup viewing platform was replaced with a revolving platform and the central column supporting the roof was replaced by a new steel truss, which now supports the roof from the outside. In order to increase the exhibition space above, visitors enter through what was originally a basement. Formal entrances, erected from 1926 to 1928, serve as boundaries between Grant Park and bordering streets lined with Victorian and early twentieth-century homes of varied sizes and styles. Notice at the southern intersection of Boulevard and Killian Street the turreted **Julius Fisher House** with its elaborate Victorian woodwork on the parapet and the window frames. A visit to Grant Park is not complete without exploring the residential district west of Cherokee Avenue, in the orthogonal network of tree-lined streets developed by Lemuel P. Grant, whose own antebellum mansion, the **Lemuel P. Grant House,** survives as a noble ruin. This district, now on the National Register, has seen periodic restoration since the early 1970s. The prevailing housing type, one-story gabled cottages painted in pastel colors and graced by a front porch, as well as the picturesque Queen Anne, Italianate, and Craftsman bungalow homes remain affordable.

SE 9   **Martin Luther King Jr. Middle School**
       582 Connally Street, S.E.
       1973: Heery and Heery, Architects and Engineers; Merrill Elam, Designer; GAAIA Award

SE 10   **Atlanta–Fulton County Stadium**
        521 Capitol Avenue, S.E.
        1965: FABRAP with Heery and Heery, Joint Venture Architects

SE 11   **Georgia Department of Archives and History Building**
        330 Capitol Avenue, S.E.
        1965: A. Thomas Bradbury and Associates, Architects

Placed in a parklike setting west of the Grant Park residential district, the 170,000-square-foot **Martin Luther King Jr. Middle School** has been totally internalized for security reasons. The forbidding, windowless exterior envelope in poured-in-place concrete belies the open interior plan

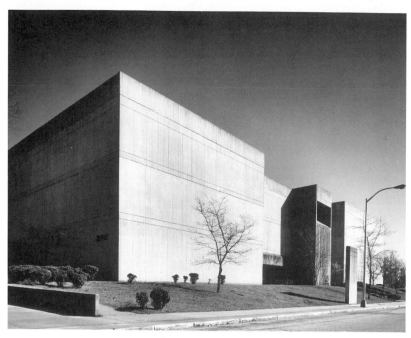

of freely arranged spaces organized around a teaching theater. Nearby, in the blasted environment bordering the highway, two monumental buildings stand out. The **Atlanta–Fulton County Stadium** is an open arena designed and built in fewer than twelve months in order to meet franchise deadlines. The main structure, formed by eighty identical sections of box steel bents, seats up to 58,000 spectators for football and baseball games, concerts, and other special events. The seventeen-story **Georgia Department of Archives and History Building** is a windowless and scaleless marble block resting on a colonnaded rectangular podium.

SE 12   George Washington Carver High School (Leete Hall)
1275 Capitol Avenue, S.W.
1920: Alexander Hamilton Jr., Architect; NR

Purchased by the Atlanta Board of Education in 1946, this high school was originally built as Leete Hall, part of Gammon Theological Seminary, a black institution founded in 1883 by the Methodist Episcopal Church and now part of the Atlanta University complex. This red brick structure stands out in its parklike environment. Its picturesque square tower, with four finials emerging from the trees, is highly visible from Interstate 75/85. Beyond the abundant and striking white accents, inspired by the late Gothic Jacobean style of England, notice the subtle lozenge-shaped brick work.

SE 13 **Atlanta Federal Penitentiary**
601 McDonough Boulevard, S.E.
Begun 1902: Eames and Young, Architects (Saint Louis, Missouri)

In 1899 Congress passed legislation authorizing the construction of three
federal penitentiaries, with Atlanta designated as one of the sites. The
prison, which was to be built within two miles of Downtown, was the

only site to be located in a metropolitan area. Two cellhouses were completed in 1902, followed by a number of auxiliary structures. Within the twenty-eight-acre complex, prisoners were virtually self-sufficient, working to supply most of their own needs. In its early years the penitentiary was one of the city's most popular landmarks for out-of-town visitors. The enclosing wall erected between 1903 and 1910 was the largest concrete construction in the United States at the time. Buildings constructed of Stone Mountain granite are purposely overpowering. Massive classical ornamentation is concentrated on the projecting entrance wing (1910), with its segmental pediment supported by columns. In her article in *Atlanta History* (Spring 1990), Barbara James stated that this maximum security facility, "modeled after the architectural and administrative style of New York's Auburn Prison," was "one of the last American prisons that perpetuated the nineteenth century penal philosophy."

Area 12

Inman Park (IP)

Begun in 1889, Inman Park was the inspiration of developer Joel Hurt and was named after his business associate Samuel Inman. Hurt operated one of the first electric streetcar lines in the United States. The line originated Downtown and ran along Edgewood Avenue. Hurt closely supervised the layout of Inman Park's 189 acres, which he had entrusted to landscape gardener J. Forsyth Johnson. To enhance his plan Hurt also envisioned a hotel and convention hall at the intersection of Euclid and Edgewood avenues. Although this layout does not have the sophistication of earlier garden suburbs by Frederick Law Olmsted and his followers, Inman Park today, with its ten-acre Springvale Park and mature trees, is not devoid of pastoral charm. The presence of large homes on relatively modest lots generates its characteristically tight residential fabric. In the teens, with the development of Ansley Park and Druid Hills, and the public perception that Victorian-style architecture was outdated, this once desirable neighborhood started to decline. Speculative builders erected modest bungalows on vacant lots that had originally been designated as interior parks; the mansions prominent Atlantans had built for themselves were transformed into rooming houses or subdivided into apartments and for the most part poorly maintained. In the 1960s some homes on Euclid Avenue and surrounding streets were demolished in anticipation of the construction of two highways that were never built. The early 1970s saw the creation of the popular Spring Festival, the Tour of Homes, and the placement of the entire neighborhood on the National Register of Historic Places. Symbolized by the butterfly banner hung in windows of restored homes, Inman Park's ongoing revitalization is the result of a remarkable community effort. For information about guided walking tours, call the Atlanta Preservation Center.

Area 12

Inman Park (IP)

1 The Trolley Barn
2 Inman Park United Methodist Church
3 Callan Castle
4 Joel Hurt Cottage
5 Joel Hurt House
6 Beath-Dickey House
7 Woodruff-Burruss House
8 George E. King House
9 Charles R. Winship House
10 Inman Park Elementary School
11 Carter Presidential Center

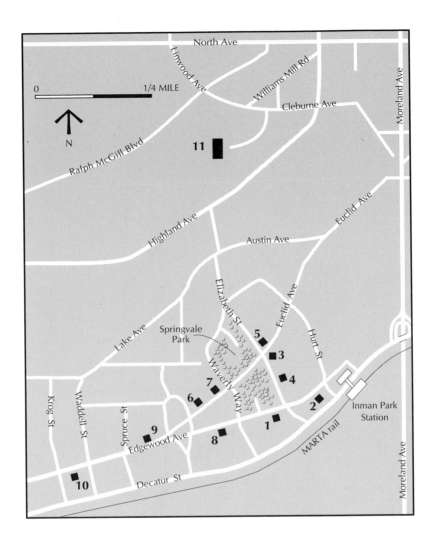

North Ave

Linwood Ave

Williams Mill Rd

Cleburne Ave

Moreland Ave

0 1/4 MILE

N

Ralph McGill Blvd

11

Highland Ave

Austin Ave

Euclid Ave

Elizabeth St

Euclid Ave

Lake Ave

Springvale Park

Hurt St

Waverly Way

5

3

4

7

6

Krog St

Waddell St

Spruce St

9

Edgewood Ave

8

1

2

Inman Park Station

MARTA rail

10

Decatur St

Moreland Ave

IP 1 **The Trolley Barn (Inman Park Street Car Barn)**
963 Edgewood Avenue, N.E.
Circa 1889: Architect Unknown; NR. Renovation 1988: Denson and
Associates, Architects; UDC Award

IP 2 **Inman Park United Methodist Church**
1015 Edgewood Avenue, N.E.
1898: Willis F. Denny, Architect; NR

The **Trolley Barn,** which was located at the terminus of the Edgewood
Avenue line, is evidence of the neighborhood's origin. With its overhanging roof, round turret, and walls covered with clapboards and
shingles (the dark paint is not original), it presents the same Victorian
features as nearby houses. After 1907 the barn was no longer used as
a transportation facility, but it has since been used in various ways, including as a basketball court, a farmers' market, and a shoe shop. The
City of Atlanta purchased the structure in 1976 and contributed to its
restoration and adaptive reuse as a public facility for the neighborhood.
The Romanesque Revival **Inman Park United Methodist Church** is an
adaptation of an English parish church. Simple and almost unadorned
masses of grey granite complement its diminutive scale and fit the tone
of the neighborhood.

IP 3 Callan Castle (Asa Candler House)
145 Elizabeth Street, N.E.
1903: George E. Murphy, Architect; NR

IP 4 Joel Hurt Cottage
117 Elizabeth Street, N.E.
Circa 1882: Architect Unknown; NR

IP 5 Joel Hurt House
167 Elizabeth Street, N.E.
1904: Walter T. Downing, Architect; NR

At fourteen thousand square feet, **Callan Castle** is one of the largest homes in Inman Park. Its formality reflects the status of its first owner, Coca-Cola magnate Asa Candler, who lived there until 1916. Splendidly addressing the street corner, its design is particularly versatile. The two-story pedimented portico is reminiscent of Greek Revival mansions; the rambling mass of the building, the asymmetrical position of the entrance doorway, and the mixture of materials are definitely Victorian in character. The delicate decor of garlands on the entablature and the Palladian motif above it are characteristic of the Colonial Revival style. Considerably more modest is the entrance portico of the **Joel Hurt Cottage,** where the developer lived during the early phase of developing Inman Park. Notice the diamond-shaped panes on the hexagonal

IP 3

tower. In 1904 Hurt moved to the **Joel Hurt House,** a half-Italianate, half-Victorian mansion in buff brick across Euclid Avenue from Callan Castle.

IP 6   **Beath-Dickey House**
       866 Euclid Avenue, N.E.
       Circa 1898: Architect Unknown; NR. Restoration 1969: Robert Griggs

IP 7   **Woodruff-Burruss House**
       882 Euclid Avenue, N.E.
       1890: Gottfried L. Norrman, Architect; NR

The **Beath-Dickey House** is a fine example of the Queen Anne style. Its massing is asymmetrical, with a deep front porch balanced by a projecting gabled wing. There are porches on every floor, including a belvedere in the turret crowned by a metal finial. The presence of high chimney stacks and the mingling of materials—granite, brick, marble, textured wood shingles, and slate—contribute to the overall picturesque effect. While the stone steps and cobblestone driveway are original, the iron gate is a later addition that does not reflect the typical relation of the

IP 6

Victorian home to the streetscape. Interior designer Robert Griggs's restoration of the Beath-Dickey House in 1969 marked the beginning of
Inman Park's gentrification. The fifteen original rooms recovered their
grandeur (see *Landmark Homes of Georgia* for illustrations of the splendid woodwork). The **Woodruff-Burruss House** is in the process of being
restored. Ernest Woodruff, who acquired the Coca-Cola Company from
the Candler family in 1919, lived in this thirty-room residence before
moving to a Downing-designed home at 908 Edgewood Avenue.

IP 8

IP 8   **George E. King House**
889 Edgewood Avenue, N.E.
1889: Architect Unknown; NR

IP 9   **Charles R. Winship House**
814 Edgewood Avenue, N.E.
1893: Architect Unknown; NR

IP 10   **Inman Park Elementary School**
729 Edgewood Avenue, N.E.
1892: Gottfried L. Norrman, Architect; NR

Named after its first occupant, the founder of the King Hardware Company, the **George E. King House,** with its construction date inscribed
on a brick panel on the right-end side, is one of the oldest houses in
Inman Park. With the exception of the circular gazebo attached to the

wraparound porch, its highly articulated masses and wood ornaments are very angular and reflect the Eastlake style. Of particular interest is the delicate lacework with its arch motifs and the way in which the triangular "pediment" marking the entrance echoes the gable above it. The **Charles R. Winship House,** which was originally painted maroon with black trim, is recognizable for its delicately carved porch and high chimney stacks placed at the corners of the gable. The stained-glass windows date from the original construction in 1893. The **Inman Park Elementary School** is interesting as one of the earliest examples of school buildings in Atlanta. The taut windows and unsophisticated brick exterior are similar to college buildings of the same era in the city. The grouping of openings and raised keyhole central motif give a sense of monumentality to this modestly scaled structure.

IP 11

IP 11   **Carter Presidential Center**
One Copenhill Avenue, N.E.
1986: Jova/Daniels/Busby with Lawton, Umemura and Yamamoto (Honolulu), Joint Venture Architects; Jova/Daniels/Busby, Interior Designers; EDAW, Landscape Architects; UDC Award

Atlanta was selected as the site of the presidential library of Jimmy Carter, who before his election as president of the United States served as governor of Georgia. Arriving through a formal entrance, the visitor to the Carter Presidential Center sees the flagged Court of the States followed by a rectangular colonnade flanked by pavilions. The sprawling composition, formed by four interconnected circular pavilions, is best seen from the garden side, which also offers a splendid view of the downtown skyline. On the southern side, one finds the presidential library and museum with orientation theaters. On the northern side are the Carter Center of Emory University and executive offices. The overall design hinges on horizontal bands of concrete. The controversial Presidential Parkway planned from the downtown connector to the Presidential Center and all the way to Ponce de Leon Avenue, has not received public support and remains unfinished. Access to the facility is from Cleburne Avenue, not Copenhill as its official street address implies.

Area 13

Virginia-Highland (VH)

This tour evokes a sense of Atlanta as it was in the roaring twenties and presents a sampling of the vernacular architecture of the Jazz Age. It begins with two recently renovated apartment buildings and continues along the much disfigured Ponce de Leon corridor to the avenue's busy, and fortunately well-preserved, intersection with North Highland Avenue, where some of the most attractive middle-class neighborhoods in Atlanta are situated. Developed in the late teens and twenties by speculative builders who took advantage of the new mobility afforded by the automobile, the northeast "bungalow districts," known as Virginia-Highland and Morningside, continued Midtown's residential growth, in terms of population and geography. One of the first subdivisions was North Boulevard Park, centered on Park Drive, which was begun in 1916 and took advantage of the proximity of Piedmont Park (AP 13). On tree-lined streets conducive to strolling, small apartment buildings blend with one-story bungalows with inviting front porches—both well suited to the narrow city lots.

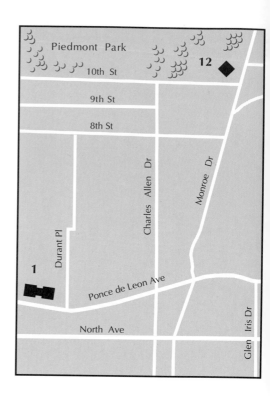

Area 13

Virginia-Highland (VH)

1 Atlanta Transitional Center
2 Sears and Roebuck Building
3 Ford Factory Square
4 Briarcliff Plaza
5 Druid Hills Baptist Church
6 Briarcliff Summit
7 Colonnade Condominiums
8 Atkins Park
9 RJ's Wine Bar Cafe
10 Highland Hardware
11 Samuel M. Inman Middle School
12 ParkSide Restaurant

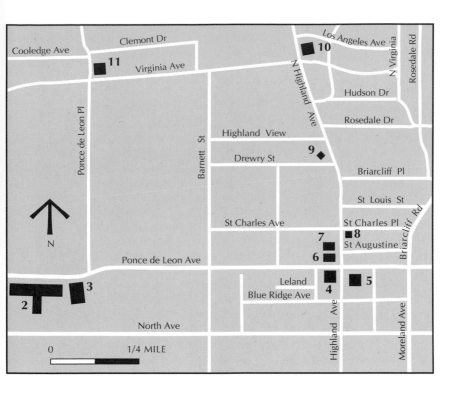

Cooledge Ave

Clemont Dr

■11 Virginia Ave

Los Angeles Ave

■10

N Virginia

Rosedale Rd

N Highland Ave

Hudson Dr

Rosedale Dr

Ponce de Leon Pl

Barnett St

Highland View

Drewry St

9 ◆

Briarcliff Pl

St Louis St

Briarcliff Rd

St Charles Ave

St Charles Pl

■8

7 ■

St Augustine

N

6 ■

Ponce de Leon Ave

Leland

5

Blue Ridge Ave

4

Highland Ave

Moreland Ave

2

■3

North Ave

0   1/4 MILE

VH 1 Atlanta Transitional Center (332 Ponce de Leon Apartments and The Rosslyn)

332 and 344 Ponce de Leon Avenue, N.E.
332 Ponce de Leon Apartments 1921: G. Lloyd Preacher, Architect. The Rosslyn 1913: Lila Ross Wilburn, Architect. Renovation 1991: Taylor-Anderson, Architects; UDC Award

Venturing down Ponce de Leon Avenue from Midtown, the visitor will see sections featuring a strange mixture of fast-food establishments and pre–World War II garden apartments in the Craftsman style. Typical of this style is what is now the Atlanta Transitional Center, which combines two such structures into a halfway house for men and women who have served time in prison. The building on the right was previously called the Rosslyn, after its designer, Lila Ross Wilburn (1885–1967), one of the few women architects in Atlanta who had an extensive residential practice. The oversized brackets supporting the roof and the unusual curved solid metal balcony rails are distinguishing features.

VH 2 Sears and Roebuck Building

677 Ponce de Leon Avenue, N.E.
1926: Nimmons, Carr and Wright, Architects (Chicago)

The truly monumental Sears and Roebuck Building stands across the street from the site of Ponce de Leon Springs, which at the turn of the century was a popular country spa that could be reached from Peachtree Street by streetcar. All Sears and Roebuck buildings throughout the country were entrusted to the same Chicago-based architectural firm; their powerful masses pierced by large glass panes were given an identical architectural treatment, generally with strong projecting piers (as is

the case here) sheathed in red brick. A landmark feature, the centrally located tower on Ponce de Leon Avenue was originally designed with setbacks. Its low pyramidal roof and stone accents were inspired by Italian villas of the Renaissance, bringing a conservative but eminently refined note to the stark structure. Originally a retail store and mail order warehouse, the building was recently purchased by the City of Atlanta for use as office space.

VH 3 Ford Factory Square (Ford Factory Building)

699 Ponce de Leon Avenue, N.E.
1916: John Graham, Designer; NR. Adaptive Reuse 1987: Bradfield Associates, Architects; UDC Award

The Ford Motor Company came to Atlanta in 1907 with a small sales and service branch. In 1914, as a result of a new regionalist policy, the company decided to concentrate its sales, service, administration, assembly, and shipping operations for four Southeastern states in Atlanta, and moved to the present site on the Ponce de Leon corridor. The following year production began on the Model T. The work of an in-house designer, this 150,000-square-foot facility resembles Ford's other regional headquarters. Offices occupied the front of the building; assembly areas were concentrated in the back. A highly articulated brick facade with terra-cotta accents was designed to face Ponce de Leon Avenue and disguise an industrial loft structure, in poured-in-place concrete, with a

central lightwell and columns supporting mushroom caps. In 1942 the Ford Factory was acquired by the United States War Department, which sold it to a private developer in 1979. Placed on the National Register in 1984, Ford Factory Square has been restored and divided into upscale one- and two-bedroom rental units, with commercial space available on the ground floor.

VH 4 **Briarcliff Plaza**
1037–1061 Ponce de Leon Avenue, N.E.
1939: George Harwell Bond, Architect. Renovation 1982: The Kirkland Group, Architects; UDC Award

VH 5 **Druid Hills Baptist Church**
1085 Ponce de Leon Avenue, N.E.
1928: Dougherty and Gardner, Architects (Nashville)

Designed to serve the Druid Hills and Atkins Park districts, **Briarcliff Plaza** was Atlanta's first automobile-oriented commercial strip, and in 1939 boasted "plentiful parking space." With a smaller group of stores at a right angle, the low structure set back from Ponce de Leon Avenue was designed in the then-popular style of commercial Art Deco that has come to be known as "streamlined moderne." The center of the plaza is marked by the multicolor fanlike motif of the theater marquee. At the intersection with North Highland Avenue, the diamond-shaped

VH 4

VH 5

sign of the drugstore espouses the curve of the continuous awning, along which runs bright neon letters. Once dilapidated, the storefronts have been revamped with tiles, glass blocks, and metal trims. On a relatively low budget, the recent renovation recaptures the mixture of glamour and neighborhood quality that makes Briarcliff Plaza a genuine Atlanta landmark. Across North Highland Avenue stands the **Druid Hills Baptist Church,** completed in 1928. With its colossal pedimented portico, this Beaux-Arts structure closely resembles the First Church of Christ, Scientist (UM 17) in Midtown by Edward Dougherty and Arthur Neal Robinson. Additions to the original square-shaped sanctuary were erected in the mid-1950s.

VH 6

VH 6 Briarcliff Summit (Briarcliff Apartments)
1050 Ponce de Leon Avenue, N.E.
1925: G. Lloyd Preacher, Architect; NR

The nine-story H-shaped structure now known as Briarcliff Summit was originally a luxury apartment hotel. Commissioned by Asa Candler, who retained a suite on the top floor and had his real estate company headquarters there, it complemented the single-family development of Druid Hills. The design superimposes an unadorned red brick shaft and a stylized lighthearted Mediterranean top on a severe two-story, cast-in-place concrete base with horizontal striations mimicking stone masonry. Walls on the upper floor are stuccoed; notice their colorful terra-cotta detailing, especially on the engaged columns with Corinthian capitals between the twin and triple arched openings. Following the general decay of the Virginia-Highland neighborhood, the hotel was vacated and abandoned in the 1960s. Converted into apartments for senior citizens, it reopened in 1979 at the time this area began to be rejuvenated.

VH 7 Colonnade Condominiums (Colonnade Court Apartments)
734 and 746 North Highland Avenue, N.E.
1918: Architect Unknown; NR

Designed in the same free-spirited manner as the surrounding bungalows, the Colonnade Condominiums are one of the best examples of garden apartments in Atlanta. Two structures, perpendicular to North Highland Avenue, frame a handsomely landscaped courtyard with Mediterranean-styled shrubbery. An Italianate flavor is further enhanced by the tiles of the boldly projecting decorative roofs and the stucco of the attic, pierced with smaller openings than the two floors below. The residential complex is well named since the dominant feature of its design is the use of overscaled white columns, strikingly detached from the red brick background framing the terraces and porches. Their Ionic capitals are repeated on top of the lamp posts in the courtyard. Notice "pre-postmodern" details, such as the broken pediments enhancing the raised doorways and the brick and terra-cotta frame of the square openings.

VH 8 Atkins Park
Saint Augustine Place, Saint Charles Place, and Saint Louis Place, N.E.
Begun 1910, NR

VH 9 RJ's Wine Bar Cafe
870 North Highland Avenue, N.E.
Circa 1920: Builder Unknown. Remodeling 1986: Roy Frangiamore, Architect; UDC Award

Atkins Park was developed by Edwin Wiley Grove, a Saint Louis pharmaceutical company owner, who took advantage of the new Ponce de Leon streetcar line. The development was given a distinctive character

VH 9

and a sense of enclosure by the "gates" (stone posts and walls) built at the intersections of its three parallel tree-lined streets—Saint Augustine Place, Saint Charles Place, and Saint Louis Place—with North Highland Avenue and Briarcliff Road. It features parallel service alleys in the middle of the two interior blocks. A medley of single-family period homes and Craftsman style bungalows, built between 1912 and the early 1930s, form a tight neighborhood fabric. Two blocks away, at the corner of Drewry Street and North Highland Avenue, an authentic cottagelike gas station was recently transformed into **RJ's Wine Bar Cafe**.

VH 10 **Highland Hardware**
1045 North Highland Avenue, N.E.
1926: Builder Unknown. Restoration 1984: Peter Hand and Associates, Architects; UDC, GAAIA Awards

VH 11 **Samuel M. Inman Middle School**
774 Virginia Avenue, N.E.
1923: Warren C. Powell, Architect

VH 12 **ParkSide Restaurant**
500 Tenth Street, N.E.
1990: Anderson/Schwartz, Architects (New York)

Recently rediscovered by young professionals, the area around the intersection of Virginia and North Highland avenues is anchored by a small shopping strip dating back to the late 1920s. Most businesses here are now directed toward entertainment; one exception, however, is **Highland Hardware**. Behind the original brick facade protected by a tile-covered parapet, exists a remodeled interior well fitted for a store specializing in woodworking materials and tools. Visitors to the area

VH 10

VH 12

should walk along Lanier Boulevard, a quiet divided parkway parallel to North Highland Avenue, which features a median planted with beautiful magnolias. Lined with bungalows and neo-Tudor homes, Lanier Boulevard extends to the Morningside district, another residential development built between the world wars. Driving on Virginia Avenue to Piedmont Park, one comes upon another "landmark," the **Samuel M. Inman Middle School,** designed in the neo-Byzantine style that characterized school construction in Atlanta in the 1920s. At the intersection of Monroe Drive and Tenth Street, the **ParkSide Restaurant** integrates a former golf-course clubhouse from the 1930s with an upscale dining facility. The visual and physical transition between the picturesque structure in Stone Mountain granite topped by a small cupola and the glazed rectangular dining room is provided by a clocktower reminiscent of one from the 1895 Cotton States Exposition.

creation of Joel Hurt. As early as
.....ck Law Olmsted, who subseqøently turned
..... over to his sons. In 1900 Hurt, unable to raise the capital
for the development, sold Druid Hills to a consortium that included
Asa Griggs Candler, whose house at 1260 Briarcliff Road is now part of
the Georgia Mental Health Institute. The fifteen-hundred-acre development opened in 1908, as the first example of comprehensive suburban
planning in Atlanta. Ponce de Leon Avenue was continued and treated
as a divided boulevard, to serve as the central focus and main artery
for the development. This "parkway" was lined by a number of elegant churches and stately homes. In the years since, it has become a
busy thoroughfare, and many of the residences are now offices. Characterized by large lots with houses situated well back from the road,
Druid Hills presents a very different character from that of Inman Park.
Here Neel Reid received some of his earliest residential commissions in
Atlanta. A country club and golf course constructed in 1924 mark the
southern limit of this National Register district, which tolerates very few
intrusions.

Druid Hills (DH)

1 Callanwolde Fine Arts Center
2 Stillwood Chase
3 Will Campbell House
4 Sigmund Montag House
5 Louis Regenstein House
6 Frank Adair House
7 The Performing Arts and Athletic Center, Paideia School
8 Oscar Strauss House
9 Joseph Neel Reid House
10 Walter Rich House
11 Smith-Benning House

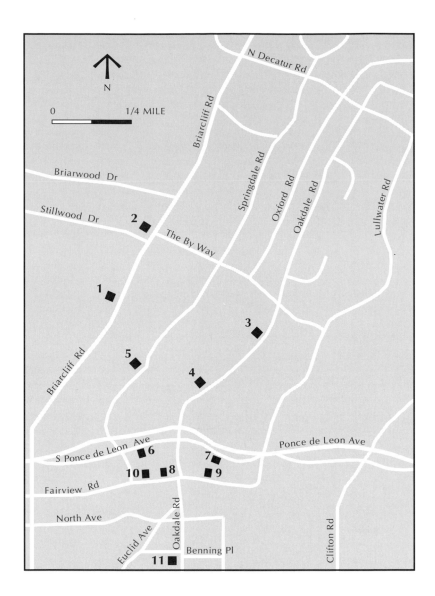

DH 1 Callanwolde Fine Arts Center

980 Briarcliff Road, N.E.
1917–1921: Henry Hornbostel, Architect (New York City and
Pittsburgh); NR

Callanwolde was built for Asa Griggs Candler's eldest son, Charles
Howard Candler (1878–1957), who was chairman of the board of the
Coca-Cola Company and of the board of trustees of Emory University.
It derives its name from Callan Castle in Ireland ("Callan" is Irish for
"Candler"), which was given to a Candler ancestor by the British crown
in the seventeenth century, and "wold," Old English for woods or forest.
Adjacent to Druid Hills, the mansion was nestled in a twenty-seven-acre
wooded tract (now reduced to twelve acres). Its style can be qualified
as "modern neo-Tudor," and, as in his Italianate buildings on the Emory
University campus, Henry Hornbostel simplified historical precedents
and incorporated modern construction methods and practical requirements into his designs. Consequently, Callanwolde is built of poured-
in-place concrete and steel. Windows and the herringbone pattern half-
timberings are much larger than in authentic Tudor homes. Battlements
and tracery are used with moderation. The irregular, rambling elevations
are unified by an uninterrupted roof plane with transverse gables of the
same height at each end. The lofty 27,000-square-foot interior, with
twenty-four rooms, offers richer and more eclectic decoration than the
exterior. Restored in the 1970s, Callanwolde now houses a Fine Arts
Center for the DeKalb County Recreation, Parks, and Cultural Affairs
Department.

DH 2 Stillwood Chase

Briarcliff Road at the By Way, N.E.
1988: Taylor and Williams, Architects

Stillwood Chase represents a noteworthy exception among current stan-
dardized and undistinguished multifamily housing projects in Atlanta.
The architects, who also acted as developers, respected the domestic

scale of the neighborhood and preserved mature trees. The thirty-four townhouses on this small, irregular, infill site are grouped in four clusters around an interior street lined with landscaped sidewalks. Atop a brick base, walls mix wood clapboards and stucco painted green, beige, and brown. Gazebos, trellises, latticed gables, and bay windows individualize the units.

DH 3 **Will Campbell House**
888 Oakdale Road, N.E.
1914: Hentz, Reid and Adler, Architects; Neel Reid, Designer

DH 4 **Sigmund Montag House**
850 Oakdale Road, N.E.
1915: Hentz, Reid and Adler, Architects; Neel Reid, Designer

DH 5 **Louis Regenstein House**
848 Springdale Road, N.E.
1917: Hentz, Reid and Adler, Architects; Neel Reid, Designer

The asymmetrical composition of the **Will Campbell House** gives evidence to Neel Reid's ability to depart from historical precedents in order to individualize his residential commissions. In pointing out that "the entrance doorway is derived from the 1700 to 1750 period; the use of two story pilasters is typical of 1750 to 1780, and the floor casement doors and sidelight are from the Federal period, 1781–1820," architectural historian James Grady has rightly stressed how Reid placed

adaptable effects above historical accuracy (*The Architecture of Neel Reid in Georgia*, p. 32). Giant Ionic pilasters divide the street facade into three parts, each of which exhibits its own tripartite arrangement (notice the unusual superimposed screened porches on the left end side). Dormer windows and chimney stacks give a vertical accent to the composition, which is rendered more abstract by the sparse ornamentation in very low relief. The shifting of the entry to the right is made all the more dramatic by the bright red hue of the entrance door. The **Sigmund Montag House** was also designed by Neel Reid. Its hipped tile roof, brick quoins, and window accents are directly inspired by the architecture of early seventeenth-century French chateaux, while precedents for the entrance motif can be found in seventeenth-century England. The **Louis Regenstein House** is one of the first Italian-inspired homes designed by Neel Reid. The profile and simplicity of its gabled street elevation and the way in which the pink stucco walls (originally a more authentic buff color) are punctured by openings are reminiscent of farmhouses in Tuscany.

DH 6   Frank Adair House
1341 South Ponce de Leon Avenue, N.E.
1911: Hentz and Reid, Architects; Neel Reid, Designer

For one of the first homes he built in Atlanta, Neel Reid drew inspiration from English domestic architecture of around 1700. However, instead of the traditional dark red facade of neo-Georgian residences, the Frank Adair House is faced in a cheerful cream brick veneer with deep mortar joints. Another departure from historical precedents is evidenced in the lateral placement of the pedimented doorway (a porte cochere adjacent to this entrance has been demolished). The unconventional composition of the central portion demonstrates Reid's masterful handling of proportions and ornamentation. The triangular rhythm, created by the vertical alignment of the pedimented dormers over the paired shutters

between windows rather than the windows themselves and the unusual placement of stone panels with swag motifs below the second-floor windowsills, alleviates the formality of the four double French doors of the living room on the ground level. Before being restored to its original grandeur, the Frank Adair House had known several owners and many years of neglect.

DH 7

DH 7 **The Performing Arts and Athletic Center, Paideia School**
1509 South Ponce de Leon Avenue, N.E.
1987: Dowling Architects and Associates, Architects; Housen and Gambino, Landscape Architects; UDC Award

Paideia School, housed in several stately homes, required a Performing Arts and Athletic Center that would include an auditorium seating 380 and a gymnasium. The three-hundred-foot-long structure, playfully designed by Dowling Architects, is sited in mid block behind two existing houses, which are also inhabited by the school, and adjusts to the residential scale without being intrusive. The volumes are broken up into smaller scale units and employ vernacular forms and materials (brick, wood trim, and shingles). Notice the varying patterns in the load-bearing masonry walls and the variety of colors used on the roof surfaces.

DH 8

DH 8 **Oscar Strauss House**
1372 Fairview Road, N.E.
1917: Hentz, Reid and Adler, Architects; Neel Reid, Designer

DH 9 **Joseph Neel Reid House**
1436 Fairview Road, N.E.
1914: Hentz, Reid and Adler, Architects; Neel Reid, Designer

Another of Neel Reid's early works, the **Oscar Strauss House** is a rare example of the architect's use of the medieval Tudor style. Features typical of this English-inspired style—dark rough brick walls, half timbering, small glass panes—receive a more stylized than historical treatment. Notice the understated doorway with a metal grille and twin terra-cotta medallions. The eclectic Reid selected the neo-Georgian style for his own home, the **Joseph Neel Reid House,** which he occupied only briefly before moving to Roswell (see RS 2). According to architectural historian James Grady, architect Charles Platt's much larger Anna Osgood House (1902) in Hadlyme, Connecticut, offered a precedent for the prominent central motif—a doorway framed by Doric pilasters and topped by a Palladian window (*Architecture of Neel Reid in Georgia*, p. 38).

DH 10

DH 10 Walter Rich House
1348 Fairview Road, N.E.
1913: Hentz, Reid and Adler, Architects; Neel Reid, Designer

The Walter Rich House, which Neel Reid designed for the owner of Rich's Department Store, qualifies as a "French manor house" based on its stuccoed walls pierced by high windows with wooden shutters, its steep roof with gabled dormers and prominent but unadorned chimney stacks, and the low stone wall framing the central doorway. The symmetrical composition is enlivened by the placement of the side dormer windows between, as opposed to directly above, the other openings. As in most of Reid's domestic designs, the ornamentation focuses on the doorway, which in this particular instance is surmounted by a Rococo-inspired carved motif and mock balcony in wrought iron.

DH 11   **Smith-Benning House**
520 Oakdale Road, N.E.
1886: Architect Unknown; NR

The Smith-Benning House is one of the oldest residences in Candler Park. Named after Asa Griggs Candler, this middle-class residential district, located south of Druid Hills, was developed around 1885, and is more akin to its neighbor to the southwest, Inman Park. The section that is on the National Register (roughly bounded by Moreland, DeKalb, McLendon, and Harold avenues, Mathews Street, and Clifton Terrace) assembles a varied housing stock. The homes, built predominantly from the 1880s to the 1920s, range from Eastlake cottages to Craftsman bungalows. The area, rediscovered in the 1970s, remains affordable and displays craftsmanship as fine as that in Inman Park's Victorian homes. Suffering from ill repair for some time, the Smith-Benning House is now undergoing much needed restoration.

Emory University (EU)

Named for Methodist bishop John Emory, Emory University has an
enrollment of approximately nine thousand students. An outgrowth of
Emory College (founded in 1836 in Oxford, Georgia), the Atlanta campus was established in 1914, when Asa Candler donated seventy-five
acres of his Druid Hills development along with a large endowment
to the school. His brother, Bishop Warren Candler, became the university's first chancellor. The Coca-Cola legacy remains a major con-
tributor to the university's growth; the most recent building campaign
was boosted by the $105 million endowment received from Ernest and
George Woodruff in 1979. Emory's first master plan was entrusted to
the Beaux-Arts-trained architect Henry Hornbostel (1867–1961), whose
firm built the Carnegie Technical Schools in Pittsburgh. The most prestigious facilities planned for the Emory campus were arranged around a
quadrangle, and the hilly terrain dictated a less formal layout for subsequent facilities. Atlanta's climate and the lush vegetation of the site led
Hornbostel to use Italian villas of the High Renaissance as a model for
academic buildings. Ivey and Crook, a local firm responsible for much
of the architecture on the 630-acre campus, continued the Italianate
style into the 1960s. This visit to Emory starts with a walking tour around
the original quadrangle and a driving tour centered on the medically
oriented "Clifton Corridor," which features, among other prestigious
institutions, the Centers for Disease Control and the American Cancer
Society National Headquarters.

Area 15

Emory University (EU)

1 Glenn Memorial United Methodist Church
2 Education Building and Little Chapel, Glenn Memorial Church
3 Rich Memorial Building
4 Michael C. Carlos Hall
5 Emory University Museum of Art and Archeology
6 Pitts Theology Library
7 William R. Cannon Chapel
8 George W. Woodruff Physical Education Center
9 R. Howard Dobbs University Center
10 Alumni Memorial Hall
11 Gambrell Hall
12 Emory University Hospital
13 Harris Hall
14 South Clinic Building, Emory Clinic
15 Scarborough Memorial Building Addition, Emory Clinic
16 Ronald McDonald Childhood Cancer Clinic
17 Robert W. Woodruff Health Sciences Center Administration Building
18 Lullwater House
19 O. Wayne Rollins Research Center
20 George and Irene Woodruff Residential Center
21 Turner Village and D. Abbott Turner Center

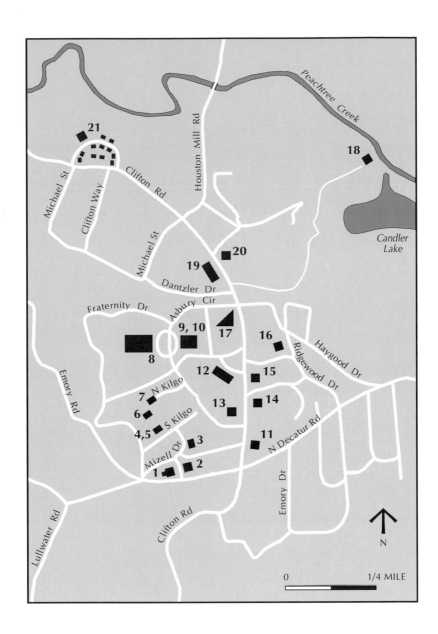

EU 1 **Glenn Memorial United Methodist Church**
1652 North Decatur Road, N.E.
1930: Hentz, Adler and Shutze, Architects; Philip Shutze, Designer

EU 2 **Education Building and Little Chapel, Glenn Memorial Church**
1660 North Decatur Road, N.E.
1940: Shutze and Armistead, Architects; Philip Shutze, Designer

EU 3 **Rich Memorial Building**
1602 Mizell Drive, N.E.
1946: Shutze and Armistead, Architects; Philip Shutze, Designer.
Addition 1975: Tippett and Taylor, Architects

An elegant transition between Druid Hills and the Emory campus is
assured by a wrought-iron gateway and the **Glenn Memorial United
Methodist Church,** which is also used as a public auditorium for the uni-

versity. Blending a number of historical precedents (the unadorned shaft is reminiscent of King's Chapel in Boston and the steeple is similar to Saint Michael's in Charleston), Philip Shutze's classical design achieves a great degree of purity. It plays on the subtle contrast between large unadorned planes of cream-colored stucco and the slender Ionic entrance colonnade detached from a rusticated background. In the **Education Building** and **Rich Memorial Building,** Shutze followed Hornbostel's Italian inspiration for Emory's original quadrangle buildings (EU 4, EU 6), but the highly sculptural motifs enhancing the entrances are personal touches. The Education Building includes the exquisitely crafted **Little Chapel,** which was inspired by Christopher Wren's Church of Saint Stephen Walbrook (1672–1679) in London.

EU 2

EU 4 Michael C. Carlos Hall (Lamar School of Law)
571 South Kilgo Circle, N.E.
1916: Palmer, Hornbostel and Jones, Architects (New York and
Pittsburgh); Henry Hornbostel, Designer; NR

EU 5 Emory University Museum of Art and Archeology
Michael C. Carlos Hall Additions and Remodeling 1984, 1993: Michael
Graves, Architect (Princeton), AIA Award

Michael C. Carlos Hall is one of the original buildings of Henry Hornbostel's 1915 master plan. The architect's initial concept was not entirely
implemented: on the main elevation, the asymmetry of the fenestration
was to be concealed by a one-story colonnade linking the quadrangle
buildings and leading to a monumental library. With its low-pitched red-
tiled roof and projecting cornice, Carlos Hall is reminiscent of Italian
villas. Rich terra-cotta motifs, inspired by Spanish Colonial architecture,
enhance the monumental doorway. Otherwise, decorative effects are
limited to an original patchwork of thin slabs of Georgia marble (these
were "leftovers" from the first sawing of rough blocks) ranging in color
from light grey to pink. Joints are hardly visible because the marble
facing, anchored by wires, was placed inside the forms of the concrete bearing walls before they were poured. On the exterior, Michael
Graves's addition for the building's conversion to the **Emory University
Museum of Art and Archeology** is limited to an unobtrusive stair tower
on the back side. Inside, this major proponent of "modern traditional-
ism" was responsible for a drastic remodeling even to the smallest detail.
Fortunately, in the entrance lobby he preserved Hornbostel's lofty spiral
staircase, silhouetted against a commanding arched window. Emory
University can be proud of its custom-made museum, with the lower
level devoted to permanent archeological collections (notice the temple
plans painted on the floors and the display cases in bird's-eye maple
veneer), and upper level intended for temporary exhibitions. Graves
masterfully carved out interior spaces, modulated wall surfaces, and
orchestrated visual sequences. His highly personal decorative syntax is
respectful of the scale and program of the museum. Neutral tones have

been used on walls and ceilings of exhibition areas, while "Gravesian" muted colors enhance the colonnaded clerestory of the bowed staircase as well as the intermediate spaces (notice in these spaces the neo–Art Deco hanging lamps and the recessed ceilings in the shape of a brass-colonnaded Greek temple). As of this writing, Michael Graves, respectful of the identity of the quadrangle, has designed a 35,000-square-foot addition in stucco and marble, doubling the existing building toward the east; its center will be marked by a colonnaded square entrance pavilion. New galleries are expected to open in 1993.

EU 6 **Pitts Theology Library (Candler School of Theology)**
505 North Kilgo Circle, N.E.
1919: Palmer, Hornbostel and Jones, Architects (New York and Pittsburgh); Henry Hornbostel, Designer; NR. Interior remodeling 1965: Paul Rudolph, Architect (New York)

EU 7 **William R. Cannon Chapel**
515 North Kilgo Circle, N.E.
1981: Paul Rudolph, Architect (New York); Tippett, Taylor and Anderson, Associated Architects

Leaving Carlos Hall (EU 4), the visitor faces its twin building across the quadrangle, also designed by Henry Hornbostel. This second building now houses the **Pitts Theology Library,** remodeled in a modernist fashion by Paul Rudolph, whose father was in the first graduating class of the Candler School of Theology. The nearby **William R. Cannon Chapel,** another Rudolph design, includes offices and meeting rooms along with

an impressive sanctuary. Rudolph is best known for his "brutalist" buildings (epitomized by the Architecture School at Yale University, 1964), but in this case his surprising design is eminently sympathetic to its surroundings. Taking advantage of a sharp drop-off at the edge of the site, cascading vaults covered in red tiles of the same color as Hornbostel's buildings, a flat steeple, and a high freestanding perpendicular vault framing an entrance emerge from the historic quadrangle. An intimate courtyard was created at the lower level. The roofline, slender pilotis, and the walls in smooth formed concrete all indicate the architect's acknowledged indebtedness to the work of Le Corbusier. The exposed structural elements, with beautifully crafted herringbone motifs, equally dominate the interior, where they successfully blend with exposed mechanical ducts.

EU 8 George W. Woodruff Physical Education Center
600 Asbury Circle, N.E.
1983: John Portman and Associates, Architects

The 187,000-square-foot George W. Woodruff Physical Education Center, which includes a sports medicine clinic on the upper level, was made as unobtrusive as possible by sliding its mass into the hillside and enclosing it with ivy berms. From the inconspicuous entrance on Asbury Circle runs a skylit concourse, opened laterally to the lower level and crossed by transverse bridges connecting the upper floor. On the left side, the multipurpose gymnasium and Olympic-size swimming pool are visible through glass planes; opposite are four levels of smaller rooms accessed through a "Portmanesque" central stair hall. Without a highly visible or competitive sports program at Emory, Portman's design needed

EU 8

to infuse excitement and a sense of community to support the facility. His simple but strongly stated idea, further articulated with the use of economical detailing, generates a successful solution to a building type rarely conducive to architectural excellence.

EU 9 **R. Howard Dobbs University Center**
605 Asbury Circle, N.E.
1986: John Portman and Associates, Architects

EU 10 **Alumni Memorial Hall**
605 Asbury Circle, N.E.
1949: Ivey and Crook, Architects. Renovation 1986: John Portman and Associates, Architects

The relatively low profile and white and pearl-grey Georgia marble veneer of the **R. Howard Dobbs University Center** enable Emory's new 91,400-square-foot student center to remain a friendly presence

225　**Emory University**

EU 9, *interior*; EU 10, *exterior*

among its older neighbors. The bold masses of the main elevation on Asbury Circle express the building's tripartite organization: the post office, kitchens, and faculty dining rooms are located behind the curved colonnade on the ground level; the bookstore on the intermediate semi-circular layer; and the food plaza inside the overhanging third level, supported by freestanding structural piers that are pulled out on the diagonal and treated as decorative elements. Like John Portman's downtown hotels, the Dobbs University Center is an introverted building in which users are led progressively toward an exciting communal space. Here the theatrical experience takes on a literal meaning. By way of a horseshoe staircase protected by a transparent rotunda, one proceeds to a skylit plaza. Several levels of tiered curvilinear balconies, which accommodate dining tables, look onto the staged neo-Renaissance entrance facade of the **Alumni Memorial Hall**.

EU 11

EU 11 **Gambrell Hall**
1722 North Decatur Road, N.E.
1972: Stevens and Wilkinson, Architects; Kemp Mooney, Designer

Housing a 450-seat auditorium and moot court, a law library, and the student lounge, as well as classrooms and offices for faculty and staff, Gambrell Hall is an abstract composition of horizontal masses that, according to Stevens and Wilkinson, "reflects the strength and stability of the law." The main entrance on North Decatur Road is framed by staircases rising to a second level podium, which is interrupted by a "moat" on the opposite side. Paradoxically the symmetry and formality of the ribbon windows and slender columns, influenced by Le Corbusier, give the structure a "neo-Beaux-Arts" character. The deep blue-green marble facing contrasts sharply against the white concrete walls of the cantilevered upper floor.

EU 12 **Emory University Hospital**
1364 Clifton Road, N.E.
1922: Hentz, Reid and Adler; Neel Reid, Designer.
A Wing (Whitehead Wing) 1945: Shutze and Armistead, Architects;
Philip Shutze, Designer. G Wing 1973: Robert and Company. Visitor
Reception Center Addition and Renovation 1987: Nix, Mann and
Associates, Architects; SARC Award

EU 13 **Harris Hall (Florence C. Harris Memorial Nurses' Home)**
1340 Clifton Road, N.E.
1928: Hentz, Adler and Shutze, Architects; Philip Shutze, Designer.
Addition 1953: Ivey and Crook, Architects

EU 14 **South Clinic Building (Eye Center and Emory Clinic Addition)**
1327 Clifton Road, N.E.
1979: Tippett and Associates, Architects

EU 15 **Scarborough Memorial Building Addition**
1365 Clifton Road, N.E.
1988: Tippett and Associates, Architects

EU 16 **Ronald McDonald Childhood Cancer Clinic**
2032 Ridgewood Drive, N.E.
1986: Thompson, Ventulett, Stainback and Associates, Architects

The original **Emory University Hospital,** designed by Neel Reid's firm in the spirit of Hornbostel's quadrangle buildings, was a U-shaped building with a low tile roof supported by prominent brackets. Designed by Philip Shutze, the Whitehead Wing, which projects toward Clifton Road and forms the main pedestrian entry to the hospital, conveys some dignity to a structure, plagued by random additions, that did not feature the refined Italianate detailing found on its neighbor **Harris Hall,** also designed by Shutze's firm and currently a dormitory. The Whitehead Wing houses conference rooms for the hospital administration and staff. The over-scaled decorative elements, especially the entrance motif with its broken pediment and date of completion (1945) engraved in Roman numerals on the lintel, bear the mark of Philip Shutze. He was also responsible for the decoration (including elaborate woodcarving executed by Her-bert Millard) of the Whitehead Memorial Room, which serves as the hos-pital's boardroom. Across the street, it is interesting to compare how one firm, Tippett and Associates, in a decade's time switched from the "neo-brutalist" treatment of large abstract concrete masses in the **South Clinic Building** to the Mediterranean-inspired forms and materials in keeping with the "Emory vernacular" of its neighbor the **Scarborough Memorial Building Addition**. In the design of the **Ronald McDonald Childhood Cancer Clinic,** the architects have broken up volumes in order to de-emphasize the institutional nature of the facility and to maintain the scale of neighboring structures.

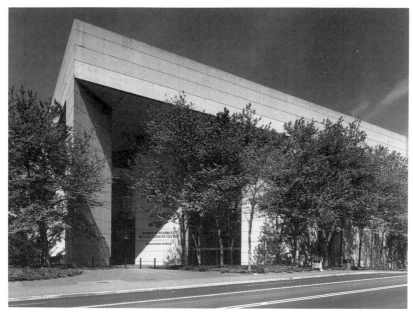

EU 17 **Robert W. Woodruff Health Sciences Center Administration Building**
1440 Clifton Road, N.E.
1976: Heery and Heery, Architects; Merrill Elam, Project Architect;
GAAIA Award

In the Robert W. Woodruff Health Sciences Center Administration
Building—a mixed-use building for the medical school—educational
facilities are located on the ancillary level, an open exhibition space
and a benefactors' room occupy the plaza level, and administrative
offices complete the two upper levels. Massive concrete forms and large
expanses of glass make the triangular structure appear larger than its
78,000 square feet. The sixty-foot-high portico enhances the monumentality of the Clifton Road entrance. The integration of roofs covered in
red clay tile above each floor scales down the diagonal elevation facing
the older part of the campus. An outdoor theater (often used by students for sunbathing) is formed by the roof of the 500-seat underground
auditorium.

EU 18 **Lullwater House (Walter Turner Candler House)**
1463 Clifton Road, N.E.
1926: Ivey and Crook, Architects; Lewis E. Crook Jr., Designer; NR

Beautifully sited on a high point overlooking a large lake and built on
185 acres of a landscaped park, the 7,500-square-foot Lullwater House
has been the residence of Emory University's presidents since 1963. At
the request of the client, one of Asa Candler's sons, the newly formed

firm of Ivey and Crook used sixteenth-century English country estates as models for the design. Gables and prominent slate roofs with high chimney stacks, walls of fieldstone quarried on the grounds, and half-timbered walls, as well as small-paned windows convey a sense of the picturesque English predecessors. Centered on an arrival court, the crenellated tower containing the main entrance articulates the L-shaped plan. The lower volumes on the left-hand side of the tower house the kitchen and the original servants' quarters, while the private quarters are located in the higher portions. The English influence continues in the interior with furnishings and detailing found in the later styles of the Elizabethan and Regency periods.

EU 19   **O. Wayne Rollins Research Center**
         1510 Clifton Road, N.E.
         1990: Rosser Fabrap International, Architects and Engineers;
         GAAIA Award

EU 20   **George and Irene Woodruff Residential Center**
         1495 Clifton Road, N.E.
         1987: Aeck Associates, Architects

Appropriately mechanistic in its architectural expression, the **O. Wayne Rollins Research Center** offers over six acres of floor space for interdisciplinary research labs to what will become a new campus for a consortium of Atlanta educational institutions. The northeast elevation forms a grid that defines the lab units within. The southwest elevation utilizes

the exterior horizontal runs of exhaust ducts for sun shading and gathers these mechanical systems into four vertical stacks that define the center's massing and give it the appearance of an electrical generating plant. Across the street, an undergraduate dormitory, the **George and Irene Woodruff Residential Center,** recalls the original architecture of the quadrangle through the repetition of the red tile roofs and simple window treatment. This semicircular building flanked by residential wings features a dining terrace with a pergola overlooking a wooded area.

EU 21 **Turner Village and D. Abbott Turner Center**
1703 Clifton Road, N.E.
Housing Renovation 1989, Community Center and Chapel 1990: Scogin, Elam and Bray, Architects; Douglas C. Allen, Landscape Architect

Turner Village provides Emory theology students with housing, a small nondenominational chapel, and a 14,000-square-foot community center, the **D. Abbott Turner Center**. The renovation of the existing two-story slablike residences was largely cosmetic: the addition of metal canopies and the raising of the upper floor, now topped by low barrel-vaulted roofs, gave these conventional units a dynamic ocean-liner look. On the northwestern part of the site, the subtle geometry of the new center and chapel is in perfect agreement with its leafy surroundings. It is based on a dynamic interplay of concave and convex lines for the walls,

overhanging roofs, and generous deck at the rear. The architects played on the contrast between heavy masonry masses of dark grey brick and opened glazed surfaces. The project's architectural and spiritual focus is to be found behind the center in the chapel, manifested in a taut, opened cylindrical spire with a slanted top. The chapel is reached through an increasingly narrow, light-filled corridor wedged between the living room and the library of the community center and downward through a curved ramp. Additional housing units for students and visiting lecturers and an association building are planned for the vacant northern section of the site.

Buckhead Residential (BR)

Buckhead has become a geographic area with very loosely defined boundaries. First to be considered are the posh residential neighborhoods and adjoining areas in the southern and western part of Buckhead which, as it is known today, extends all the way from Brookwood Station (UM 32) and the Interstate 75/85 connector in the south to the exclusive West Paces Ferry Road area, six miles north of Downtown. In the teens and twenties, its development was made possible by the advent of the automobile and the desire of Atlanta's elite to find more secluded precincts than Ansley Park or Druid Hills. The district includes several private real-estate ventures, such as Tuxedo Park, Haynes Manor, and Peachtree Heights East, as well as Peachtree Heights Park, a National Register District that was developed by E. Rivers and W. P. Andrews and laid out by the renowned New York firm of Carrère and Hastings. With the exception of West Paces Ferry Road, which has become such a busy thoroughfare that walking from one estate to another is risky indeed, quiet winding roads are lined with grand period homes. Most mansions occupy a commanding position on their large lots and are highly visible from the street. Front yards feature sweeping manicured lawns and natural stands of trees. The abundance of dogwoods and native shrubs makes a spring visit a pure delight. Secluded backyards shelter box gardens and swimming pools. Some estates have been subdivided recently into tight clusters of elaborate homes, which are caricatures of their stately neo-Georgian or Italianate neighbors.

Area 16

Buckhead Residential (BR)

1 Luxemburger House
2 Philip Junger House
3 Peachtree Post
4 E. Rivers Elementary School
5 Evans-Cucich House
6 Randolph-Lucas House
7 160 Rumson Road, N.E.
8 Second Ponce de Leon Baptist Church
9 North Fulton High School
10 Garden Hills School
11 Crestwood
12 Henry B. Tompkins House
13 D. Lurton Massee Jr. House
14 C. C. Case House
15 Lawrence P. Klamon House
16 Morris Brandon School
17 American Security Insurance Company Building
18 Trinity School
19 Andrew Calhoun House
20 Winship Nunally House
21 Villa Lamar
22 Patterson-Carr House
23 Joseph D. Rhodes House
24 James Dickey House
25 Governor's Mansion
26 Southern Center for International Studies
27 Harry L. English House
28 Knollwood
29 Albert E. Thornton House
30 Cherokee Town Club
31 H. W. Beers House
32 Floyd McRae House
33 Edward Van Winkle House
34 T. M. Watson House
35 Livingston Wright House
36 William F. Manry House
37 Philip McDuffie House
38 Ryburn Clay House
39 Bolling Jones House
40 Jesse Draper House
41 Henry Newman House
42 Robert Alston House
43 Stuart Witham House
44 Vaughn Nixon House
45 Swan House
46 Tullie Smith House

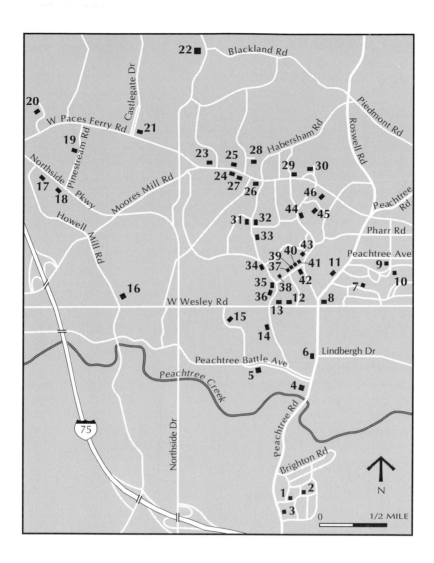

22■ Blackland Rd

20♦ W Paces Ferry Rd **■21**
Castlegate Dr

19♦
Pinestream Rd

Northside Pkwy

17♦ **23**■ **25**■ **28**■ Habersham Rd
18♦ Moores Mill Rd **24**■■ **29**■ **30**■
Howell Mill Rd **27**■ **26**■ **46**♦
44♦ **45**♦ Peachtree Rd

31■ **32**■ Pharr Rd
33■ Peachtree Ave
43♦ **9**■
39♦**40**♦ **11**♦
34■ **37**♦ **41** **10**■
35■ **42**■
16■ **38**■ **7**■
W Wesley Rd **36**■ **12**■ **8**■
13■
15♦
14■
Lindbergh Dr
Peachtree Battle Ave **6**■
5■
Peachtree Creek **4**■
Northside Dr
75
Brighton Rd

1■ **2**■
3■

N

0   1/2 MILE

BR 1   **Luxemburger House**
14 Palisades Road, N.E.
1922: Hentz, Reid and Adler, Architects; Neel Reid, Designer

BR 2   **Philip Junger House**
60 Palisades Road, N.E.
Remodeling 1985: Philip Junger, Architect

BR 3   **Peachtree Post (Micro Mart Computer Product Showroom)**
1781 Peachtree Street, N.E.
1981: Richard Rauh and Associates, Architects; GAAIA Award

Planned under the supervision of B. F. Burdette, the Brookwood Hills
District was developed in several phases from 1922 to 1930 and is listed
on the National Register. Situated on rolling terrain, this residential enclave features shady winding streets (notice the brick median marking
the intersection between Palisades and Brighton roads and Peachtree
Street) and a large recreation area incorporating a natural spring. Period
homes, such as Neel Reid's neo-Georgian **Luxemburger House,** and
bungalows form a dense fabric. While there are very few intrusions, one
of the most damaging was a ranch style house built in the late 1960s at
the corner of Palisades Road and Parkdale Way. With masonite siding,
large aluminum sliding doors, and an oversized concrete base, the **Philip
Junger House** before it was remodeled was considered an anomaly
in the neighborhood. Afterward, however, the use of shingle siding, a
gabled front facade, and a band of paired Doric columns, as well as a

reduction in the scale of the openings have unified the structure and made it more appropriate to its commanding site. The white colonnade that fills the original overhang leads to the new stair addition and recessed entry. Returning to busy Peachtree Street, the visitor will encounter the **Peachtree Post,** originally designed as a computer product showroom and now used as a video production studio. The highly articulated high-tech facade features elegant proportions in a variety of sleek materials.

BR 4   E. Rivers Elementary School

8 Peachtree Battle Avenue, N.W.
1949: Stevens and Wilkinson, Architects

The first Georgia school designed using the vocabulary of the International Style, the E. Rivers Elementary School attracted national attention
and was featured in *TIME Magazine* as one of the nation's outstanding
schools. According to the April 1951 issue of *Architectural Forum*, it
"proved that the well-known school building ingredients—concrete,
brick, glass block and a standard 'finger plan'—can be combined in
a fine piece of architecture," and "demonstrated to other Southern
communities that modern schools can be cheerful, handsome and inexpensive." The E. Rivers School became a prototype for a number of
schools designed by Stevens and Wilkinson and by other architects in
the Atlanta area. Its exposed white concrete frame (which is continued
by a cantilevered canopy on the entrance facade) is clearly differentiated
from the cherry-red brick walls enlivened by the yellow casements of the
large windows. A detached auditorium is used for community functions.

BR 5   Evans-Cucich House

306 Peachtree Battle Avenue, N.W.
1935: A. F. N. Everett, Architect

In sharp contrast with its revivalist Peachtree Heights Park neighbors,
the flat-roofed Evans-Cucich House is one of the few Art Deco homes
in Atlanta. Sheathed in limestone, its formal raised facade on Peachtree Battle Avenue features monochromatic and stylized ornamentation
in low relief (notice the "pyramid" motif on the central top window,
reminiscent of the profile of setback skyscrapers of the 1920s). The overall decorative effect is rather severe and, in the instance of the fluted
pilasters surrounding the doorway, borders on classicism.

BR 6 **Randolph-Lucas House**
2494 Peachtree Road, N.W.
1924: P. Thornton Marye, Architect; HB

Encroached on by commercial development, this mansion, in red brick with stone accents, is said to have been patterned after the eighteenth-century Virginia home built by an ancestor of the original owner, Hollins Nicholas Randolph. Its simple mass, topped by a steep slate roof and lateral chimney stacks, is effectively reminiscent of plantation houses in the Georgian style. The large entry porch with fan and sidelights framing a large doorway more closely resembles slightly later examples of the so-called Federal style.

BR 7   **160 Rumson Road, N.E.**
1925: Burge and Stevens, Architects

BR 8   **Second Ponce de Leon Baptist Church**
2715 Peachtree Road, N.E.
1937: George Harwell Bond, Architect. Addition 1990: Peter Hand and
Associates, Architects

BR 9   **North Fulton High School**
2890 North Fulton Drive, N.E.
1932: Hentz, Adler and Shutze; Philip Shutze, Designer

BR 10   **Garden Hills School**
285 Sheridan Drive, N.E.
1938: Tucker and Howell, Architects

The simple but nicely detailed and proportioned red brick house at **160
Rumson Road,** which combines classical and Tudor stone accents, is
one of the period homes that line the major artery of Garden Hills. Rumson Road has other variations on the Tudor style by Burge and Stevens
(178 Rumson Road), and Ivey and Crook (125 Rumson Road), as well
as white frame Dutch Revival houses with gambrel roofs. The upper-
middle-class neighborhood of Garden Hills was developed by lawyer
Philip McDuffie starting in 1925 and is now on the National Register. The picturesque landscaping, which included Sunnybrook Park,
shows the enduring influence of Frederick Law Olmsted's concepts in
Atlanta. The depression during the 1930s saw the erection of smaller
period homes. Garden Hills includes some apartment buildings, like the

moorish Alhambra Apartments at 2855 Peachtree Road, but very few modern intrusions. From the 1930s onward, Garden Hills operated as a self-sufficient district with its commercial strip along Peachtree Street. The neocolonial **Second Ponce de Leon Baptist Church** (now with a compatible postmodern addition), Philip Shutze's **North Fulton High School,** and the classically inspired **Garden Hills School** are noteworthy structures in this area dating from that period.

BR 11   **Crestwood (Canton Apartments)**
2840 Peachtree Road, N.W.
1928: Architect Unknown; NR. Renovation 1984: Porter Associates, Architects; UDC Award

In the three-story Crestwood building, now converted to condominiums, one finds the same stone classical and mannerist ornaments that Philip Shutze used in the Hotel Peachtree Manor (LM 24) and Reid House (UM 23) in Midtown. The unknown designer of the Crestwood, who some believe was Philip Shutze, had to resort to artifice in order to alleviate the monotony created by elongated surfaces of red brick with unadorned paired and single sash windows. Quoins divide the long Peachtree Street elevation into three bays. The truly "heroic" two-story rusticated doorway, the pediment of which is broken by an overwhelming cartouche surmounted by a scrolled bracket and an open shell, is echoed by more modest swag motifs above the side entrances and balustrades that interrupt the parapet line. The renovation and conversion of the Canton Apartments into the Crestwood condominiums attests to the growing attraction of luxury apartment living in Buckhead.

BR 12 **Henry B. Tompkins House**
125 West Wesley Road, N.W.
1922: Hentz, Reid and Adler, Architects; Neel Reid, Designer; NR

Beautifully sited on a knoll, the Henry B. Tompkins House is an adaptation of classical English residential designs. The massing is simple and elegant, with a center block flanked by short symmetrical wings. Smooth stucco walls and unadorned sash windows contrast sharply with the heroic doorway framed by rusticated pilasters and crowned by the impressive broken segmental pediment of the projecting entrance. Neel Reid was commissioned to design this house by his friends the Tompkinses, who also entrusted the designer with the interior decoration and landscaping.

BR 13 **D. Lurton Massee Jr. House**
157 West Wesley Road, N.W.
Street Facade Renovation 1978; Pool House Addition 1986: Surber, Barber, and Mooney, Architects; Kemp Mooney, Designer; Philip Hauswirth, Landscape Architect

It is difficult to believe that the well-balanced facade of the D. Lurton Massee Jr. House, nestled in lush vegetation, is in fact a drastic renovation of an asymmetrical and bland house. The existing profile of the right-end-side pavilion served as a base to restore a symmetrical char-

acter, strengthened by the new windows whose large mullions create a geometrical interplay on the facade. Duplicating the proportions of the first-floor openings, an ornamental screen extends from the left-end side into the bushes. The doorway, now painted red to contrast with the grey and white synthetic stucco coating on the facade, was emphasized with the addition of a formal staircase framed by a retaining wall that runs the length of the house. The landscaped forecourt completes the formal and symmetrical harmony. With the new facade approximately 2,500 square feet of space was added, as well as a neoclassical pool house in the back.

BR 14 C. C. Case House
2624 Habersham Road, N.W.
1921: Hentz, Reid and Adler, Architects; Neel Reid, Designer

According to architectural historian James Grady, Neel Reid at his client's request fashioned the street facade of the C. C. Case House after Tintinhull House, a medieval manor house in Somerset County, England, which was given a classical face-lift around 1720 (*Architecture of Neel Reid in Georgia*, p. 72). The simplicity and elegance of the central pedi-

mented pavilion framed by pilasters, the segmental pediment above
the doorway, and the mullioned windows with small panes of leaded
glass are uplifted by the presence of two eagles surmounting the piers
of the entrance wall, which were also inspired by Tintinhull. Notice the
intricate concentric paving of the circular courtyard.

BR 15 **Lawrence P. Klamon House**
2665 Dellwood Drive, N.W.
1983: Surber, Barber and Mooney, Architects; Kemp Mooney,
Designer; SARC Award

The Lawrence P. Klamon House, a custom-made home of relatively
modest size, is located on a deep, narrow lot surrounded by homes of
the 1930s. Announced by a formal central driveway, the symmetrical
street facade looks all the more impressive because it is well set back
from, and raised above, Dellwood Drive. It is centered on an overscaled
Palladian doorway-exedra. This motif, intended as a response to classical details on surrounding homes, was used by Claude-Nicolas Ledoux
in his Paris gate houses of the 1780s and emulated by Thomas Jefferson
at the University of Virginia. Echoing the curvature of the doorway, the
magnified west-facing "dormer window" floods the barrel-vaulted central stair hall and the two-story central living area with sunset light (the
master suite of less formal massing is located in the back and has an intimate deck). The small square openings on the ground floor correspond
to the utility rooms, the large ones above them to two guest bedrooms.
The effect of a *piano nobile* raised on a base is enhanced by the differen-
tiation in tone of the synthetic stucco applied to the wood frame. In sum,
the Klamon House, with thoroughly modern materials and abstracted

classical forms blended into a subtle geometry, presents an idiosyncratic public image in refreshing contrast to the mass-produced eclectic cluster mansions often found in Northwest Atlanta.

BR 16

BR 16 Morris Brandon School
2741 Howell Mill Road, N.W.
1947: Tucker and Howell, Architects

Sited at a major intersection, the Morris Brandon School impresses the visitor with its stern but elegant Art Deco entrance facade. While interesting neo-Byzantine educational buildings of the 1920s and Bauhaus-inspired structures of the 1950s and 1960s are numerous in Atlanta, well-preserved examples of this transitional style, which was popular during the New Deal years, are exceptional. The sculptural masses of white painted concrete are well differentiated and proportioned (notice the subtle contrast between the terraced roofs and the slight "pediment" of the back pavilion). The central entrance block is made more dynamic by the curvature of its right corner and entrance canopy. Except for a few striations, the walls are left bare of any ornament and the decorative effect relies mostly on the rhythm and delicate divisions of the casement windows. The classroom block at the back features large functional bays.

BR 17   **American Security Insurance Company Building**
3290 Northside Parkway, N.W.
1969: Taylor and Collum; Richard Taylor, Designer; GAAIA Award

A nicely proportioned four-story office building overlooking Northside Parkway, the American Security Insurance Company Building was the first steel-frame structure constructed in Atlanta to use liquid coolant as a fireproofing device (the exterior structural columns are filled with water). The purpose of this feature was to allow the actual structural members to remain exposed rather than being concealed underneath a coating of sprayed-on fireproofing and decorative sheathing. The system works by interconnecting all water-filled members so that convection currents within them will circulate cooling water to any area heated by fire, thus delaying the deformation and failure of structural members subjected to extreme heat. An interesting facade treatment is generated by the exposed weathering steel overhangs and vertical baffles that provide passive solar heat gain control.

BR 17

BR 18

BR 18 **Trinity School**
3254 Northside Parkway, N.W.
Renovation and Addition 1984–1988: Lord and Sargent, Architects;
Terry Sargent, Designer; GAAIA, SARC, AIA Awards

Trinity School, a private academy for five hundred students from pre-
school to sixth-grade, was first housed in a former public school. The
innovative renovation and whimsical additions to that once bland two-
story structure have been widely featured and highly praised in the
architectural press. The administrative wing, which the visitor sees first,
has been expanded in order to provide a covered drop-off and pick-up
area with additional offices above. Its curvature and the way in which
the concrete columns are made of skewed stacked cubes gives the
two-story entrance colonnade a very unusual kinetic quality. Reached
through the existing school, the multipurpose facility added to the east
and housing non-classroom activities takes advantage of the forty-foot-
deep gorge where the 10,000-square-foot gymnasium, which doubles
as an auditorium, is partially buried. Rooftops and terraces, contained
by odd-shaped retaining walls that continue the design, serve as outdoor
playgrounds. A medieval-looking tower visible from Northside Parkway
anchors the composition and shelters a storytelling well and a reading
room. The rough-textured masonry of beautifully crafted ocher-colored
concrete blocks, with a few overscaled geometric openings and an array
of glass bricks arranged in a square pattern, are in sharp contrast with
the entirely glazed stairwell and other large glass planes animated by
colorful mullions. Both outside and inside, these two additions are pic-

turesque and playful, yet rational and monumental; their design strikes the viewer as a very personal and successful answer to a complex set of building parameters and a difficult site.

BR 19 **Andrew Calhoun House**
3418 Pinestream Road, N.W.
1923: Hentz, Reid and Adler, Architects; Philip Shutze, Designer; NR

BR 20 **Winship Nunally House**
1311 West Paces Ferry Road, N.W.
1923: Hentz, Reid and Adler, Architects; Neel Reid, Designer

BR 21 **Villa Lamar**
801 West Paces Ferry Road, N.W.
1912: George O. Totten Jr., Architect (New York)

BR 22 **Patterson-Carr House**
3820 Northside Drive, N.W.
1939: Hentz, Adler and Shutze, Architects; Philip Shutze, Designer

In the winter it is possible from the street to see the elaborate rooftops of the neo-Baroque **Andrew Calhoun House** through the usually dense foliage of the trees. Once thought to have been designed by Neel Reid, it has since been reattributed to Philip Shutze by architectural historian Elizabeth Dowling, who used it as the cover illustration for her monograph *American Classicist*. Reid's **Winship Nunally House** is not visible from West Paces Ferry Road because it is now located in the middle of a condominium development, which has taken its character from the original house. As architectural historian James Grady writes, the design for this "romantic" and rambling stuccoed home "is medieval in feeling but abstractly handled without precise English or French detailing" (*The Architecture of Neel Reid in Georgia*, p. 124). The **Villa Lamar,** which is also not usually visible from the street because of the lush vegetation, features a large central Palladian vestibule and a tile roof with a protruding cornice supported on brackets. The composition was directly inspired by the casino of the Villa Medici (1574–80) in Rome. The **Patterson-Carr House** demonstrates Philip Shutze's developing interest during the 1930s in early American residential architecture. Although much less formal than his earlier works of Georgian or Italian inspiration, the massing of this brick, clapboard, and stucco structure (painted in pale yellow) is carefully composed and stabilized by the central gabled portion, which features symmetrical openings. In order to preserve the pastoral beauty of the sweeping lawn, the driveway, bordered by a quaint white picket fence, is on the right side of the property. The paved arrival court leads to an enclosed garden (its low walls are disguised by shrubbery), bordered by a gallery and a higher latticed entrance porch supported by slender columns.

BR 21

BR 22

251 **Buckhead Residential**

BR 23 **Joseph D. Rhodes House**
541 West Paces Ferry Road, N.W.
1926: Hentz, Adler and Shutze, Architects; Philip Shutze, Designer

The Joseph D. Rhodes House should be regarded as a collaborative design effort between Neel Reid, who died before its completion, and his
successor, Philip Shutze. According to architectural historian Elizabeth
Dowling (*American Classicist*, p. 86), Shutze drew his inspiration for the
two-story central portion of the facade on West Paces Ferry Road from
the Scuola dei Tiraoro e Battiloro (1711), a small baroque edifice built
on the Grand Canal in Venice (direct borrowings are found in the curves
and countercurves of the broken pediment and the frames of the central
doorways and window). Compared to its precedent, the central portion
of the Rhodes House was stretched one bay on each side and flanked by
a one-story side wing on the right and a symmetrical porte cochere on
the left. Originally the stuccoed walls were painted reddish pink, providing a dramatic contrast with the white accents in high relief. To provide
an authentic Italian flavor, Shutze had stipulated that cypress trees be
planted along the central driveway; they did not thrive, however, and
eventually were replaced by dogwoods.

BR 24 **James Dickey House**
456 West Paces Ferry Road, N.W.
1917: Hentz, Reid and Adler, Architects; Neel Reid, Designer

BR 25 **Governor's Mansion**
391 West Paces Ferry Road, N.W.
1968: A. Thomas Bradbury and Associates, Architects

BR 24

The **James Dickey House** was one of the first residences to be constructed along West Paces Ferry Road and is the largest wood frame
house that Neel Reid designed. The most obvious precedent for the
monumental two-story porch supported by ultra-thin Tuscan columns
is the Mount Vernon portico (1799), which had also served as a design source for New York architects McKim, Mead and White a decade
earlier. Across the street, on a site that was formerly part of the Robert
Foster Maddox estate, stands the new **Governor's Mansion**. More closely
resembling a Mississippi plantation house than an antebellum mansion
in Georgia, this large red brick rectangle is wrapped by a white Doric
portico. The front entrance is said to be based on an 1830s design by
Asher Benjamin.

BR 26   **Southern Center for International Studies (James J. Goodrum House)**
320 West Paces Ferry Rd, N.W.
1929: Hentz, Adler and Shutze, Architects; Philip Shutze, Designer

BR 27   **Harry L. English House**
426 West Paces Ferry Road, N.W.
1929: Hentz, Adler and Shutze, Architects; Philip Shutze, Designer

The **Southern Center for International Studies,** formerly the James J.
Goodrum House, abandons the Italian Baroque idiom for a more sedate
and stately English Regency style, indicating a new phase in Philip
Shutze's work. The exterior, originally painted pale yellow to enhance
the white portico and green shutters, is now modernized in a cream-
white tone. The ornamentation focuses on the central portion, with the
pristine Palladian motif and wrought-iron railing above the doorway.
The residence's rich interior includes murals and a dining room emu-
lating the eighteenth-century taste for Chinese decor. The house was so

well regarded at the time of its completion that it received an honorable mention from the Architectural League of New York and extensive coverage in the July 1932 issue of *Architecture*. Its elegant and restrained interiors can be viewed by appointment with the Center. The **Harry L. English House,** designed at the same time and in the same style as the Goodrum House, is enhanced by a pedimented porch and looks deceptively small from West Paces Ferry Road. In fact it is almost square and the back facade has two projecting wings. Notice the two elegant niches with urns that frame the fanlit doorway.

BR 28   **Knollwood (W. H. Kiser House)**
3351 Woodhaven Road, N.W.
1929: Hentz, Adler and Shutze, Architects; Philip Shutze, Designer

BR 29   **Albert E. Thornton House**
205 West Paces Ferry Road, N.W.
1938: Hentz, Adler and Shutze, Architects; Philip Shutze, Designer

BR 30   **Cherokee Town Club (Grant House)**
155 West Paces Ferry Road, N.W.
1921: Walter T. Downing, Architect

According to architectural historian Elizabeth Dowling, the very formal **Knollwood,** one of Philip Shutze's "earliest fully developed American works" evolved from his study of Chatham (1765) in Stratford County, Virginia: "He translated the original stucco house into a brick Geor-

gian mass with a one-story portico that spans the curving arrival drive"
(*American Classicist*, p. 199). Shutze's more modest **Albert E. Thornton
House** can be regarded as a "synthetic" interpretation of the English
Regency style. The curvature of the attached entrance pavilion is echoed
by the unusual (almost postmodern) shape of the dormer window above
it. Unexpected also are the stepped gables framing the wings. Also along
West Paces Ferry Road, the English manor that now houses the **Cherokee Town Club** demonstrates how the beautiful natural setting of this
popular thoroughfare enables very diverse styles to blend.

BR 31   **H. W. Beers House**
3066 Habersham Road, N.W.
1940: Pringle and Smith, Architects

BR 32   **Floyd McRae House**
3053 Habersham Road, N.W.
1929: Hentz, Adler and Shutze, Architects; Philip Shutze, Designer

BR 33   **Edward Van Winkle House**
3031 Habersham Road, N.W.
1939: Hentz, Adler and Shutze, Architects; Philip Shutze, Designer

Period homes of great architectural quality overlook Habersham Road
by the dozen. The **H. W. Beers House,** by Pringle and Smith, boasts
a horseshoe staircase, common in Charleston, which leads to a pedimented loggia supported by Tuscan columns. The main rooms are on

the second floor. Philip Shutze modeled the **Floyd McRae House** after Mrs. McRae's childhood home on Lakeshore Drive in Chicago. A few details, such as the high chimney stacks and the high pitched gables, convey the style of an English manor. The greyish stuccoed walls and stone quoins, the slate roofs and the gates at the end of the driveway contribute to an authentic Old World flavor, but as always in Shutze's work, picturesque effects comply with a harmonious composition. Shutze's neo-Georgian **Edward Van Winkle House** features a pediment at the columned portico that echoes the roof-level pediment above.

BR 34 **T. M. Watson House**
2888 Habersham Road, N.W.
1921: Hentz, Reid and Adler, Architects; Neel Reid, Designer

BR 35 **Livingston Wright House**
2820 Habersham Road, N.W.
1922: Hentz, Reid and Adler, Architects; Neel Reid, Designer

BR 36 **William F. Manry House**
2804 Habersham Road, N.W.
1921: Hentz, Reid and Adler, Architects; Neel Reid, Designer

These three neocolonial frame houses by Neel Reid show his versatility in one of his favorite idioms. The **T. M. Watson House** is a relatively massive composition with symmetrical side porches, an eclectic doorway (notice the arch within the framed opening), and a prominent unadorned central pediment. The **Livingston Wright House** is approached via a picturesque winding cobblestone drive that Reid designed. Notice the "rusticated" wood blocks detailing the one-story porches that frame the neocolonial central portion. Under the fluted Doric pilasters of the doorway, a mock stone veneer was also designed.

Next door, the **William F. Manry House** (as well as the garden and the interior) was designed by Reid for close friends. In this frame house, the architect boldly, but masterfully, incorporated asymmetrical openings while maintaining a tripartite rhythm for the facade. On the pedimented central block, notice the off-center entrance with sidelights framed by delicate pilasters and entablature; and on the right wing, the recessed side porch surmounted by a single window.

BR 37   **Philip McDuffie House**
        7 Cherokee Road, N.W.
        1922: Hentz, Reid and Adler, Architects; Neel Reid, Designer

BR 38   **Ryburn Clay House**
        21 Cherokee Road, N.W.
        1922: Pringle and Smith, Architects

BR 39   **Bolling Jones House**
        5 Cherokee Road, N.W.
        1926: Pringle and Smith, Architects

BR 40   **Jesse Draper House**
        3 Cherokee Road, N.W.
        1922: Hentz, Reid and Adler, Architects; Neel Reid, Designer

BR 41   **Henry Newman House**
        1 Cherokee Road, N.W.
        1921: Hentz, Reid and Adler, Architects; Neel Reid, Designer

Commissioned by and named after the developer of the Garden Hills District, the **Philip McDuffie House** is one of the largest homes designed by Neel Reid. The street elevation features a sophisticated and

highly personal orchestration of classical stone accents on the red brick background. Its horizontality, stressed by the way in which the lintel surmounting the doorway aligns with the cornice of the side porches, is balanced by the vertical thrust of the four Ionic pilasters on the central portion which houses a monumental stair hall. This formal arrangement does not systematically reflect the interior layout. While the three bays of the left wing all denote a living porch, the opposite side reflects an interior arrangement that devotes two bays to a sun porch and one to the dining room; on the second floor the third sash window from the left lights a tiny closet and two out of three of the end windows on the right are fake. At the rear, the facade is equally symmetrical but less formal, and the boxwood garden is also said to be by Reid. Distinguished neighbors are the neo-Georgian **Bolling Jones House** and the neocolonial **Ryburn Clay House,** both designed by Pringle and Smith, and the **Jesse Draper House** and **Henry Newman House,** two white frame houses with dark shutters designed by Reid. The Draper House has a relatively narrow facade and looks almost cottagelike (in effect, rooms extend to the back). On the basic colonial structure of the street elevation, one finds Greek Revival ornamentation (a style that Reid rarely used) in particular the central loggia with freestanding Ionic columns and the narrow openings cut into the entablature. In the Newman House, which is loosely patterned after examples of the Federal period (c. 1800), notice the slender columns attached to the central portion, which give the illusion of supporting the central pediment, and the equally "thin elegance," as architectural historian James Grady terms it, of the details of the central doorway and arcades of the side porches (*Architecture of Neel Reid in Georgia*, p. 78).

BR 42   **Robert Alston House**
2890 Andrews Drive, N.W.
1923: Hentz, Reid and Adler, Architects; Neel Reid, Designer

BR 43   **Stuart Witham House**
2922 Andrews Drive, N.W.
1926: Hentz, Reid and Adler, Architects; Neel Reid, Designer

BR 44   **Vaughn Nixon House**
3083 Andrews Drive, N.W.
1926: Hentz, Reid and Adler, Architects; Neel Reid, Designer

Stately Andrews Drive features no fewer than three homes designed by Neel Reid. With its red brick facade pierced by simple sash windows, hipped roof, dormer windows, and end chimneys, the main block of the **Robert Alston House** is derived from English precedents of the early eighteenth century. Its mass is continued by two-story recessed wings, which are themselves flanked by one-story projecting porticoes. These templelike structures, along with the entrance doorway framed by Doric columns and entablature, bring a pristine white clarity to the composition. The subtle articulation provided by the side wings, with their single arcaded bay on the ground level and stringcourse placed at the same height as the entablature of the end pavilions, is particularly effective. Architectural historians have offered clues to the precedents Reid freely blended. According to James Grady (*Architecture of Neel Reid in Georgia*), such an unusual blend of a Georgian structure with Greek Revival accents can be found in England around 1800. For Catherine Howett (*The Colonial Revival in America*), the temple fronts of the end pavilions appear to be inspired by the architecture of Thomas Jefferson. In the nearby **Stuart Witham House,** Neel Reid flanked another neo-Georgian central block with recessed wings of the same height. The prominent doorway, with its fluted Corinthian pilasters and scroll pediment, ap-

BR 42

pears closely related to one at Westover in Virginia. The pronounced quoins, stringcourse, and segmental windows enliven an otherwise faithfully executed Georgian facade. Completed after Neel Reid's death, the **Vaughn Nixon House** was the architect's last residential design. According to architectural historian James Grady, Reid modeled it after the Hammond-Harwood House (1774) in Annapolis, paying particular attention to the delicate ornamentation of the raised pedimented doorway, the carved frame of the window above it, and the oculus of the pediment. While its precedent was built in brick with stone accents, the Nixon House employed a coating of white stucco. The plan and other facades are Reid's inventions (especially the garden facade with a central columned loggia and terraced end pavilions that are visible from Andrews Drive).

BR 45 Swan House (Edward H. Inman House)

3101 Andrews Drive, N.W. (Atlanta History Center)
1926: Hentz, Adler and Shutze, Architects; Philip Shutze, Designer;
NR, LB

The Swan House is Philip Shutze's best-known work for several reasons: it is open to the public; it is at once spectacular and exquisite; and it has an authentic Old World flavor. This ambience was requested by the clients, Edward Hamilton Inman, entrepreneur and heir to a thriving cotton brokerage, and his wife, Emily. Mrs. Inman worked closely with Shutze on the interior decoration and dictated the swan motif from

BR 45

which the house derives its name. The Swan House has all the comforts
of an English country home in a landscaped twenty-five-acre Italian
park. Shutze played on the contrast between the lush greenery and the
soft tones of the stuccoed garden facade facing Andrews Drive as he
orchestrated sequences leading to the central portion of the house: the
side box gardens, the cascade (directly influenced by the cascade of
the Villa Corsini in Rome, which he had studied during his tenure at the
American Academy), and the horseshoe staircase. The grand segmental
entrance motif and the broken pediment framed by allegorical sculp-
tures of Summer and Autumn (all four seasons were represented in an
earlier, more ambitious proposal) on the eve line reinforce the Italian
villa feeling. In contrast, the entrance facade on the arrival court borrows
stylistically from English eighteenth-century neo-Palladian architecture
(Marcus Binney believes the Doric portico derives from William Kent's
Ducombe Park in Yorkshire). The grand interior, designed by Shutze to
accommodate Mrs. Inman's collection of antiques, remains humane. Of

great prominence is the elegant flying staircase and beautifully crafted moldings. Throughout the house decorative elements in high relief cast expressive shadows. The Swan House was purchased by the Atlanta Historical Society in 1976 after Mrs. Inman's death.

BR 46

BR 46　**Tullie Smith House**
3099 Andrews Drive, N.W. (Atlanta History Center)
Circa 1836: Architect Unknown; NR; UDC Award

Built by cotton planter Robert Hiram Smith, this antebellum farmhouse bears the name of the last member of the family who occupied it. Originally located in DeKalb County—on the site now known as Executive Park (BL 18) on North Druid Hills Road—it was moved to the grounds of the Atlanta History Center in 1969. A rare example of the so-called plantation plain style in the Atlanta metropolitan area, the Tullie Smith House should be regarded as more typical of everyday life on the frontier than Roswell's Greek Revival mansions. The simple wooden frame structure, covered with clapboards, features tall brick chimneys on each of the gable ends. The one-story front porch is supported by chamfered posts and closed at one end, creating a "parson's room" to accommodate travelers. The house is one room deep—its simple plan did not call for a central hallway—with a rear shed room and a freestanding kitchen in the back in order to prevent fires from spreading to the main house. Concern for authenticity was considered tantamount in the restoration of the structure itself, the interior furnishings, and the landscaping of the immediate surroundings.

Buckhead, Lenox Square (BL)

This tour focuses on the Buckhead commercial area—once a homey retail and entertainment center, but now a section dominated by more image conscious developments—and the area around Lenox Square, Atlanta's first regional shopping mall. Many office towers and a few highrise condominiums (a living formula that slowly gains acceptance in Atlanta) generate an ever-changing and increasingly glitzy skyline at the expense of single-family-home neighborhoods, which disappear from the map weekly. Even though this district, which is rapidly becoming Atlanta's new financial center, is inside the city limits, uncontrolled and clustered growth, as well as a disregard for pedestrian activities, make it look more suburban than urban. And even though its density is increasing, it will look even more suburban when traffic congestion is alleviated by a new parkway extending Georgia Route 400 from the perimeter highway to the north past Lenox Square to the Interstate 85 connector to the south.

Area 17

Buckhead, Lenox Square (BL)

1 Buckhead Plaza
2 Bank South, Buckhead Branch
3 Buckhead Library
4 Oxford Book Store at Buckhead
5 The Tower at Tower Place
6 Piedmont Center, Buildings One through Twelve
7 Herman Miller Showroom
8 Atlanta Financial Center
9 Second Church of Christ, Scientist
10 Lenox Square
11 Swissôtel Atlanta
12 D&B Software Building
13 Phipps Plaza
14 Resurgens Plaza
15 Atlanta Plaza
16 Corporate Square Office Park
17 Honeywell Office Building
18 Executive Park
19 Capital City Country Club
20 Oglethorpe University
   Phoebe Hearst Hall
   Lupton Hall
   Lowry Hall
   Hermance Stadium

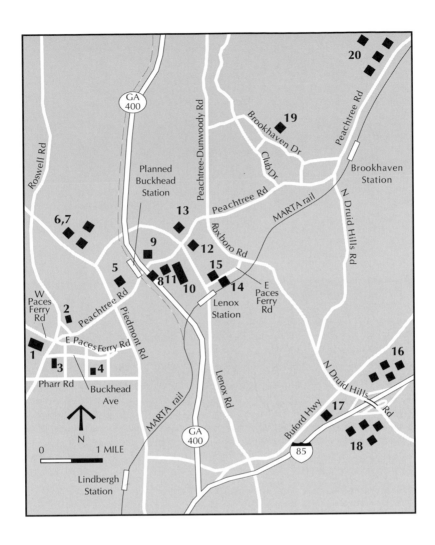

GA 400

Roswell Rd

Planned Buckhead Station

Peachtree-Dunwoody Rd

Brookhaven Dr

19

Club Dr

Peachtree Rd

MARTA rail

Peachtree Rd

Brookhaven Station

N Druid Hills Rd

20

6,7

13

9

Roxboro Rd

12

5

Peachtree Rd

Piedmont Rd

8 11

10

15

14

E Paces Ferry Rd

Lenox Station

W Paces Ferry Rd

2

E Paces Ferry Rd

1

3

4

Pharr Rd

Buckhead Ave

MARTA rail

Lenox Rd

GA 400

N

0   1 MILE

Lindbergh Station

N Druid Hills Rd

16

Buford Hwy

17

18

85

BL 1

BL 1   **Buckhead Plaza**
3060 Peachtree Road, N.W.
1988: Thompson, Ventulett, Stainback and Associates, Architects

BL 2   **Bank South, Buckhead Branch**
3116 Peachtree Road, N.E.
1987: Jova/Daniels/Busby, Architects

Located on a prime site in the traditional heart of Buckhead, **Buckhead Plaza** is a multi-use development on more than seventeen acres. Characteristic of Buckhead's transformation in recent years, this posh project replaces a twenty-year-old Sears retail store. Three additional towers, using the same facade treatment as the existing nineteen-story building, and a four-hundred-room hotel are planned. The major plaza and freestanding lowrise retail and restaurant space address the major intersection of Peachtree Street and West Paces Ferry Road. The office tower is a long and narrow rectangle with a gabled top. Its finely crafted, non-structural, precast concrete exterior features infill panels in pink polished Canadian granite (the same material used as paving for the plaza) and green reflective glass. "Flying buttresses" adorn setbacks that are used as terraces for prime office space. The neo-Gothic feeling they convey is continued in the high pitched gables of the satellite pavilions. The two-level lobby is a successful interpretation of palatial entry spaces of the Baroque Age. At an equally conspicuous Buckhead location, the **Bank South, Buckhead Branch** is notable for its striped marble veneer, abstracted neoclassical window pattern, and large atrium. Its design is an attempt to renew the tradition of great "civic" architecture common to turn-of-the-century banking establishments.

BL 3

BL 3 **Buckhead Library**
269 Buckhead Avenue, N.E.
1989: Scogin, Elam and Bray, Architects; UDC, GAAIA Awards

BL 4 **Oxford Book Store at Buckhead (RBM of Atlanta)**
360 Pharr Road, N.E.
1968: Bruce Goff, Architect (Brattlesville, California)
Adaptive Reuse 1989: Eatman, Gauff and Company, Architects

The 20,000-square-foot **Buckhead Library** created an outcry among Buckhead residents for being intrusive, an odd claim when one witnesses the aesthetic and urban chaos reigning in this commercial strip. In its own "deconstructionist" way, this enigmatic narrow rectangle topped by a gently slanting roof answers the designer's idea of a library as a tool to "communicate with speed and clarity." Along Buckhead Avenue the tripartite canopy reaches out to both the sidewalk and the parking lot. The building's floor plan follows a simple linear organization. The circulation desk (marked on the outside by a conical tower), the reference area, and the main reading room form a unified fluid space, while special functions such as the children's and periodical libraries and the public meeting room are located in lateral "saddle bags," which form low masses protruding from the main volume. In the reading area users can take full advantage of a spectacular view of Downtown through the glass plane running the entire width and height of the Pharr Road facade. Diagonally hung dark grey slate shingles imported from France clad the steel frame structure. Two blocks away, **Oxford Book Store at Buckhead,** Atlanta's largest bookstore, is housed in a former car dealership formed of three two-story circular buildings joined on the second floor by a triangular block. The modest design seems fairly "tame" for an architect as unconventional as Bruce Goff. The adaptive reuse as a bookstore has preserved the hyperbolic ceiling of the original glassed-in automobile showroom and the cedar siding of the original garage. The entrance pavilions were added in 1989.

BL 5

BL 5 **The Tower at Tower Place**
3340 Peachtree Road, N.E.
1975: Stevens and Wilkinson, Architects; Kemp Mooney and Jim
Kortan, Designers

Tower Place was the first large real estate venture in Buckhead, a district
that in the mid-1970s was becoming a prime retail and entertainment
center but was not yet the urban office center (and the alternative to
Downtown) that it has now become. Tower Place, like the multi-use
Colony Square (UM 9) complex in midtown (which developed at about
the same time), became the magnet for a new corporate district. Anchored by the Tower at Tower Place, a highly visible twenty-nine-story
office building, the complex includes a two-story shopping mall with
movie theaters, a 230-room hotel, a renovated low-rise office building,
and extensive parking decks. Clad entirely in energy-saving reflective
glass, the office building has an inverted tapered shape and faceted exterior, which provide an exceptionally large number of corner offices in
high demand on the leasing market. The floor sizes increase from bottom
to top, so that the premium-rate upper floors include sixty-eight facets.

BL 6

BL 6 **Piedmont Center, Buildings One through Twelve**
3565 (Buildings 1–4), 3525 (Buildings 5–8), and 3495 (Buildings 9–12)
Piedmont Road, N.W.
1975–1979, 1981, 1984: Cooper Carry and Associates, Architects

BL 7 **Herman Miller Showroom**
Piedmont Center, Building 2, Suite 200
1988: Scogin, Elam and Bray, Architects; GAAIA Award

The master plan for **Piedmont Center,** a high-density, lowrise office development, called for three 550,000-square-foot, seven-story clusters
of buildings in cast-in-place concrete with grey insulated glass. Each

BL 6

cluster has been broken into four elements connected at ground level
and at the top two floors, offering the advantage of flexible rental spaces
up to 90,000 square feet on a single floor. The site planning minimized
changes in the original topography and landscape, with existing trees
preserved in the central sunken courtyards (often used for business-
related functions) and parking decks sheltered behind the existing slope.
According to the designers of the **Herman Miller Showroom** in Piedmont Center, the spectacular and highly sculptural architecture of the
10,000-square-foot office furniture display space "radiates and swirls"
from the front doors: the geometric design of the show areas is generated
by an intricate network of points, lines, and surfaces, in much the same
way as an abstract painting by Wassily Kandinsky.

BL 8

BL 8 **Atlanta Financial Center**
3333, 3343, and 3353 Peachtree Road, N.E.
South Tower 1982: Smallwood, Reynolds, Stewart, Stewart and
Associates, Architects. Center Tower 1987, North Tower 1989: Stevens
and Wilkinson, Architects

BL 9 **Second Church of Christ, Scientist**
3372 Peachtree Road, N.E.
1986: Toombs, Amisano and Wells, Architects; Joseph Amisano,
Designer

The one-million-square-foot **Atlanta Financial Center** comprises three
towers of dark reflective glass resting on a precast concrete base and
connected by multilevel bridges. Its easily identifiable pyramid massing is striking, even awe-inspiring when seen from Peachtree Road:
two obliquely placed twelve-story wings frame a nineteen-story faceted
block with a gabled top, which is built on a bridge to allow the extension of Georgia Route 400 to pass underneath. This type of architecture,
as well as the layout of the multilevel parking decks in back is not unlike
recent suburban office complexes along Interstate 285. Catering to financial institutions, it has attracted investment, banking, and accounting
firms to the Buckhead area. Opposite Peachtree Road stands the small
but assertive **Second Church of Christ, Scientist,** with its straightforward masses of horizontally striated poured-in-place concrete. Preceded
by a rectangular lobby, the square sanctuary with slanted corners and
clerestory windows seats 350. The room is designed in such a way that
the acoustics adapt to the needs of the speaker, who can be heard even
when addressing the congregation from locations other than on the
platform.

BL 10 Lenox Square
3393 Peachtree Road, N.E.
1959: Toombs, Amisano and Wells, Architects; Sasaki, Dawson,
DeMay, Landscape Architects (New York); Julian Harris, Sculptor; AIA
Award. Neiman-Marcus Department Store 1972: John Carl Warnecke,
Architects (New York). Plaza Court Expansion 1981: Greenberg Farrow
Architecture, Architects. Lenox Square Theaters 1982: Nix, Mann and
Associates, Architects; GAAIA Award

BL 11 Swissôtel Atlanta
3391 Peachtree Road, N.E.
1991: Rabun Hatch and Associates, Architects

When it opened in 1959 **Lenox Square** was the first regional mall in the
Southeast, and through growth has remained one of the region's largest.
As first built, the project included fewer than sixty stores on two levels,
medium-sized branches of the two downtown department stores, and
only six thousand parking spaces on the seventy-two-acre site. Because
Lenox Square has been much altered and enlarged over the years, the
original structures are now hardly identifiable. The Peachtree Road
facade was first limited to the low concrete colonnade supporting pyramid roof units (the Rich's block on its left was not part of the original
scheme). It was bisected by a fifty-five-foot-wide open-air pedestrian
walkway with sculpturally shaped canopies and arches in white concrete, wall infills in yellow Georgian brick, planting boxes, fountains,
sculpture, and seating alcoves. Covered and "upgraded," the mall has
not retained any of its intimacy and "its fine treatment . . . with particular
reference to natural lighting and shelter," which was commended by
the 1960 AIA Award Committee. Today Lenox Square's major archi-

tectural focus is the multilevel skylit food court to which theaters and retail shops have been added. The entire development is scheduled to undergo a vast renovation in the near future that promises to revive the architectural vitality it had in the 1960s. The mall itself has attracted considerable development around its perimeter including several upscale hotels and office structures. The recently completed **Swissôtel Atlanta,** clad in white aluminum panels and seemingly sliced open by an intruding black granite "flying beam," is the stylistic descendent of Richard Meier's High Museum of Art (UM 20).

BL 12 **D&B Software Building (Cities Service Building)**
3445 Peachtree Rd., N.E.
1969: Toombs, Amisano and Wells, Architects; Joseph Amisano,
Designer; Ross H. Bryan, Structural Engineer (Nashville); GAAIA Award

BL 13 **Phipps Plaza**
3500 Peachtree Road, N.E.
1969: FABRAP, Architects. Renovation and Additions 1992: Thompson,
Ventulett, Stainback and Associates, Architects

Modest and understated compared to its more recent and showy neighbors, the thirteen-story **D&B Software Building** was one of the first large
office structures built on the Lenox Square perimeter. The exterior of
this monolithic and minimalist structure features a geometric pattern of
pink-colored reflective glass panels measuring thirty-one feet in height
by as much as fifty-six feet in width. Its distinctive feature is the structural frame—post tensioned girders every third floor each carry two
suspended floors below. This allows one third of the floors throughout
the building to be free of interior columns, while the "tension columns"
that interrupt the interior of the other floors are smaller than standard
compression columns would be. **Phipps Plaza,** the poshest shopping
mall in Atlanta, has undergone numerous renovations since opening in
1969. The most recent, still under construction at this writing, promises
to be even more glamorous, in keeping with its tenants and clientele.

BL 14

BL 14 **Resurgens Plaza**
945 East Paces Ferry Road, N.E.
1988: Smallwood, Reynolds, Stewart, Stewart and Associates, Architects

The twenty-seven-story Resurgens Plaza office building is built atop the
MARTA Lenox Square Station passenger concourse. Responsible for the
design of a number of sleek modernist structures on the Lenox Square
perimeter—among them Atlanta Plaza (BL 15) across the street—the
firm of Smallwood, Reynolds, Stewart, Stewart and Associates ventured
here into postmodern classicism, an idiom regarded as attractive to
status-conscious executive clients. The setback massing is reminiscent of
skyscraper designs of the 1920s, and the facades, constructed of precast
concrete panels complete with mock rustications, consoles, and keystones, bear a noticeable kinship to those of Spanish architect Ricardo
Boffil's French housing projects. At Resurgens Plaza, form definitely does
not follow function: the two-story lobby is located on the eleventh and
twelfth floors, the first ten "floor" levels being used as parking decks and
the impressive ground-floor arcaded bays as automobile access. The design of the elevated lobby reveals the same yearning for timeless prestige
as the exterior envelope: the horseshoe staircase and polished marble
floors evoke Versailles; the mahogany paneling, cozy English clubs.

BL 15 **Atlanta Plaza**
950 East Paces Ferry Road, N.E.
1986: Smallwood, Reynolds, Stewart, Stewart and Associates, Architects

Linked to the rapid-transit station by an elevated pedestrian walkway, the thirty-four-story Atlanta Plaza office tower was the first phase of a proposed mixed-use development. A second tower with the same profile, but boasting ten additional floors, and a four-hundred-room hotel were originally planned for the surrounding site but will probably not be built. In order to give what they call a "prismatic quality" to the building, the designers carved the curtain wall of silver reflective glass with setbacks both in height and in depth on the top five floors, creating space for "executive balconies." The resulting silhouette is easily recognizable on the skyline but hardly visible from ground level. In marked contrast is the horizontal rhythm of the polished granite and black glass on the southwest side, where the use of glass was minimized. As is common of this building type, Atlanta Plaza features a grand lobby with an outpouring of marble. More unusual is the use of two Aubusson tapestries and a sculpture by Henry Moore, *Reclining Figure, Prop*, at the front entrance.

BL 16

BL 16 **Corporate Square Office Park**
Buford Highway at Corporate Boulevard, N.E.
Begun 1964: Toombs, Amisano and Wells, Architects

BL 17 **Honeywell Office Building**
2801 West Druid Hills Drive, N.E.
1978: Thompson, Ventulett, Stainback and Associates, Architects;
GAAIA Award

BL 18 **Executive Park**
North Druid Hills Road at Executive Park Drive, N.E.
Begun 1966: Stevens and Wilkinson, Barrett and Associates, Architects;
Sasaki, Dawson and DeMay, Landscape Architects (New York)

Compared to recently developed complexes in the Cumberland Mall and Perimeter Mall areas, the relatively small and inconspicuous suburban office parks of the 1960s seem to belong to bygone eras. Erected on what was then a treeless abandoned site, **Corporate Square,** a low-budget speculative venture, remains a remarkably cohesive office park, despite the fact that its buildings were added over a period of years. The minimalist but elegantly proportioned facade treatment, consisting of horizontal bands of white precast concrete and ribbons of dark glass, was prescribed by the designers for all buildings, as was the alignment of buildings along a simply but finely landscaped pedestrian outdoor mall, hidden from any view of the outlying parking areas. The same "traditional" corporate spirit was adopted in the 1978 **Honeywell Office Building**. Nestled in the trees and taking advantage of the presence of Peachtree Creek, it has, like the nearby Corporate Square buildings, a simple horizontal rhythm of ribbed precast concrete panels and tinted glass, but breaks with its orthogonal precedents by incorporating a gently curving facade facing the wooded area that buffers it from the parking lot. A less formal but equally understated layout was adopted in **Executive Park,** with its unobtrusive modernist structures along tree-lined roads graced by manicured landscaping.

BL 19

BL 19 **Capital City Country Club (Brookhaven Country Club)**
53 West Brookhaven Drive, N.E.
1928: Burge and Stevens, Architects

Owned by the same organization that established the downtown Capital City Club (PC 13) the Capital City Country Club was built in what is called the French Provincial style. Few of the picturesque details are historically correct, although the architecture of Normandy farmhouses did inspire timber framing and the dovecote-shaped turret. What counts is the impression of cozy informality given by the irregularity of the building's masses and the hodgepodge of rustic materials—stucco, local stone, and variegated slate. South of the clubhouse is the historic Brookhaven District, which is on the National Register and comprises three residential subdivisions. Built between 1910 and 1940, period homes—Colonial, Georgian, and Tudor—set well back from the street, are located on long and narrow lots forming the first country club community in Atlanta.

BL 20, Lupton Hall

BL 20 **Oglethorpe University**

4484 Peachtree Road, N.E.
Phoebe Hearst Hall (Administration Building) 1915, Lupton Hall 1925,
Lowry Hall 1929, Hermance Stadium 1931: Morgan and Dillon,
Architects

Chartered in 1835 as the Presbyterian College for Men in Midway near
Milledgeville, Georgia, Oglethorpe University moved to downtown
Atlanta after the Civil War. Closed in 1872, it reopened in the fall of
1916 on its present site, 135 acres of land bequeathed by the Silver
Lake Park Company. The landscape design, entrusted to Charles W.
Leavitt of New York City, features oaks, pines, and expansive lawns.
Oglethorpe's oldest buildings are grouped around a quadrangle reminiscent of Corpus Christi College in Cambridge, England, where General
James Oglethorpe attended school. They were all designed by Morgan
and Dillon, a local firm, in the Tudor style with slate roofs and blue
granite walls with limestone accents. Gabled or crenellated projections
and mullioned windows with small panes of glass add to the medieval
feeling. The oldest building on campus is Phoebe Hearst Hall, renamed
after the mother of newspaper tycoon William Randolph Hearst; it has
kept its great hall in the English fashion and serves as the Administration Building. Lupton Hall is named after the Chattanooga Coca-Cola
bottling magnate and benefactor of the university, John Thomas Lupton,
and features an exposed carillon atop its crenellated tower. Lowry Hall

currently houses the university's library, but was originally constructed as the School of Commerce and Banking from funds left to the school by Colonel Robert James Lowry and his wife, Emma Markham. The original plan for Hermance Stadium, named for Harry Hermance, a Woolworth executive, called for an arena with 50,000 seats, but was scaled down to 5,000 during the depression of the 1930s.

Cumberland Mall (CM)

This driving tour focuses on one of Atlanta's major hubs for corporate highway architecture. Viewed as a natural continuation of the growth to the north, the Cumberland Mall area deserves such attention. A phenomenon characteristic of the rapidly growing cities of the 1980s and aimed at a discriminating clientele, speculative suburban office centers such as those in the Cumberland Mall area provide suburban living and easy access to Interstate 285, Atlanta's perimeter highway completed in 1969, and to Hartsfield Atlanta International Airport. Their conspicuous and towering buildings offer panoramic views of the downtown skyline and actually contain more office space, though fewer employees, than Downtown. In some ways acting as corporate "billboards" along the highway, these abstract structures are often difficult to reach; however, this difficulty is counteracted by a plethora of amenities provided to tenants and visitors: health clubs, restaurants, convenience services, and regional shopping malls as well as nearby hotels. These self-contained business facilities (some of which do not particularly invite outside visitors) attract tenants through the use of expensive interior and exterior materials, luxurious lobbies, large atriums, and conscious consideration of the parking deck as an integral component of the overall design. Their carefully planned landscaping usually includes an artificial lake (a body of water for this type of facility is most desirable and now forms a prevalent feature) and is meant to help compose a picturesque setting for the often dramatic abstract forms. The sleek and highly polished structure, without emphasis on the ground-level entrance, is a manifestation of the slick image often longed for by developers and marketing professionals.

Cumberland Mall (CM)

1 IBM U.S. Marketing and Services Headquarters
2 Overlook III
3 Cumberland Center II
4 Courtyard by Marriott, Cumberland Center
5 Riverwood 100
6 The Galleria
  Galleria 100
  Galleria 200
  Galleria 300
7 Georgia U.S. Corporate Center
8 Wildwood 2300 Building
9 Wildwood 2500 Building
10 Wildwood 3100 Building
11 Wildwood Plaza
12 Hewlett-Packard Building
13 National Institutional Food Distributor Associates (NIFDA) Building
14 John Knox Presbyterian Church

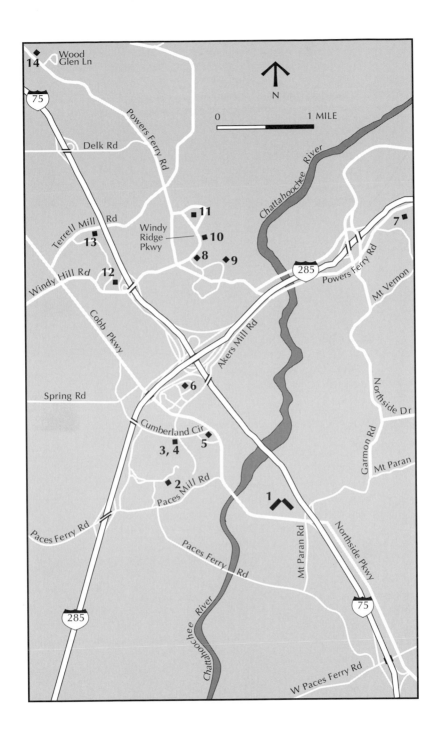

Wood
14 Glen Ln

75

Delk Rd

Powers Ferry Rd

Chattahoochee River

11

Terrell Mill Rd

13

Windy
Ridge
Pkwy

10

8

9

7

285

Powers Ferry Rd

Mt Vernon

Windy Hill Rd

12

Cobb Pkwy

Akers Mill Rd

Northside Dr

Garmon Rd

Spring Rd

6

Cumberland Cir

3, 4

5

Mt Paran

2

Paces Mill Rd

1

Mt Paran Rd

Northside Pkwy

Paces Ferry Rd

Paces Ferry Rd

Chattahoochee River

75

285

W Paces Ferry Rd

N

0   1 MILE

283   **Cumberland Mall**

CM 1 IBM U.S. Marketing and Services Headquarters
4111 Northside Parkway, N.W.
Lakeside 1977, Hillside 1987: Thompson, Ventulett, Stainback and
Associates, Architects; Roy Ashley and Associates, Landscape
Architects; GAAIA Award

Concern for the environment was the prime consideration in the design of the IBM U.S. Marketing and Services Headquarters compound,
planned to include eventually one million square feet of workspace and
built on a wooded and hilly 110-acre site near the Chattahoochee River
(access is from Northside Parkway near Mount Paran Road). Phase one,
known as Lakeside, is a 375,000-square-foot, eleven-story rectangular
structure spanning two hillsides over a 3.5-acre man-made lake (which
also controls water run-off). Access is from the narrow southern side of
the rectangle with visitors entering the two-story lobby from a covered
drive-through motor lobby. Varied openings respond to different functions housed on each level: superimposed are two floors of classrooms,
a balconied cafeteria with a sawtooth configuration of floor-to-ceiling
glazing, a blind service zone, six office floors with deeply recessed window walls supplemented by sun-screens, and finally the computers
and mechanical equipment evidenced on the upper level by a narrow
median slot. The elegant rhythm of the cast-in-place exposed concrete
structure and horizontal voids, stabilized by slender evenly spaced and
slightly recessed columns, is enhanced at the base by wood trims and
planters. Phase two, now called Hillside, a 400,000-square-foot addition
using the same architectural expression and placed at a right angle, is
linked to the earlier facility by glazed bridges.

CM 2

CM 2 **Overlook III**
2859 Paces Ferry Road, N.W.
1987: Smallwood, Reynolds, Stewart, Stewart and Associates,
Architects; Laubmann Reed and Associates, Landscape Architects

The Overlook Complex occupies an eighty-acre site overlooking the
old town of Vinings. The largest of its office buildings is the twenty-
story, 450,000-square-foot Overlook III office tower, which exemplifies
the typological features of recent corporate highway architecture. The
prismatic mass, curved on both ends and ornamented with extensive
setbacks (used as balconies) is topped with a shallow glass pyramid,
which provided a spectacular office for the developer's top executive. Its
streamlined exterior is sheathed in silver reflective glass with dynamic
horizontal white marble trim of two different widths. The 1,400-space
covered parking facility is linked to the main lobby by a gallery featuring

retail services and a health club. Attention was given to the architectural treatment of the marble-clad public areas, with walls featuring insets of hand-milled white oak paneling and beveled glass, and a lobby focused on the distant view of the downtown skyline.

CM 3 **Cumberland Center II**
3100 Cumberland Circle, N.W.
1989: Cooper Carry and Associates, Architects

CM 4 **Courtyard by Marriott, Cumberland Center (Compri Hotel)**
3000 Cumberland Circle, N.W.
1987: Whatley and Partners, Architects

The sixteen-story **Cumberland Center II** office building has an unusual and highly distinguishable silhouette that plays on the bold contrast of masses and materials: two half-cylinders of reflective glass are grafted to a conventional rectangular core, sheathed in polished Spanish granite and pierced by square openings that are slightly recessed on the end rows and next to last floor to create a frame. The composite shaft is crowned by a sixty-foot-high pitched copper roof. Access to the two-story entrance colonnade leading to the grand lobby is through a formal forecourt framed on the opposite side by the 182-room **Courtyard by Marriott** hotel, whose overwise plain forecourt and Cumberland Circle facades are enlivened by neo–Art Deco Gravesian central projections in high relief.

CM 4, *left;* CM 3, *right*

CM 5 Riverwood 100

100 Cumberland Circle, N.W.
1989: John Portman and Associates, Architects

Riverwood is being developed by Portman-Barry Investments as "an integrated whole." At this time, however, only Riverwood 100, the first of two twenty-four-story towers of the symmetrical master plan, has been completed. With its future twin tower, it will serve as a powerful gateway framing a grand tree-lined boulevard, extended by two lower office buildings and terminated by a curved hotel facing a circular piazza. When completed, this formally designed enclave will provide an astonishing contrast with the untouched natural surroundings. The existing tower is sheathed in dark reflective glass. It has marked setbacks on the side of the future boulevard, some of which are topped by barrel vaults (notice how, at each horizontal recess, the bands of grey granite are interrupted by square "quoins" in pink granite topped by perforated metal ornaments). The Portman touch is carried at the ground level by the massive triangular entrance motif and the vaulted tubular canopies that frame it and channel vehicular access. The parking structure has been recessed into an existing ravine beneath the buildings.

CM 6 The Galleria

Cobb Parkway at Galleria Parkway, N.W.
Galleria 100 1982: Smallwood, Reynolds, Stewart, Stewart and Associates, Architects; Keller Smith, Project Architect. Galleria 200 1984: Smallwood, Reynolds, Stewart, Stewart and Associates; Keller Smith, Project Architect. Galleria 300 1987: JPJ Architects (Dallas); Laubmann Reed and Associates, Landscape Architects

Master planned by Smallwood, Reynolds, Stewart, Stewart and Associates along with landscape architects Laubmann Reed and Associates, the Galleria is an eighty-five-acre, mixed-use development by Trammel Crow Corporation with a specialty retail mall complementing neighboring Cumberland Mall. Its luxury hotel and office towers line a landscaped park whose major feature is a cascading waterfall topped by an unusual carillon. The horizontal emphasis on the facades of the eighteen- to twenty-story office towers functions as a unifying feature, while monotony is avoided through the use of variations in detailing and choice of materials: travertine marble cladding and insulated solar glass for Galleria 100, precast spandrels faced with pink polished granite and silver reflective glass for Galleria 200, and an unobtrusive gabled top on Galleria 300.

CM 7 Georgia U.S. Corporate Center (Life of Georgia Corporate Center)

5770 and 5780 Powers Ferry Road, N.W.
1985: Thompson, Ventulett, Stainback and Associates, Architects; Philip Junger, Project Manager; GAAIA Award

Life of Georgia, a major regional insurance company, moved its headquarters from midtown Atlanta (see LM 11) to the present steeply sloped, wooded thirty-nine-acre site in 1985. Local zoning board requirements and the proximity to residential areas dictated the low profile of the Georgia U.S. Corporate Center, which consists of the seven-story 314,000-square-foot Corporate Center Building and the six-story 128,000-square-foot Pavilion placed at a right angle to it. The Pavilion was designed primarily as shell space for expansion of corporate offices. The skylit and colonnaded entrance canopy is the main feature of a formal plaza that provides access to both structures. With their square

CM 6

CM 7

289   **Cumberland Mall**

openings and alternation of matte and polished pink granite aggregate spandrel panels, these entrance facades express, in the designers' own words, "stability, permanence and quality without ostentation." At the back, the longer north-facing facade of the Corporate Center Building overlooks the woods. It has a more straightforwardly modern expression with a full height window wall open to the three-story lobby. Its curved masonry retaining walls in split face granite integrate the natural contours of the site with the building form (the appendage houses the cafeteria and a fitness center). Walls built in the same coarse stone work define major parking and drive areas throughout the site.

CM 8

CM 8 **Wildwood 2300 Building**
2300 Windy Ridge Parkway
1986: Cooper Carry and Associates, Architects; Sanford Nelson,
Designer; Gibbs Landscape Company, Landscape Architects

CM 9 **Wildwood 2500 Building**
2500 Windy Ridge Parkway
1985: Smallwood, Reynolds, Stewart, Stewart and Associates, Architects

CM 10 **Wildwood 3100 Building**
3100 Windy Ridge Parkway
1984: Cooper Carry and Associates, Architects

The 270-acre Wildwood office park is a joint venture of IBM Corporation and Cousins Properties. It is anchored by the highly visible eleven-story, 715,000-square-foot **2300 Building,** which stretches across a knoll overlooking the Chattahoochee River National Park. On the highway elevation, a grid of pink South Dakota granite projecting from the gabled curtain wall in dark reflective glass forms a triangular motif framing the clear glass atrium. The entry procession is given a quasi-surrealistic dimension by the semicircular retail court framed by a radial concrete parking structure for 1,850 cars. Equally effective visually is the slick, curved blue-glass facade of the fourteen-story **2500 Building**. On the other hand, the **3100 Building** disappears under the trees. This low structure, spanning a deep ravine, is anchored by a barrel vaulted atrium and is used exclusively by IBM as a training facility.

CM 11

CM 11 **Wildwood Plaza**
3200 Windy Ridge Parkway
1991: I. M. Pei and Partners, Architects

The abstract design of the twin fifteen-story wings of Wildwood Plaza, which are clad in grey granite and reflective glass, is a stunning example of the architect's penchant for dealing with the relationship of geometrical forms in plan and elevation. Notice how the towers, which appear independent due to the juxtaposition of their facades in the front, are actually part of the same circular form as seen from the back. The glazed half pyramid, which I. M. Pei and Partners designed as a connecting space, looks like a much-reduced version of the firm's entrance pyramid for the Louvre Museum in Paris.

CM 12   **Hewlett-Packard Building**
North by Northwest Office Park
2015 South Park Place
1986: Durfee and Hughes, Architects; Douglas Allen, Landscape
Architect

CM 13   **National Institutional Food Distributor Associates (NIFDA) Building**
North by Northwest Office Park
1665 Terrell Mill Road
1977: Durfee and Hughes, Architects; GAAIA Award

Located north of the Cumberland Mall area, North by Northwest is a
traditional landscaped enclave of relatively modest office structures distributed along wide ring roads. From the Windy Hill Road entrance, just
west of Interstate 75, the visitor will see the **Hewlett-Packard Building,**
a 70,000-square-foot, three-story structure resting on a rough granite
base. Like the northern facade, the southern entrance facade of light
grey porcelain panels and glass, steps back on the left and rounds its
corner on the right. Notice the refined color treatment of the curved
solar screen with tubular railings, echoing those that flank the entrance
portal in polished granite. In the same office park but set in a ravine and
accessed directly from Terrell Mill Road, the 15,000-square-foot **NIFDA
Building,** built in the late 1970s, is as modest and understated as the
Cumberland Mall area "dinosaurs" of the 1980s are spectacular and
showy: the western-cedar-sheathed one-story entrance facade is hardly
visible; at the back, a two-story balconied space opens on a lake visible
through pine trees that otherwise conceal the building.

CM 14

CM 14 **John Knox Presbyterian Church**
505 Powers Ferry Road
1967: Toombs, Amisano and Wells, Architects; Joseph Amisano,
Designer; AIA Award

Set in the outskirts of Marietta, the non-intrusive but powerful design of
the John Knox Presbyterian Church respects the residential scale of this
northern portion of Powers Ferry Road. Resting on a low square base
of rough-hewn grey stone in random ashlar, the sanctuary is topped by
a high roof covered in wood shingles and crowned by a square tower
sheathed in the same material. The all-wood roof structure, left exposed
inside the church, allows light to filter in from the notched openings of
the tower. The square walled courtyard, which Joseph Amisano based
on parish churches of medieval England, was meant as an out-of-doors
gathering place, sheltered from the parking lot, for the family-oriented
congregation. Unfortunately, this grass-planted enclosure is not well uti-
lized because it is not on a direct path from the sanctuary to the parking
lot. Amisano's design for a central bell tower was never implemented.

Perimeter Mall (PM)

This area, which has grown up around another of Atlanta's regional malls, constitutes the eastern anchor to what is sometimes known as "the Golden Crescent," that stretch of the perimeter highway along which the most intense and visible development has taken place. Unlike the Cumberland Mall area—the Crescent's western anchor—the Perimeter Mall area is characterized by towering skyscrapers set in lush gardens with surrounding midrise office blocks acting as vantage points for observing the man-made "natural" settings. Here the office parks tend to be more cohesive, with the majority of their individual buildings having been designed by a single architectural firm according to a master plan, while at Cumberland, the office parks are generally collections of various buildings, by different architects, arranged in landscaped settings without regard for neighboring structures.

The Perimeter Mall area is critically situated near the intersection of Georgia 400 North-South Parkway and the perimeter highway, a location easily accessed from the residential communities of Roswell and Alpharetta to the north and the business development in Buckhead and Downtown to the south. Significant to this area's vitality is the location of three major hospitals and their surrounding support facilities at this same intersection. This medical complex suffers from a lack of overall cooperative master-planning but will continue to attract new development to this already congested area.

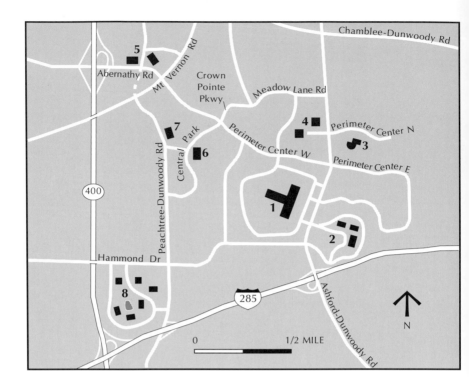

Area 19

Perimeter Mall (PM)

1 Perimeter Mall
2 One, Two, and Three Ravinia Drive
3 HBO & Company
4 The Terraces at Perimeter Center
5 400 and 500 Northpark Town Center
6 7000 Central Park
7 9000 Central Park
8 Concourse at Landmark Center
9 Korean Church of Atlanta

PM 1　**Perimeter Mall**
　　　　4400 Ashford-Dunwoody Road
　　　　1971: Katzmann and Associates, Architects. Macy's Wing Addition
　　　　1982: Hallmuth, Obata and Kassabaum, Architects. Rich's Furniture
　　　　Showroom Addition 1986: Smallwood, Reynolds, Stewart, Stewart and
　　　　Associates, Architects; Dan Carrithers, Interior Designer

PM 2　**One, Two, and Three Ravinia Drive**
　　　　1, 2, 3 Ravinia Drive, N.E.
　　　　1981–1991: Kevin Roche, John Dinkeloo and Associates, Architects
　　　　(Hamden, Connecticut); Roy Ashley and Associates, Landscape
　　　　Architects

Perimeter Mall is Atlanta's first regional mall to be designed from the
outset as an enclosed pedestrian space. It also had the unique distinction
of being completely designed, including the department store anchors,
by one architectural firm, which accounts for its initial visual unity. (The
usual practice is for each department store to supply its own design

PM 2

team.) Though substantial additions have kept the mall competitive with more recent rivals (it is metropolitan Atlanta's second largest regional retail and entertainment center after Lenox Square), its scaled down pedestrian hallways seem cramped by today's standards. Located on a forty-two-acre site across from Perimeter Mall, Ravinia was developed by Gerald Hines Interests of Houston, Texas, in 1981. The thirty-one-story tower (**Three Ravinia Drive**) and similar midrise buildings (**One and Two Ravinia Drive**), with their emphatic horizontal lines of aluminum sunshades and reflective glass windows, recall prehistoric animal shapes from a landscape in the nineteenth-century tradition of Frederick Law Olmsted. The newly completed tower, with its seven-story interior arboretum and conspicuous use of more glass than its predecessors on the site, houses MCI and Holiday Inn as its principal tenants.

PM 3

PM 3 HBO & Company (Perimeter 301)
301 Perimeter Center North
1982: Thompson, Ventulett, Stainback and Associates, Architects

Completed in 1982, the six-story, 162,000-square-foot HBO & Company office building was the first of the elegant but dematerialized metal and glass office buildings at Perimeter Center Office Park. At the time, HBO & Company's "crisp, slick" image (as described by the architects) was distinct from that of other suburban development in Atlanta. Visible from Ashford-Dunwoody Road, the conspicuous curving facade of insulated brushed stainless steel panels and solar grey glass is notched at the location of the lateral entrances. The partial ellipse, a form that also creates a reduction of annual cooling loads, orchestrates changing reflections and provides a striking contrast to the surrounding natural landscape. The flat north elevation offers filtered views into the shady adjacent wooded areas. The building has recently been joined by a similarly detailed, but less geometrically interesting, companion to the northeast.

PM 4

PM 4 **The Terraces at Perimeter Center**
400 Perimeter Center Terrace (North Terrace)
115 Perimeter Center Place (South Terrace)
1983: Skidmore, Owings and Merrill, Architects (Chicago); Bruce Graham, Designer

Each of the twin eleven-story office buildings that comprise the Terraces at Perimeter Center is composed of two wings connected by bridges spanning a nature-filled central atrium. On the outside, their distinctive architectural feature is the detached structural grid, "ornamented" by solar fins providing shading for the recessed glazed offices. With set-backs creating a series of terraces from the seventh to the eleventh floors, the concrete frame becomes a kind of Sol LeWitt's three-dimensional minimalist sculpture. The grounds are graced by ponds and spanned by a cable-suspended wooden footbridge. Plans call for the parking structures to become overgrown with vines.

PM 5   **400 and 500 Northpark Town Center**
1000 and 1100 Abernathy Road
Begun 1984: John Portman and Associates, Architects

Northpark Town Center is a 100-acre mixed-use development by
Portman-Barry Investments. Planned to include all amenities for everyday living, such as an upscale retail shopping mall and entertainment
facilities to complement the two existing office towers, 400 and 500
Northpark Town Center, the development features an imposing combination of straight slabs and irregular setbacks emphasizing vertical
rhythms. Different from but not antithetical to Portman's downtown
architecture, this on-going project also incorporates pedestrian plazas
and bridges. Buildings utilize bronze vision glass, glass spandrel panels
with grey-pink granite, and granite entry portals. Plans call for a future
structure of fifty-five stories to be added to the complex along with two
additional midrise towers.

PM 6 **7000 Central Park**
7000 Central Park
1989: Cooper Carry and Associates, Architects; Roman Stankus, Project
Designer; SWA Group, Landscape Architects (Houston, Texas)

PM 7 **9000 Central Park**
9000 Central Park
1989: Cooper Carry and Associates

Master planned by Cooper Carry and Associates, Central Park is a sixty-
acre mixed-use development. At this time, two of its twelve projected
buildings, which eventually will include a 350-room hotel, have been
erected. The first office building, **7000 Central Park,** is an eighteen-
story, 400,000-square-foot, long slab animated by a slanted roof and
numerous vertical and horizontal setbacks. It rests on a slightly recessed
base housing a three-story lobby. Its precast concrete structural grid is
also to be found in the 1,200-space parking structure tucked back in the
trees. Both the curtain wall and the roof are in reflective glass of various
shades of blue. Adorned with three fountains, the man-made lake at its
foot features an accessible jetty ending in a "gazebo," which will mark
the axis of symmetry for a twin tower to the south. An identical faceted
facade treatment is applied to the eight-story, 200,000-square-foot **9000
Central Park** located at the edge of the property.

Concourse at Landmark Center
1 through 8 Concourse Parkway
Hotel and Office Buildings 1985–1991: Thompson, Ventulett, Stainback
and Associates, Architects; Ray Hoover, Partner in Charge; Roy Ashley
and Associates, Landscape Architects. Office Buildings 1985–1991:
Associated Space Design, Interior Designers. Hotel 1987: Hirsch-Bedner
and Associates, Interior Designers. Athletic Club 1988: Ohlson Lavoie
Corporation, Architects (Denver). Bridge 1986: Scogin, Elam and Bray,
Architects; Mack Scogin, Designer; GAAIA Award

Thompson, Ventulett, Stainback and Associates worked closely with
landscape architect Roy Ashley to establish the seventy-acre Concourse
at Landmark Center as an office complex within a parklike environment.
Buildings, with facades utilizing transparent glass for the lofty nature-
filled atriums and several tones of green reflective glass for the office
spaces, are connected by a tree-lined pedestrian pathway. The development, which includes three lowrise office buildings, the twenty-story
Doubletree Hotel, and an athletic club, focuses on two thirty-one-story
towers. These are the tallest buildings in the area and are given more
prominence by their faceted shapes, which allow up to sixteen column-
less corner offices per floor, and their setback tops crowned by unusual
crossed open beams and arches. Back on the ground, Mack Scogin conceived the foot bridge linking the hotel to the lowrise office buildings as
a passageway of pleasure and enjoyment. The architect has described
it as "an unreasonable combination of bridge parts, unnecessary and

PM 8, hotel, *left;* office buildings

suggestive, demanding the attention of the crosser." This bridge "defies reason and easy access." Most disquieting is the presence of a rock, alluding to natural bridges, at the highest point of this slender structure. A singular oversized truss, with stylized "insect wings" on one side and a cable abutment system acting as a guardrail on the other, creates the image of a giant dragonfly emerging from the water.

Korean Church of Atlanta
2197 Peeler Road
1989: James Mount, Architect

Located along a residential suburban road northeast of Perimeter Mall, the Korean Church of Atlanta is a relatively small structure resting on a concrete base which is made even more dramatic by its conspicuous siting in a large clearing and its massive entrance staircase. Topped by freestanding open-timber construction, which culminates in a pedimented "pavilion," the concrete steps lead to a central lobby. This space has pastel-colored walls and gives access to the light-filled, fan-shaped sanctuary, whose steel structural members are highlighted in grey, and to the lower office wing. In his highly original synthesis of oriental and deconstructionist influences, James Mount was inspired by the regulating role of the circle in oriental architecture. Specifically Korean are the five-square motifs found on the exterior wooden balustrade and the interior doors of the sanctuary.

Area 20

Roswell (RS)

Founded in 1839 by Roswell King and his son, Barrington, the City of Roswell lies twenty-one miles north of downtown Atlanta and offers the nearest examples of antebellum architecture. General Sherman's troops burned the Kings' cotton and woolen mills because they supplied goods to the Confederacy but spared their homes as well as those of friends who had come to Roswell from coastal Georgia. At a time when its popularity started to wane, Willis Ball, a carpenter from Windsor, Connecticut (Roswell King's birthplace), designed and built the major buildings of this Georgian "frontier town" in a Greek Revival idiom. The town has since prospered as an Atlanta suburb due to the extension of the expressway system (Georgia 400) north and is now courting business and industry on its own as the sixth most populated city in Georgia. Tours of Roswell's historic district are available through the Roswell Historical Society.

Area 20

Roswell (RS)

1 Bulloch Hall
2 Mimosa Hall
3 Barrington Hall
4 Roswell Presbyterian Church
5 Herman Miller, Roswell Facility
6 Saint Andrew Catholic Church

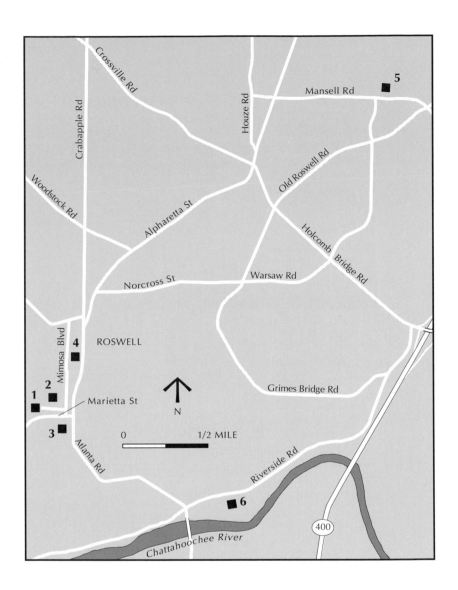

RS 1   **Bulloch Hall**
180 Bulloch Avenue, Roswell
Circa 1840: Willis Ball, Builder; NR

RS 2   **Mimosa Hall (Phoenix Hall)**
127 Bulloch Avenue, Roswell
Circa 1840: Willis Ball, Builder

RS 3   **Barrington Hall**
60 Marietta Street, Roswell
1842: Willis Ball, Builder; NR

Built by Major James Stephens Bulloch of Savannah, who was Theodore
Roosevelt's grandfather and Eleanor Roosevelt's great grandfather, **Bulloch Hall** is perched on a lawn at the terminus of a quiet tree-lined
cul-de-sac. This simple but elegant white clapboard house has a full
pedimented portico supported by four massive Doric columns. The
lofty central hall, combined with large windows and high ceilings, was
designed to catch summer breezes. Bought by the City of Roswell in
1978, it was restored and is now used as a cultural center. It is the only
antebellum home in Roswell open to visitors. **Mimosa Hall,** whose leafy
portico is preceded by a long alley, was constructed for Major John Dun-
woody, James S. Bulloch's brother-in-law and one of the first settlers of
Roswell. The original wood building was accidentally set on fire during the housewarming party but was rebuilt immediately of stuccoed
brick scored to resemble stone (hence its former name Phoenix Hall).
Revivalist architect Neel Reid, who lived there from 1916 until his death,
was responsible for changes to the interior and grounds. Set back from
the street on a hill, **Barrington Hall** is a temple-shaped house built by
Barrington King, president of the Roswell Manufacturing Company, with

RS 2

pine and poplar hewn at the King sawmill and brick from King Brick
Company. Damaged by fire in 1987 and subsequently restored, it is surrounded on three sides by a wide gallery supported by two-story Doric
columns. Notice the lantern—or "widow's walk"—on the hipped roof
and the simple six-pane transom marking the entrance door. The influence of Asher Benjamin's pattern books is noticeable both outside and
inside. Willis Ball copied the dining room and parlor chimney pieces
from examples in the *Practical House Carpenter* (1835).

RS 3

RS 4 **Roswell Presbyterian Church**
755 Mimosa Boulevard, Roswell
1840: Willis Ball, Builder; NR

Designed by Willis Ball, the Roswell Presbyterian Church, in white painted wood, adopts the same unaffected temple shape and pleasant proportions as Ball's residential constructions. Its slightly raised portico is supported by four fluted Doric columns. A finely molded entablature runs along the top of the side walls, whose clapboard siding is also to be found on the entrance pediment and square belfry. Notice the contrast between the large windows and the understated central front door.

RS 5   **Herman Miller, Roswell Facility**
        1000 Mansell Road, Roswell
        1981: Heery & Heery, Architects; Mack Scogin, Designer; SARC,
        GAAIA Awards

RS 6   **Saint Andrew Catholic Church**
        675 Riverside Road, Roswell
        1987: Nix, Mann and Associates, Architects; GAAIA Award

The **Herman Miller, Roswell Facility** is dramatically sited on a grassy
knoll overlooking a man-made pond. The first of several buildings to
occupy the site, this structure was designed for the assembly and distribution of office furnishings, which are showcased in use by the company
in the open-office portion of the facility. The slick facades, constructed
of clear, anodized, insulated aluminum panels, are embellished by
winged canopies, painted red, designed to shade the low-level operable
windows of the production areas and induce air movement through
them. The sophisticated design responds well to the company's image
and demonstrates Roswell's duality as a historic country town and modern progressive city. Similarly, the **Saint Andrew Catholic Church** at the
southern extreme of the city, takes a classical vocabulary and makes a
thoroughly contemporary statement. The plan is based on a Greek cross
(one with four equal arms) and though stripped of ornamentation, the
facades and interior are reminiscent of Italian Renaissance churches in
Florence and Venice.

Decatur (DC)

Incorporated in 1822, Decatur is actually older than Atlanta. The seat of DeKalb County, it suffered greatly during the Civil War. Located six miles east of Five Points, downtown Decatur can easily be reached by MARTA. Many of its fine pre–World War II commercial structures have been replaced by parking decks and modern administrative and office buildings. Still, Decatur has miraculously preserved its small-town feeling, which carries the visitor miles and decades away from Peachtree Center.

Decatur (DC)

1 Old DeKalb County Courthouse
2 Pythagoras Masonic Temple
3 Decatur Town Center, Buildings One and Two
4 One West Court Square
5 MARTA Decatur Transit Station
6 Avondale Estates Historic District
7 Agnes Scott Hall, Agnes Scott College
8 Buttrick Hall, Agnes Scott College
9 McCain Library, Agnes Scott College
10 Charles A. Dana Fine Arts Center, Agnes Scott College
11 Community Center of South Decatur
12 East Lake Country Club
13 Gentry-McClinton House

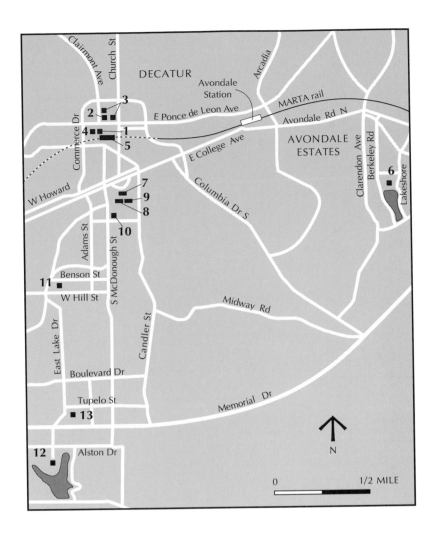

Clairmont Ave
Church St
Commerce Dr
DECATUR
Avondale Station
Arcadia
MARTA rail
E Ponce de Leon Ave
Avondale Rd N
AVONDALE ESTATES
E College Ave
Clarendon Ave
Berkeley Rd
Lakeshore
W Howard
Columbia Dr S
Adams St
S McDonough St
Benson St
W Hill St
East Lake Dr
Candler St
Midway Rd
Boulevard Dr
Tupelo St
Memorial Dr
Alston Dr
N
0   1/2 MILE

2 **3** **4** **1** **5** **7** **9** **8** **10** **11** **13** **12** **6**

DC 1

DC 1 **Old DeKalb County Courthouse**
101 East Court Square
1917: Walker and Chase, Architects; NR

DC 2 **Pythagoras Masonic Temple**
108 East Ponce de Leon Avenue
1925: William J. Sayward, Architect; NR

DC 3 **Decatur Town Center, Buildings One and Two**
150 East Ponce de Leon Avenue
125 Clairemont Avenue
1987: Thompson, Ventulett, Stainback and Associates in Association
with Urban Design Associates, Architects

DC 4 **One West Court Square**
1 West Court Square
1971: Toombs, Amisano and Wells, Architects; GAAIA Award

DC 5 **MARTA Decatur Transit Station**
Church Street at Sycamore Street
1978: Edwards and Kelsey (Newark) with Stevens and Wilkinson, Joint
Venture Architects

Like other county seats in Georgia, Decatur grew outward from its
courthouse square, which unfortunately has been much altered over
the years. The first DeKalb County Courthouse was a log cabin erected

around 1823 on the site of the present **Old DeKalb County Courthouse,** which is built of cut Stone Mountain granite. Its current appearance remains essentially as designed in 1917 when, following a disastrous fire, Atlanta architects Walker and Chase transformed a structure built some fifteen years earlier into a larger classical building with wings and pedimented porticoes supported by unfluted Corinthian columns on the northern and southern elevations. These entrance motifs look ill-proportioned and unstable because their thin columns rest on very high bases, which rise from the entrance steps. Interiors, which now house the DeKalb Historical Society, are decorated with Alabama marble; the neoclassical main courtroom has been made into a meeting room. The city block on the opposite side of Ponce de Leon Avenue includes the **Pythagoras Masonic Temple,** whose heroic entrance betrays the influence of Philip Shutze's mannerist-inspired buildings, and the two recent four- and five-story office buildings of the **Decatur Town Center**. Their design, with small openings in walls sheathed with patterned brick and low-pitched clay tile roofs, reflects a more contextual approach than that of the "minimalist" **One West Court Square** office building, built at a time when the use of reflective glass was regarded as a proper way to minimize the bulk of a building in the vicinity of a historic structure. The glazed pyramid marking one of the entrances to the unobtrusive underground **MARTA Decatur Transit Station** emerges from the landscaped grounds south of the old courthouse while a glazed shed marks the eastern portal.

DC 5

DC 6 **Avondale Estates Historic District**
Begun 1924: Robert Cridland, Landscape Architect (Philadelphia)

Located a mile and a half east of Decatur and developed during the period between 1924 and 1941, the historic district of Avondale Estates, a small town chartered in 1926, extends south of Avondale and Covington roads from Fairfield to Lakeshore drives and all the way down to the man-made Avondale Lake. It represents only a third of the "new town" envisioned in the 1920s by entrepreneur George F. Willis. Compared with earlier Olmsted-influenced residential districts in Atlanta, Avondale Estates retained a picturesque character, but adopted a more comprehensive approach to planning, following recent East Coast precedents such as Forest Hills Gardens in Queens, New York. Coming from downtown Decatur, visitors will notice the unusual arched gate to Fairfield Drive on the south side of Avondale Road. Proceeding farther on the northern corridor, they will discover on either side of Clarendon Avenue a 1925 two-story shopping strip animated by picturesque gables. Its neo-Tudor style, very fashionable at the time for this type of building, was in tune with the overall English touch imposed by Willis and was also adopted for the clubhouses of the two large parks (all these communal structures were entrusted to the architect Arthur Neal Robinson). The street pattern, featuring landscaped medians, traffic islands, and circles, was laid out by a local civil engineer, O. F. Kauffman, who had worked on the late phase of Druid Hills. Philadelphia-based Robert Cridland was responsible for the landscaping featuring small parks in the middle of three of the residential blocks reached by way of pedestrian paths. On the small manicured lots, single-family houses in the English medieval idiom pleasantly mix with Craftsman bungalows and homes inspired by the Dutch Colonial and Spanish Mission styles.

DC 6

DC 7 **Agnes Scott Hall, Agnes Scott College**
141 East College Avenue, Decatur
1891: Bruce and Morgan, Architects

DC 8 **Buttrick Hall, Agnes Scott College**
141 East College Avenue, Decatur
1930: Edwards and Sayward, Architects

DC 9 **McCain Library, Agnes Scott College**
141 East College Avenue, Decatur
1936: Edwards and Sayward, Architects

Renamed after the mother of Colonel George W. Scott, a wealthy manufacturer and benefactor, this private liberal arts college for women was
established in 1889 as the Decatur Female Seminary by members of
the local Presbyterian church. Agnes Scott College currently enrolls six
hundred students. Although of different styles, the twenty-five structures
on the 105-acre campus are harmonized by their dark brick exterior
with stone accents. They form relatively informal clusters around lawns
crisscrossed by brick alleys and planted with mature trees. Parking areas
are well hidden from view. First built was **Agnes Scott Hall,** which faces
East College Avenue in the direction of the courthouse square and currently houses administrative offices and dormitories on the upper floors.
Its landmark tower crowned by a steep slate roof, Romanesque Revival entrance porch (notice the nice detailing of the coupled columns
supporting the recessed arch), taut windows, and decorative brick and

terra-cotta work are all features typical of Victorian campus architecture. A pleasant domestic note is brought to the design by the side porch and hexagonal turret on the right end side. Behind Agnes Scott Hall lies the main quadrangle (the gazebo was originally a well house) bordered on the opposite side by the neo-Gothic **Buttrick Hall** and **McCain Library** (the reading room is well worth a glance with its beautifully crafted timber framing).

DC 10

DC 10   **Charles A. Dana Fine Arts Center, Agnes Scott College**
1965: Edwards and Portman, Architects; John Portman, Designer. Renovation 1989: Bailey and Associates, Architects

An early John Portman design, the Charles A. Dana Fine Arts Center is used by Agnes Scott's art and drama departments. It provides a modernist yet contextual response to the surrounding structures in the Collegiate Gothic style. A courtyard separates the openwork red brick screen wall, featuring taut ribbed lancet motifs, evenly spaced concrete "buttresses," and a central arched gateway, from the arts center itself. This low glazed structure is surmounted by steep slate-covered zigzagging "dormers" providing northern light to the studios located on the "floating platform" of the upper third floor. Taking East Dougherty Street to the east, the visitor can explore South Candler Street, which is lined by fine Victorian and early-twentieth-century period homes and bungalows.

DC 11 **Community Center of South Decatur (Scottish Rite Hospital for Crippled Children)**
321 West Hill Street, Decatur
1920: Hentz, Reid and Adler, Architects; Neel Reid, Designer; NR

Widely publicized in the 1920s (it was then the major children's hospital in the Southeast) this pavilion complex was the first of the philanthropic "Shriner's" hospitals built in the United States by Scottish Rite Consistories and became a prototype for many more to follow. The original building, which is now the Community Center of South Decatur, consisted of the two-story administration building and flanking one-story ward buildings, with detached connecting passageways at the rear. The eastern addition, now the Oakhurst Community Center, was built as a nurse's residence in the 1940s. Neel Reid treated the central pavilion in his favorite neo-Georgian style, with a classical arched doorway, red brick quoins, and window frames contrasting with the stuccoed walls. Along the entire southern facade of the wards, notice the simple but beautifully detailed glassed-in porches, which reflect contemporary hygienist trends emphasizing the availability of fresh air and sunlight. The landscaped grounds for exercise and convalescence were conceived as a transition to the surrounding residential neighborhood. The complex was sold in 1976, when a new Scottish Rite Hospital was built in the suburbs, and now serves as a multipurpose community and health center.

DC 12

DC 12 **East Lake Country Club**
2575 Alston Drive, S.E.
1914: Hentz and Reid, Architects; Neel Reid, Designer. Interior Remodeling circa 1927: Philip Shutze, Architect

DC 13 **Gentry-McClinton House (Virginia Manor)**
132 East Lake Drive, S.E.
1914: P. Thornton Marye, Architect; LB

Graced with a large pond, the **East Lake Country Club** was originally a subsidiary of the Atlanta Athletic Club. Its thirty-six-hole golf course, frequented by Bobby Jones, was regarded as one of the finest in town. The exterior of the Neel Reid–designed clubhouse, in stucco and red brick, was fashioned in a modified Tudor style, with prominent gables, high chimney stacks, and crenellations. Its elegant proportions have since been altered by additions. After a fire in 1926, the interior was renovated in the classical style by Philip Shutze, who in 1914 had designed the details of the original dark paneled living room. The **Gentry-McClinton House,** built for William T. Gentry, then president of the Southern Bell Telephone and Telegraph Company, is a stately two-story home using Greek Revival features such as a full height pedimented portico supported by Doric columns. Subdivided into eight apartments in the 1960s, it was restored in the late 1970s. Both of these structures, completed in 1914, were expected to boost the slow development of the East Lake district but failed to do so.

Area 22

South Side (SS)

Atlanta's South Side encompasses a vast area that has been largely ignored by developers who have concentrated on the affluent North Side. Characterized by manufacturing concerns, warehouses, and light industrial facilities, the area has been included in this guidebook mainly in order to call attention to some of its widely scattered and diverse architectural landmarks.

Dominating the South Side is Hartsfield Atlanta International Airport and surrounding ancillary functions: hotels, airline corporate offices, and shipping and receiving facilities. Creating employment opportunities for more than thirty-one thousand people, the airport is the driving force behind the South Side's economic well-being. It is also the only part of the city seen by the majority of the arriving passengers. Seventy percent of the passengers flying into Hartsfield simply change planes for their final destination.

Two historically significant sites, Fort McPherson and Lakewood Fairgrounds, also draw architectural interest for their rare, intact examples of styles imported to Atlanta in the late nineteenth and early twentieth centuries. Fort McPherson, especially, is well worth the trouble it takes to gain access to the military base. Visitors should first register at the main gate off Lee Street.

In order to include one of the metropolitan area's nationally recognized buildings—the Clayton County Headquarters Library—the South Side area has been stretched southward almost to Jonesboro. Visitors to this site may wish to contrast the library's contemporary design with the traditional Old South architecture found in Jonesboro itself.

Area 22

South Side (SS)

1 Clayton County Headquarters Library
2 Hartsfield Atlanta International Airport
3 Staff Row, Fort McPherson
4 Barracks, Fort McPherson
5 Lakewood Fairgrounds Exhibition Halls
6 Lakewood Amphitheatre

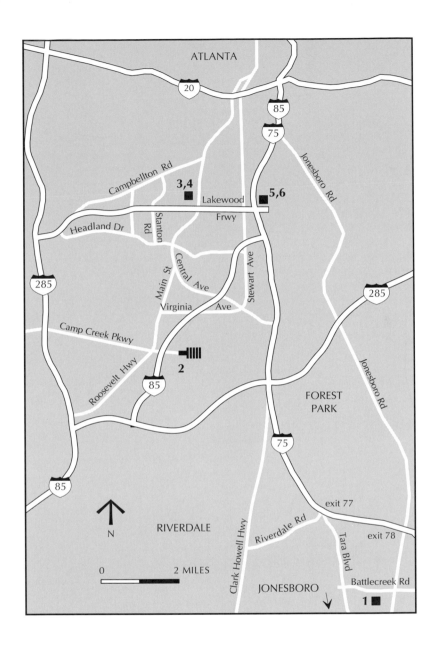

ATLANTA

20

85

75

Jonesboro Rd

Campbellton Rd

3,4

Lakewood

5,6

Headland Dr

Stanton Rd

Frwy

285

Main St

Central Ave

Stewart Ave

Virginia Ave

Camp Creek Pkwy

285

Roosevelt Hwy

2

85

Jonesboro Rd

FOREST
PARK

75

85

N

exit 77

RIVERDALE

Clark Howell Hwy

Riverdale Rd

Tara Blvd

exit 78

0   2 MILES

Battlecreek Rd

JONESBORO

1

SS 1   Clayton County Headquarters Library

865 Battlecreek Road, Jonesboro
1988: Scogin, Elam and Bray, Architects; Merrill Elam, Chief Designer;
SARC, AIA Awards

In the architects' own words, the much-praised and widely published 3,300-square-foot Clayton County Headquarters Library was conceived as "a K-Mart for information." Its design takes into account easy access to "cultural goods" (as exemplified by the neon signage), as well as an undistinguished site lying between a low density residential suburb and a rapidly growing shopping strip. The exterior, highly articulated in glass and corrugated steel (painted with black and white patches magnifying the pattern found in old school notebooks), reflects the functional interior organization along two axes meeting at the circulation desk, which is surmounted by a square skylight. Originating with the aedicula in the parking lot, the entrance axis materializes in a hallway that separates the lower office wing from the public spaces with their curved roofs rising up; the children's library is located in the lowest part. The perpendicular axis pierces the lateral facade with the lower volumes of the director's office and the genealogy room. Other secondary elements of the building requirements, such as the gently curved storytelling corner, opened to the wooded creek, and vaulted study cubicles at the rear, are given clear expression on the outside. To comply with budgetary constraints, the architects incorporated industrial materials and equipment, such as stadium light fixtures in the reading room. Both inside and outside the detailing is very crisp and abstract, but without a dehumanized high tech atmosphere: in fact, the ambient lighting and details such as the light-colored wood accents in the trellis beams, furniture, and partitions do quite the opposite.

SS 2 **Hartsfield Atlanta International Airport**
Interstate 85 and Camp Creek Parkway
1980: Stevens and Wilkinson; Smith, Hinchman and Grylls (Chicago), and Minority Airport Architects and Planners, Architects; Tom Ramsey, Chief Designer; Roy Ashley and Associates, Landscape Architects

Serving fifty-five million passengers each year, Hartsfield Atlanta International Airport is the world's largest terminal complex and second busiest airport after Chicago's O'Hare. Named after William Hartsfield, Atlanta's mayor for more than twenty years (1937–1940, 1942–1961), it is the fourth terminal built by the city on a former racetrack site purchased from Asa Candler in 1929 (previous structures were completed in 1932, 1948, and 1961). The unique and highly functional scheme was first developed by Stevens and Wilkinson. It follows a simple rectilinear organization that lends more to efficiency than to architectural grandeur. A bifurcated midfield terminal complex (which includes an international concourse and a MARTA station) is placed perpendicular to four long satellite gate concourses located between the runways. All these elements are connected by an underground transit system and people-mover spine. A large budget was devoted to art works intended to enliven an otherwise utilitarian scheme.

SS 2

SS 3 **Staff Row, Fort McPherson**
1 through 20 Wheeler Drive
1889–1910: Architect Unknown; NR

SS 4 **Barracks, Fort McPherson**
56 through 62 Cobb Street
1889–1891: Architect Unknown

Established in 1867, Fort McPherson is located on five hundred acres
four miles southwest of downtown Atlanta. Named after a Union general
killed in the battle of Atlanta, it became a permanent artillery garrison

in 1885. Selected as one of the posts where housing improvements for army personnel were tested, Fort McPherson is, along with Inman Park, the most distinguished Victorian residential ensemble in Atlanta. Today it serves as headquarters of the United States Army Forces Command. Facing the parade ground, the **Staff Row** comprises fifteen double and four single units for officers, and was laid out by Captain Joshua W. Jacobs, the army's quartermaster, who also played a significant role in overseeing the design and construction of these buildings. The bright red brick facades are animated by white accents, gables, and porches, and enhanced by lush vegetation. Most interesting is the Commanding Officer's Quarters (No. 10), in the Queen Anne style, with its wrapping porch, unusual window frames, and decorative chimney stack extending the entire height of one of the wings (the original one-foot-high numerals indicating its construction date, 1889, were set in the brick masonry but were replaced in 1922 by the present plaque bearing the same date). Also of interest is the Field Officer's Quarters (No. 5), which features a semi-oval turret surmounted by a balcony. Its intended twin on lot 15 was never built. The double units feature brickwork not unlike that found in Baltimore Row (LM 1). Across the parade ground, the **Barracks,** a long and narrow brick structure with a finely crafted two-story portico, is crowned by projecting pediments located above the entrances. Other Victorian nonresidential buildings—the former headquarters and the chapel—as well as Pershing Hall, a smaller residential unit, can be seen along Hardee Avenue.

SS 5 **Lakewood Fairgrounds Exhibition Halls**
2000 Lakewood Avenue, S.W.
1916: Edwards and Sayward, Architects

SS 6 **Lakewood Amphitheatre**
2002 Lakewood Avenue, S.W.
1989: Sustata and Associates, Architects (Houston)

Formerly the site of the City Waterworks, which was relocated to the
Chattahoochee River in 1893, the area became an amusement park
on 370 acres with a racetrack, midway, roller rink, bowling alley, and
a large artificial lake for boating. An elevated portion of the grounds
served as the site for the agriculturally oriented Southeastern Fair. For
many years Atlanta's largest annual event, held during the first week
of October, the fair boasted livestock as well as machinery exhibits.
The two major **Lakewood Fairgrounds Exhibition Halls**—long, narrow sheds with wooden roofs and concrete walls—form a quadrangle
completed by a smaller restaurant structure. Their sober but picturesque beige stucco exterior, with terra-cotta color accents and tile roofs,
was treated in the Spanish Colonial Revival style adopted for the 1915
Panama-California exhibition in San Diego. End gables are modeled
after the facades of eighteenth-century California mission churches, with
twin-domed towers. Notice their central arcaded entrances framed by
columns supporting statues. While the buildings themselves are in fairly
good condition, the grounds have not been well maintained. The recently constructed **Lakewood Amphitheatre** has brought new activity
into this once declining area. The facility's iron gates by metal sculptor and blacksmith Ivan Bailey depict Georgia's main rivers and add a
decorative statement to its otherwise functional expression.

Works Cited

Ames, Anthony. *Five Houses*. Princeton, N.J.: Princeton Architectural Press, 1987.

Atlanta Urban Design Commission. *Atlanta's Lasting Landmarks*. Atlanta: Atlanta Urban Design Commission, 1987.

Dowling, Elizabeth Meredith. *American Classicist: The Architecture of Philip Trammel Shutze*. New York: Rizzoli, 1989.

Garrett, Franklin M. *Yesterday's Atlanta*. Miami: E. A Seeman, 1974.

Grady, James. *The Architecture of Neel Reid in Georgia*. Athens: University of Georgia Press (for the Peachtree-Cherokee Trust), 1973.

Howett, Catherine. "A Georgian Renascence in Georgia: The Residential Architecture of Neel Reid." In *Colonial Revival in America,* edited by Alan Axelrod, 122–38. New York: Norton, 1985.

Lyon, Elizabeth. *Atlanta Architecture: The Victorian Age, 1837–1918* (Exhibition Catalog). Atlanta: Atlanta Historical Society, 1976 (reprint 1986).

Martin, Van Jones, and William R. Mitchell, *Landmark Homes of Georgia, 1733– 1983: Two Hundred and Fifty Years of Architecture, Interiors, and Gardens*. Savannah: Golden Coast, 1982.

Poling, Clark V. *Henry Hornbostel. Michael Graves* (Exhibition Catalog). Atlanta: Emory University Museum of Art and Archeology, 1985.

Reed, Henry Hope. "America's Greatest Living Classical Architect: Philip Trammel Shutze of Atlanta, Georgia." *Classical America* 5 (1977): 5–46.

Schneider, Jane F., ed. *From Plantation to Peachtree: A Century and a Half of Classic Atlanta Homes*. Atlanta: Design Editions, 1987.

Glossary

adaptive reuse   Preservation or restoration of a building's appearance while completely changing its function to meet contemporary needs.

aedicula   Originally, a templelike structure consisting of columns or piers supporting an entablature or pediment, used as a shrine, but now more generally the decorative framing of a window or doorway with such a templelike motif.

ashlar   Stone work utilizing masonry units with cut and squared edges laid in horizontal courses, usually with random vertical joints.

balustrade   A series of small, usually decorative, posts or columns (known as balusters) supporting a railing or coping, often found along rooflines as well as balconies and monumental staircases.

belvedere   A small, open-sided but roofed structure located in a landscape or atop a roof affording a view of the surrounding area. Garden versions are sometimes called gazebos.

board-and-batten   Wide vertical boards applied as siding on the exterior of a building with narrow boards applied over the joints.

bow window   A curved projection on a facade containing several windows. A bay window with three sides is a form of bow window.

caducei   Insignias bearing staffs with wings and intertwined snakes symbolizing the medical profession.

campanile   Italian term for bell tower, usually applied to freestanding structures as opposed to those attached to a main building.

carillon   A set of bells, usually played from a keyboard.

cartouche   An ornament in the form of a shield, oval, or scroll with curling edges, usually bearing an inscription.

caryatid   A sculptured female figure used as a column.

casino   A summer or garden pavilion, usually ornamental in character, found on the grounds of a larger house.

castellated   Adorned with battlements, alternating indentions in a parapet originally intended to afford defense of a fortified castle.

chamfer   The diagonal surface made by cutting off the sharp edge formed where two surfaces of a cut stone or piece of lumber meet at an angle.

Chicago School   Popularized by Chicago architects practicing between 1880 and 1910, this style features multistory building designs characterized by expressed structural frames (emphasizing the vertical rather than horizontal members) and windows that fill the voids between them.

ciborium   A canopy structure, usually a dome atop four columns, erected over a high altar or tomb, sometimes called a baldachino.

clapboard   Horizontal, overlapping wedge-shaped boards covering a building's exterior, also called weatherboard.

coffer   A decorative, recessed panel, rectangular or polygonal in form, used to define and ornament ceilings, domes, and vaults.

console   A decorative bracket generally utilizing a scroll or volute motif and usually taller than its projection.

corbelling   Projecting courses of masonry, usually brick, each one slightly beyond the one below, used as a decorative element to accent chimney-stacks, parapets, arches, vaults, or other architectural features.

cornice   In classical architecture, the top-most portion of an entablature which projects over the frieze and architrave forming an eave, also the decorative, overhanging moulding that crowns a wall or facade.

crenellation Alternately raising and lowering the level of a parapet at regular intervals to create battlements, also known as castellation.

crocket In Gothic architecture, the decorative projecting spur of carved stone foliage adorning the edges of spires, pinnacles, gables, and canopies at regular intervals along their lengths.

cupola A small, hemispheric dome usually surmounting a circular or polygonal turret atop a larger dome or roof structure.

cyclopean blocks Very large, irregular masonry units, usually rough-hewn to appear as if used directly from the quarry.

dentils Small, rectangular blocks, regularly spaced like teeth, used as decorative elements in classical cornices.

dovecote A small, compartmentalized house or box used for raising domestic pigeons.

eclectic Utilizing stylistic elements from more than one historical precedent.

entablature In classical architecture, that portion of an order above the column which consists of the architrave, frieze, and cornice.

exedra In classical Greek architecture, a recessed alcove with a raised seat. The term is now used to describe an apse or niche that opens to a larger space, either exterior or interior.

FABRAP The Atlanta architectural firm of Finch, Alexander, Barnes, Rothschild and Paschal, now part of Rosser Fabrap International.

fenestration The arrangement of windows and other openings on the facade of a building.

finial The decorative, ornamental termination of a pinnacle, spire, gable, post, or other architectural feature.

frieze In classical architecture, the band of an entablature below the overhanging cornice and above the architrave, usually decorated with continuous or paneled, low-relief sculpture but left plain in more simplified orders such as Doric and Tuscan.

Gibbs, James (1662–1754) Influential London architect whose Italian-inspired designs and drawings have been copied on both continents, especially his church designs such as St. Martin-in-the-Fields in London (1722–26), which combined a classical Roman temple portico with a steeple springing from the roof.

Kahn, Albert (1869–1942) German-born architect who emigrated to the United States and became the leading designer of industrial buildings, including automobile factories for Ford and General Motors, in the early 1900s.

lancet window A rectangular window with a pointed arched top, typical of Gothic architecture.

lantern A small turretlike construction with windows on all sides placed atop a dome or at the crossing point of intersecting pitched roofs.

Latrobe, Benjamin (1764–1820) The United States' first formally educated architect who brought engineering and design skills to his Greek and Gothic Revival buildings in Philadelphia, Baltimore, New Orleans, and Washington, D.C., where his work included the U.S. Capitol.

Le Corbusier (1887–1966) French architect whose white, cubist, open plan private residences and heavy, sculptural, exposed concrete commercial and institutional structures have made him one of the most influential architects of the twentieth century. (Also known as Charles Edouard Jeanneret and Corbu.)

loggia A gallery, room, or structure characterized by an open colonnade or arcade on one or more sides.

lunette A semicircular window or recessed wall panel usually set into a vaulted, coved, or domed ceiling or roof.

marquee A canopy projecting over an entry.

mastaba In ancient Egypt, a rectangular funerary mound which preceded the great pyramids and was formed of brick or stone with a flat top and battered sides marking the site of a burial chamber deep underground.

Mies van der Rohe, Ludwig (1886–1969) German-born architect whose pioneering minimalist designs, which relied on proportion, open spatial composition, and exquisite detailing of fine materials, were the epitome of the International Style.

mullions Thin, vertical dividing bars in a window or other opening.

oculus A circular opening in a wall or dome.

order In classical architecture, the composition of column (with base, shaft, and capital) and entablature which conforms in detail and proportion to one of the accepted Greek or Roman designs (Doric, Ionic, Corinthian, Composite, and Tuscan).

Palladian Of a style derived from the designs of Italian architect Andrea Palladio (1508–1580), who synthesized the architecture of ancient Rome into the quintessential Renaissance formula. Often used to describe a window or doorway motif made popular by Palladio which places two rectangular openings beside a larger arched opening.

palazzo Italian for "palace."

parti French term for scheme or design solution, generally used in reference to a building's plan.

pastiche A composition imitating the style of a previous work or made up of motifs borrowed from several different works.

pediment The geometric form, usually above a portico, window, or doorway, created by a low-pitched roof gable. Pediments can be classical (triangular), segmental (part of a circle), and broken (discontinuous at the apex or base).

pendentive Triangular concave device that serves as a transition from a square or polygonal room shape to a circular, domed ceiling.

pergola A canopied open structure covering a garden walk, usually overgrown with vines or shrubs.

peristyle An array of columns encircling a courtyard or an entire building.

piano nobile The main floor of a residence which contains the principal rooms but is raised above the ground or semi-recessed basement level.

piazza Italian term for an open space, generally paved and rectangular, surrounded by buildings.

pilotis French term for stilts, used to describe the posts that support a building raised above an open ground floor.

Piranesi, Giovanni Battista (1720–1778) Italian engraver and architectural theorist whose naturalistic depictions of ancient Rome and writings on its architectural supremacy fostered a new appreciation for antiquity that led to the neoclassical and Romantic movements of the late eighteenth century.

porte cochere A covered porch adjoining an entryway which allows the passage of wheeled vehicles.

putti Italian term for an architectural motif depicting children, often with wings.

quoins The accentuated blocks or stones, usually alternating between large and small faces, stacked at the corners of masonry walls.

Richardson, Henry Hobson (1838–1886) Boston architect whose personalized use of the Romanesque style, heavy rustication, and careful attention to composition and proportion was widely imitated and helped to establish a base for American architectural expression in the late nineteenth century, independent of revivalism then predominant in Europe.

roundel A small, circular panel or window.

rose window A circular window with tracery similar to the spokes of a wheel, also known as a wheel window.

rosette A decorative feature, usually round or oval in shape, sometimes decorated with rose petals or acanthus leaves.

rustication A recessed and exaggerated groove used to accent the joints in smooth or rough-hewn masonry or poured-in-place concrete.

segmental A portion of a circle, less than a semicircle, with one straight side and one curved side.

Soane, Sir John (1753–1837) English architect whose highly personal and occasionally eccentric use of the neoclassical style was at times severe and rudimentary while at other times romantic and picturesque.

stringcourse A projecting horizontal band, either moulded or plain, which runs continuously along the face of an exterior wall.

swag A carved or cast ornament, depicting a garland of flowers or bundle of cloth suspended between supports at each end.

synthetic stucco Commonly referred to as Exterior Insulation and Finishing System (EIFS), this modern material appears similar to stucco but is thinly applied to a layer of rigid, expanded foam insulation.

term A tapered pedestal supporting or merging into a human or animal figure.

terra-cotta Fired, cast clay units, usually ornamental in nature and set in brick or other masonry construction along with standard units.

torchère An ornamental bracket for a light source.

tripartite Composed of three parts, usually a base, middle, and top or a center with two sides.

turret A small, slender tower attached to a main structure.

Venturi, Robert (b. 1925) Leading American proponent of postmodern architecture, whose writings (*Complexity and Contradiction in Architecture* and *Learning from Las Vegas*) and designs substitute irrational, playful, and intricate forms for the rational, pure, and simple ones of the International Style.

Vierendeel truss Named for its inventor, a flat truss, with top and bottom chords parallel, which uses perpendicular, rigidly connected cross members rather than diagonal, pin-connected ones.

volute The spiral scroll motif, similar to a nautilus shell, usually associated with Ionic column capitals.

General Index

(Including architects, designers, developers, builders, and organizations)

References to major discussions are indicated in boldface type; references followed by the letter *m* indicate pages containing maps; page numbers for illustrations are in italics.

Ackerman, Charles, 90
Aeck Associates
  George and Irene Woodruff
    Residential Center, Emory
    University, 218m, **231**
AI Group
  The Suite Hotel at Underground
    Atlanta (Connally Building), 2m, **4**
Aiken and Faulkner
  Atlanta Life Insurance Company
    Building, 72m, **76**, *76*
Alexander, Cecil A.
  Wachovia Bank of Georgia Building
    (First National Bank Building),
    20m, **22**, *22*
Leon Allain and Associates
  Graves Hall, Morehouse College,
    162m, **166**, *167*
Allen, Douglas C.
  Frank W. Hulse IV House and Pool
    Pavilion, 138m, **141**, *141*
  Turner Village and D. Abbott Turner
    Center, Emory University, 218m,
    232, *233*
  Hewlett-Packard Building, 282m,
    292, *292*
Ames, Anthony
  Frank W. Hulse IV House and Pool
    Pavilion, 138m, **141**, *141*
  Garden House, Atlanta Botanical
    Garden, 138m, **143**, *143*
Amisano, Joseph
  MARTA Peachtree Center Station,
    46m, **48**, *48*
  Peachtree Summit, 46m, **61**, *61*
  Robert W. Woodruff Library, 162m,
    166, *166*
  Second Church of Christ, Scientist,
    264m, **271**
  D&B Software Building (Cities
    Service Building), 264m, **274**,
    274
  John Knox Presbyterian Church,
    282m, **293**, *293*

Anderson/Schwartz
  ParkSide Restaurant, 196m,
    204, *205*
Andrews, W. P., 235
Ansley, Edwin P., xxii, 137
Armistead, J. Warren
  Clark Howell Homes, 148m, **153**
Arquitectonica
  Rio Shopping Mall, 86m, **90**, *90*
Roy Ashley and Associates
  Underground Atlanta, 2m, **4**, *5*
  IBM U.S. Marketing and Services
    Headquarters, 282m, **284**, *284*
  One, Two, and Three Ravinia Drive,
    296m, **298**, *298*
  Concourse at Landmark Center,
    296m, **303**, *303*, *304*
  Hartsfield Atlanta International
    Airport, 326m, **329**, *329*
Askins, Norman D.
  Alonzo F. Herndon Home, 162m,
    165, *165*
Associated Space Design
  Hurt Building, 20m, **42**, *42*
  Concourse at Landmark Center,
    296m, **303**, *303*
Atlanta Botanical Garden, 143–44
Atlanta Historical Society, 261
Atlanta Land and Annuity Company
  Baltimore Row (Baltimore Block),
    86m, **88**, *88*
Atlanta Landmarks, 99
Atlanta Preservation Center, 1, 19, 71,
  100, 161, 176, 185
Atlanta University Center, xxi, 154,
  161–68

Bailey, Ivan, 332
Bailey and Associates
  Charles A. Dana Fine Arts Center,
    Agnes Scott College, 316m,
    322, *322*
Baker, Debra
  Rio Shopping Mall, 86m, **90**, *90*

Ball, Willis, 307
   Bulloch Hall, 308m, **310,** *310*
   Mimosa Hall (Phoenix Hall), 308m,
      310, *311*
   Barrington Hall, 308m, **310,** *311*
   Roswell Presbyterian Church, 308m,
      312, *312*
Barber, Donn
   Capital City Club, 46m, **56,** *56*
Barili, Alfredo, Jr.
   Martin Luther King Jr. Federal
      Building (United States Post
      Office), 2m, **14,** *14*
Barrett and Associates
   Executive Park, 264m, **277**
Welton Becket Associates
   MARTA Civic Center Station, 46m,
      61, *61*
Bedford-Pine Development
   Corporation, 90–91
Bond, George Harwell
   Briarcliff Plaza, 196m, **200,** *201*
   Second Ponce de Leon Baptist
      Church, 236m, **242**
Bond and Ryder
   Martin Luther King Jr. Center for
      Nonviolent Social Change, 72m,
      80, *80*
A. Thomas Bradbury and Associates
   Georgia Department of Archives and
      History Building, 174m, **181**
   Governor's Mansion, 236m, **252**
Bradfield Associates
   GlenCastle (Atlanta Stockade),
      174m, **178,** *178*
   Ford Factory Square, 196m,
      199, *200*
Braley, Scott
   Georgia Dome, 64m, **69,** *69*
Breuer, Marcel
   Atlanta–Fulton County Public
      Library, 20m, **34,** *34*
Brisbin, Brook and Beynon
   Flatiron Building (English-American
      Building), 20m, **31,** *31*
Brown, A. Ten Eyck
   Fulton County Courthouse, 2m, **12**
   The Counsel House (Bass Furniture
      Building), 2m, **13,** *13*
   Martin Luther King Jr. Federal
      Building (United States Post
      Office), 2m, **14,** *14*
   Ten Park Place South Building
      (Thornton Building), 20m, **42**
   Peachtree-Pine Building (United

   Motors Service Building), 86m,
      89, *89*
   Clark Howell Homes, 148m, **153**
   The Roosevelt (Franklin D.
      Roosevelt High School), 174m,
      179, *179*
Bruce and Everett
   First Congregational Church, 72m,
      74, *74*
Bruce and Morgan
   Concordia Hall, 2m, **13**
   NationsBank Building (Citizens and
      Southern National Bank Building;
      Empire Building), 20m, **24,** *24, 25*
   Grant Building (Grant-Prudential
      Building), 20m, **28,** *29*
   Healey Building, 20m, **28,** *28*
   Fire Station No. 6, 72m, **81**
   North Avenue Presbyterian Church,
      86m, **92,** *92*
   All Saints Episcopal Church, 86m,
      95, *95*
   Administration Building, Georgia
      Tech, 148m, **155,** *155*
   Agnes Scott Hall, Agnes Scott
      College, 316m, **321,** *321*
Bryan, Cecil E.
   Abbey Mausoleum, Westview
      Cemetery, 162m, **170,** *170*
Bryan, Ross H.
   D&B Software Building (Cities
      Service Building), 264m, **274,** *274*
Burdette, B. F., 238
Burge and Stevens. *See also* Stevens
   and Wilkinson
   West Wing, Georgia Baptist Medical
      Center, 72m, **83**
   Techwood Homes, 148m, **153,** *153*
   160 Rumson Road, N.E., 236m,
      242, *242*
   178 Rumson Road, N.E., 242
   Capital City Country Club
      (Brookhaven Country Club),
      264m, **278,** *278*
Burgee, John
   One-Ninety-One Peachtree Tower,
      46m, **50,** *50*
   One Atlantic Center (IBM Tower),
      112m, **121,** *121*
Burnham, Daniel, 31
Burnham and Root
   Equitable Building (1892), 42
Bush-Brown, Gailey and Heffernan
   Hightower Textile Engineering
      Building, Georgia Tech, 148m,
      157, *157*

Architecture Building, Georgia Tech,
148m, **157,** *158*
Price Gilbert Memorial Library,
Georgia Tech, 148m, **157,** *158*
William Vernon Skiles Classroom
Building, Georgia Tech, 148m,
157

Campbell, William
Alonzo F. Herndon Home, 162m,
165, *165*
Candler, Asa Griggs, 39, 171, 189,
202, 207, 216, 217, 329
Candler, Charles Howard, 210
Candler, Warren, 217
Candler, William, 104
Carpenter, J. E. R.
Hurt Building, 20m, **42,** *42*
Carrère and Hastings, 235
Carrithers, Dan
Perimeter Mall, 296m, **298**
Carson, Lundin and Shaw
Trust Company Bank Building, 20m,
42, *43*
Carter, Jimmy, 192
Cavender Associates
Baptist Student Center, Georgia State
University (Dixie Coca-Cola
Bottling Company), 72m, **75,** *75*
Central Atlanta Progress, 90
Chastain and Tindel
Forty Marietta Building (First Federal
Savings and Loan Association
Building), 20m, **26,** *26*
Cheek, John
First Union Plaza (999 Peachtree
Building), 112m, **116,** *116*
Chow, James
Cyclorama, 174m, **180,** *180*
Clayton, Robert M.
Atlanta Water Works, Hemphill
Pumping Station, 148m, **160,** *160*
Coca-Cola Company, 6, 39, 75, 147,
150–53, 191, 217
Collier, George Washington, 137, 143
Constantine, Augustus
The Granada All Suite Hotel
(Granada Apartments), 112m,
122, *122*
Cooper Carry and Associates
Underground Atlanta, 2m, **4,** *5*
MARTA Garnett Street Station, 2m,
18, *18*
NSI Center (National Service
Industries Headquarters Building),
112m, **131**

Architecture Building, Georgia Tech,
148m, **157,** *158*
Piedmont Center, Buildings One
through Twelve, 264m, **269,**
269, 270
Cumberland Center II, 282m,
286, *286*
Wildwood 2300 Building, 282m,
290, *290*
Wildwood 3100 Building, 282m,
290
7000 Central Park, 296m, **302,** *302*
9000 Central Park, 296m, **302**
Corput and Bass
Georgia Railroad Freight Depot, 2m,
6
Cousins, Tom, 63
Cousins Properties, 291
Cridland, Robert
Avondale Estates Historic District,
316m, **320,** *320*
Crook, Lewis E., Jr. *See also* Ivey
and Crook
Saint Mark United Methodist
Church, 86m, **102,** *102*
Lullwater House (Walter Turner
Candler House), Emory
University, 218m, **230,** *231*

Daley, Vincent
Wigwam Apartments, 72m, **81,** *82*
D'Ascenzo Studios, 129
Daugherty, Edward L.
Garden House, Atlanta Botanical
Garden, 138m, **143,** *143*
DeKalb Historical Society, 319
Denny, Willis F.
First United Methodist Church of
Atlanta, 46m, **60**
Saint Mark United Methodist
Church, 86m, **102,** *102*
Rhodes Hall, 112m, **132,** *132*
Inman Park United Methodist
Church, 186m, **188**
Denson and Associates
The Trolley Barn (Inman Park Street
Car Barn), 186m, **188,** *188*
Dinkeloo, John. *See* Kevin Roche, John
Dinkeloo and Associates
Dobson, Jack
Coca-Cola Technical Center, 148m,
151, **152**
Dodd, Bobby, 154
Dougherty, Edward
First Church of Christ, Scientist,
112m, **126,** *126*

Dougherty and Gardner
  Campbell-Egan Educational
    Building, 2m, **8**
  Druid Hills Baptist Church, 196m,
    200, *201*
Dowling Architects and Associates
  Performing Arts and Athletic Center,
    Paideia School, 208m, **213,** *213*
Downing, John Francis
  Cyclorama, 174m, **180,** *180*
Downing, Walter T.
  Trinity United Methodist Church,
    2m, **10**
  Eiseman Building, 17
  Healey Building, 20m, **28,** *28*
  Sacred Heart Church (Church of the
    Sacred Heart of Jesus), 46m,
    60, *60*
  Shellmont Bed and Breakfast Lodge
    (William P. Nicholson House),
    86m, **106,** *106*
  Atlanta Woman's Club (Wimbish
    House), 112m, **117,** *117*
  First Presbyterian Church, 112m,
    128, *129*
  Frank S. Ellis House, 138m,
    140, *140*
  Joel Hurt House, 186m, **189**
  Cherokee Town Club (Grant House),
    236m, **254**
Durfee and Hughes
  Catholic Center, Georgia Tech,
    148m, **156,** *156*
  Hewlett-Packard Building, 282m,
    292, *292*
  National Institutional Food
    Distributor Associates (NIFDA)
    Building, 282m, **292**

Eames and Young
  Atlanta Federal Penitentiary, 174m,
    183, *183*
Eatman, Gauff and Company
  Oxford Book Store at Buckhead
    (RBM of Atlanta), 264m, **267**
EDAW
  Carter Presidential Center, 186m,
    192, *192*
Edbrooke and Burnham
  Georgia State Capitol, 2m, **9,** *9*
Edwards, William A.
  Odd Fellows Building, 72m, **77,** *77*
Edwards and Kelsey
  MARTA Decatur Transit Station,
    316m, **318,** *319*

Edwards and Portman.
  Peachtree Center Tower, 46m, *51,*
    53
  Atlanta Merchandise Mart, 46m, **54**
  Hyatt Regency Atlanta Hotel
    (Regency Hyatt House Hotel),
    46m, **56,** *57*
  Charles A. Dana Fine Arts Center,
    Agnes Scott College, 316m,
    322, *322*
Edwards and Sayward
  University Homes, 154
  The Roosevelt (Franklin D.
    Roosevelt High School), 174m,
    179, *179*
  Buttrick Hall, Agnes Scott College,
    316m, **321**
  McCain Library, Agnes Scott
    College, 316m, **321**
  Lakewood Fairgrounds Exhibition
    Halls, 326m, **332,** *332*
Elam, Merrill. *See also* Scogin, Elam
    and Bray
  Georgia Power Company Corporate
    Headquarters, 46m, **62,** *62*
  Martin Luther King Jr. Middle
    School, 174m, **181,** *182*
  Robert W. Woodruff Health Services
    Center Administration Building,
    Emory University, 218m,
    230, *230*
  Clayton County Headquarters
    Library, 326m, **328,** *328*
Everett, A. F. N.
  Evans-Cucich House, 236m,
    240, *241*

FABRAP. *See also* Finch-Heery; Rosser
    Fabrap International
  Central Presbyterian Church, 2m,
    8, *8*
  Wachovia Bank of Georgia Building
    (First National Bank Building),
    20m, **22,** *22*
  Southern Bell Center, 86m, *97,* **99**
  Coca-Cola North Avenue Tower,
    148m, **152,** *152*
  Coca-Cola Enterprises Building (One
    Coca-Cola Plaza), 148m, **152**
  Coca-Cola Technical Center, 148m,
    151, **152**
  Cyclorama, 174m, **180,** *180*
  Atlanta–Fulton County Stadium,
    174m, **181**
  Phipps Plaza, 264m, **274**

Finch-Heery
  MARTA Five Points Station, 2m,
    17, *17*
Frangiamore, Roy
  RJ's Wine Bar Cafe, 196m, **203,** *204*
French, Daniel Chester, 135
Friedberg, Paul
  Fulton County Government Center,
    2m, **12,** *12*

Gardner, Eugene Clarence, and Sons
  Georgia Hall, Grady Memorial
    Hospital, 72m, **78,** *78*
Georgia Trust for Historic
    Preservation, 132
Gibbs Landscape Company
  Wildwood 2300 Building, 282m,
    290, *290*
Gilbert, Bradford
  Flatiron Building (English-American
    Building), 20m, **31,** *31*
Goff, Bruce
  Oxford Book Store at Buckhead
    (RBM of Atlanta), 264m, **267**
Gone with the Wind, xxvi, 37, 101,
    108, 117
Gordy, Frank, 97
Grady, Henry W., 78, 170
Graffin, Daniel, 58
Graham, Bruce
  The Terraces at Perimeter Center,
    296m, **300,** *300*
Graham, John
  Ford Factory Square (Ford Factory
    Building), 196m, **199,** *200*
Grant, Lemuel P., 180–181
Graves, Michael
  Ten Peachtree Place, 112m,
    114, *115*
  Emory University Museum of Art
    and Archeology (Michael C.
    Carlos Hall), 218m, **222,** *223*
Greenberg Farrow Architecture
  Plaza Court Expansion, Lenox
    Square, 264m, **272,** *272, 273*
Greene, W. Lane
  Wren's Nest, Joel Chandler Harris
    House, 162m, **169,** *169*
Grey, Jules
  The Varsity, 86m, **97,** *97*
Griggs, Robert
  Beath-Dickey House, 186m,
    190, *190*
Grove, Edwin Wiley, 203
Gullstedt, G. Lars, 85, 104, 120

Hallmuth, Obata and Kassabaum
  Perimeter Mall, 296m, **298**
Hamilton, Alexander, Jr.
  George Washington Carver High
    School (Leete Hall), 174m,
    182, *183*
Peter Hand and Associates
  Highland Hardware, 196m,
    204, *205*
  Second Ponce de Leon Baptist
    Church, 236m, **242**
Harrington Engineers
  Georgia Dome, 64m, **69,** *69*
Harris, Joel Chandler, 169, 170
Harris, Julian
  Lenox Square, 264m, **272**
Harris, Oscar
  Fulton County Government Center,
    2m, **12,** *12*
Harris and Partners
  Atlanta City Hall, 2m, **10,** *10, 11*
Hartsfield, William B., xxii, 170, 329
Harvey, Hellington and Day
  Abbey Mausoleum, Westview
    Cemetery, 162m, **170,** *170*
Hauswirth, Philip
  D. Lurton Massee Jr. House, 236m,
    244, *245*
Haverty, J. J., 33
Havis, Barney
  The Granada All Suite Hotel
    (Granada Apartments), 112m,
    122, *122*
Hawkins, Frank, 43
Healey, Thomas G., 23
Healey, William T., 28
Hedrick, Wyatt C.
  Bank South Building (Fulton
    National Bank Building), 20m,
    27, *27*
Heery and Heery. *See also*
    Finch-Heery
  Georgia Power Company Corporate
    Headquarters, 46m, **62,** *62*
  Martin Luther King Jr. Middle
    School, 174m, **181,** *182*
  Atlanta–Fulton County Stadium,
    174m, **181**
  Robert W. Woodruff Health
    Sciences Center Administration
    Building, Emory University,
    218m, **230,** *230*
  Herman Miller, Roswell Facility,
    308m, **313,** *313*

Heery Architects and Engineers
  Georgia Dome, 64m, **69,** *69*
  First Union Plaza (999 Peachtree
    Building), 112m, **116,** *116*
  One Atlantic Center (IBM Tower),
    112m, **121,** *121*
  Dorothy Chapman Fuqua
    Conservatory, Atlanta Botanical
    Garden, 138m, **144,** *144*
  Coca-Cola Company Corporate
    Headquarters, Central Reception
    Building, 148m, **150,** *150*
  Coca-Cola USA Building, 148m,
    150, *151*
Heery Interiors
  The Coca-Cola Company Corporate
    Headquarters, Central Reception
    Building, 148m, **150,** *150*
Heffernan, Paul M.
  Hightower Textile Engineering
    Building, Georgia Tech, 148m,
    157, *157*
  Architecture Building, Georgia Tech,
    148m, **157,** *158*
  Price Gilbert Memorial Library,
    Georgia Tech, 148m, **157,** *158*
  William Vernon Skiles Classroom
    Building, Georgia Tech, 148m,
    157
  Wesley Foundation, Georgia Tech,
    148m, **157**
Helmle, Corbett and Harrison
  Crum and Foster Building, 86m,
    103, *103*
Henderson, Edith
  Techwood Homes, 148m, **153,** *153*
Hentz, Adler and Shutze
  NationsBank Building (Citizens and
    Southern National Bank Building;
    Empire Building), 20m, **24,** *24, 25*
  Macy's Department Store (Davison-
    Paxon Department Store), 46m,
    48, *49*
  Spring Hill Mortuary, 112m,
    114, *114*
  Reid House (Garrison Apartments),
    112m, **130,** *130*
  Clark Howell Homes, 148m, **153**
  Glenn Memorial United Methodist
    Church, 218m, **220,** *220*
  Harris Hall (Florence C. Harris
    Memorial Nurses' Home), Emory
    University, 218m, **228**
  North Fulton High School, 236m,
    242

  Patterson-Carr House, 236m,
    250, *251*
  Joseph D. Rhodes House, 236m,
    252, *252*
  Southern Center for International
    Studies (James J. Goodrum
    House), 236m, **253,** *254*
  Harry L. English House, 236m, **253**
  Knollwood (W. H. Kiser House),
    236m, **254,** *255*
  Albert E. Thornton House, 236m,
    254
  Floyd McRae House, 236m, **255**
  Edward Van Winkle House, 236m,
    255
  Swan House (Edward H. Inman
    House), 236m, **260,** *260, 261*
Hentz, Hal
  Reid House (Garrison Apartments),
    112m, **130,** *130*
Hentz, Reid and Adler
  Rich's Department Store, 2m, **15,**
    15, 16
  Muse's Building (George Muse
    Clothing Company Building),
    20m, **30,** *30*
  Atlanta History Center, Downtown
    Office (Hillyer Trust Company
    Building), 20m, **33**
  Steiner Building, Grady Memorial
    Hospital (Albert Steiner Ward),
    72m, **78**
  Hotel Peachtree Manor (696
    Peachtree Apartments), 86m,
    105, *105*
  The Temple, 112m, **133,** *133, 134*
  Brookwood Station (Peachtree
    Southern Railway Station), 112m,
    135, *135*
  David Black House, 138m, **140**
  Robert Crumley House, 138m, **140**
  Stephen S. Lynch House, 138m, **140**
  The Villa, 138m, **142**
  The Sisters Chapel, Spelman
    College, 162m, **167,** *167*
  Tapley Hall, Spelman College,
    162m, **168**
  Will Campbell House, 208m,
    211, *212*
  Sigmund Montag House, 208m, **211**
  Louis Regenstein House, 208m, **211**
  Oscar Strauss House, 208m, **214,**
    214
  Joseph Neel Reid House, 208m, **214**
  Walter Rich House, 208m, **215,** *215*

Emory University Hospital, 218m,
228, *228*
Luxemburger House, 236m,
238, *238*
Henry B. Tompkins House, 236m,
244, *244*
C. C. Case House, 236m, **245,** *246*
Andrew Calhoun House, 236m, **250**
Winship Nunally House, 236m, **250**
James Dickey House, 236m,
252, *253*
T. M. Watson House, 236m, **256**
Livingston Wright House, 236m,
256, *257*
William F. Manry House, 236m, **256**
Philip McDuffie House, 236m,
257, *258*
Jesse Draper House, 236m, **257**
Henry Newman House, 236m, **257**
Robert Alston House, 236m, **259,**
259
Stuart Witham House, 236m, **259**
Vaughn Nixon House, 236m, **259**
Community Center of South Decatur
(Scottish Rite Hospital for
Crippled Children), 316m,
323, *323*
Hentz and Reid
John Wesley Dobbs Building
(Southern Schoolbook Depository
Building), 72m, **76**
Phelan Apartments, 86m, **108**
Frank Adair House, 208m, **212,** *213*
East Lake Country Club, 316m,
324, *324*
Herndon, Alonzo F., 76, 165
High, Harriett, 128
Gerald Hines Interests, 299
Hirsch-Bedner and Associates
Doubletree Hotel, Concourse at
Landmark Center, 296m,
303, *303*
Historic Facade Program, 14, 76
Hooker, L. J., 114
Hoover, Ray
Promenade Two, 112m, **124,** *124*
Concourse at Landmark Center,
296m, **303,** *303*
Hopson, Charles H.
Peachtree Christian Church, 112m,
133
Hornbostel, Henry, 217
Habersham Memorial Hall, 138m,
145
Callanwolde Fine Arts Center,
208m, **210,** *210*

Michael C. Carlos Hall (Lamar
School of Law), Emory University,
218m, **222,** *222*
Pitts Theology Library (Candler
School of Theology), Emory
University, 218m, **223**
Housen and Gambino
Performing Arts and Athletic Center,
Paideia School, 208m,
213, *213*
Houseworth, Marvin
CNN Center (Omni International),
64m, **66,** *67*
Howington, Frank, 102
Humphreys, J. W.
Martin Luther King Jr. Federal
Building (United States Post
Office), 2m, **14,** *14*
Hunt, Sheila A.
The Coca-Cola Company Corporate
Headquarters, Central Reception
Building, 148m, **150,** *150*
Hurst, Sam T.
Wesley Foundation, Georgia Tech,
148m, **157**
Hurt, Joel, xxii, xxv, 42, 185, 189,
190, 207

IBM Corporation, 121, 284, 291
Inman, Samuel, 185, 204
Ivey and Crook, 217
Olympia Building, 20m, **42**
Crum and Foster Building, 86m,
103, *103*
Clark Howell Homes, 148m, **153**
Alumni Memorial Hall, Emory
University, 218m, **225,** *226*
Harris Hall, Emory University,
218m, **228**
Lullwater House (Walter Turner
Candler House), Emory
University, 218m, **230,** *231*
125 Rumson Road, N.E., 242

Jacobs, Joshua W., 330
Jennings, Wilmer, 172
Johnson, J. Forsyth, 185
Johnson, Philip, 111
One-Ninety-One Peachtree Tower,
46m, **50,** *50*
One Atlantic Center (IBM Tower),
112m, **121,** *121*
Jones, Bobby, 176, 324
Jones and Thompson
MARTA Garnett Street Station, 2m,
18, *18*

Jova/Daniels/Busby
  Atlanta City Hall, 2m, **10**, *10, 11*
  Academy of Medicine, 86m,
    107, *107*
  Colony Square, 112m, *118,*
    119, *119*
  William C. Wardlaw Jr. Center,
    Georgia Tech, 148m, **154,** *154*
  L. W. "Chip" Robert Alumni and
    Faculty House (John D.
    Rockefeller YMCA Building),
    Georgia Tech, 148m, **154**
  Carter Presidential Center, 186m,
    192, *192*
  Bank South, Buckhead Branch,
    264m, **266**
JPJ Architects
  The Galleria, 282m, **288,** *289*
Junger, Philip
  Philip Junger House, 236m,
    238, *239*
  Georgia U.S. Corporate Center (Life
    of Georgia Corporate Center),
    282m, **288,** *289*
Kahn, Albert, 159
Katzmann and Associates
  Perimeter Mall, 296m, **298**
Kauffman, O. F., 320
Keck, Charles, 172
King, Martin Luther, Jr., 14, 71,
    80–82, 181
Kirkland Group, The
  Briarcliff Plaza, 196m, **200,** *201*
Kling, Vincent
  MARTA Five Points Station, 2m,
    17, *17*
Kortan, Jim
  The Tower at Tower Place, 264m,
    268, **269**

Lamberson, Plunkett, Shirley and
    Wooddall
  One Georgia Center (Life of Georgia
    Building), 86m, **95,** *96*
Laubmann Reed and Associates
  Overlook III, 282m, **285,** *285*
  The Galleria, 282m, **288,** *289*
Lawton, Umemura and Yamamoto
  Carter Presidential Center, 186m,
    192, *192*
Le Corbusier, 81, 119, 129, 141, 224,
    227
LeMaire, Eleanor
  Rich's Store for Men, 2m, **15**
Leonard, Peter
  Atlanta Woman's Club (Wimbish

House), 112m, **117,** *117*
Life of Georgia Insurance Company,
    96–97, 288
Lind, Edmund G.
  Central Presbyterian Church, 2m,
    8, *8*
Lipphold, Richard, 57
Lockwood-Greene
  Garnett Station Place (Southern
    Belting Company Building), 2m,
    18
Lord, Aeck and Sargent
  Manufacturing Research Center,
    Georgia Tech, 148m, **159,** *159*
Lord and Sargent
  Atlanta History Center, Downtown
    Office (Hillyer Trust Company
    Building), 20m, **33**
  Trinity School, 236m, **249,** *249*
Lowry, Eugene E.
  Reid House (Garrison Apartments),
    112m, **130,** *130*

Maddox, Robert Foster, 253
Marlatt, David
  Piedmont Arbors, 138m, **145,** *146*
Marye, Alger and Vinour
  AT&T Communications Building
    (Southern Bell Telephone
    Company Building), 20m, **40,** *41*
  Fox Theater, 86m, **99,** *99, 100*
Marye, P. Thornton
  Randolph-Lucas House, 236m,
    241, *241*
  Gentry-McClinton House (Virginia
    Manor), 316m, **324**
Marye and Alger
  Atlanta Woman's Club (Wimbish
    House), 112m, **117,** *117*
Franz Mayer Studios, 103
McCord, Edward and Debra
  Shellmont Bed and Breakfast Lodge
    (William P. Nicholson House),
    86m, **106,** *106*
McDuffie, Philip, 242, 257
W. S. McDuffie and Associates
  Booker T. Washington High School,
    162m, **171,** *171*
McMillan, Ferdinand
  The Castle, 112m, **123,** *123*
Meier, Richard, 111, 273
  High Museum of Art, 112m,
    128, *128*
Mies van der Rohe, Ludwig, 33
Miles, F. B., 39
Miller, Roger

NSI Center (National Service Industries Headquarters Building), 112m, **131**

Minority Airport Architects and Planners
  Hartsfield Atlanta International Airport, 326m, **329**, *329*

Mion, Charles
  174 The Prado, 138m, **140**

E. R. Mitchell Construction Company
  John Wesley Dobbs Building (Southern Schoolbook Depository Building), 72m, **76**

Mitchell, Margaret, 34, 117, 176

Mooney, Kemp. *See also* Surber, Barber and Mooney
  Gambrell Hall, Emory University, 218m, **227**, *227*
  D. Lurton Massee Jr. House, 236m, **244**, *244*
  Lawrence P. Klamon House, 236m, **246**, *247*
  The Tower at Tower Place, 264m, *268*, **269**

Morgan, Dillon and Lewis
  Cornerstone Building (J. P. Allen Building), 46m, **52**, *52*

Morgan and Dillon. *See also* Bruce and Morgan
  Fulton County Courthouse, 2m, **12**
  Walton Place (Georgia Railway and Power Building), 20m, **27**
  Fire Station No. 11, 86m, **94**, *94*
  Fire Station No. 7, 94
  L. W. "Chip" Robert Alumni and Faculty House (John D. Rockefeller YMCA Building), Georgia Tech, 148m, **154**
  Oglethorpe University, 264m, **279**, *279*

Mount, James
  Korean Church of Atlanta, 296m, *304*, **305**

Muldawer + Moultrie
  Atlanta City Hall, 2m, **10**, *10*, *11*

Murphy, George E.
  Callan Castle (Asa Candler House), 186m, **189**, *189*

Murphy and Stewart
  Candler Building, 20m, **39**, *39*

Nelson, Sanford
  Underground Atlanta, 2m, **4**, *5*
  Wildwood 2300 Building, 282m, **290**, *290*

Nevelson, Louise, 38

New South Design Associates
  Underground Atlanta, 2m, **4**, *5*

Nimmons, Carr and Wright
  Sears Roebuck Building, 196m, **198**, *199*

Nix, Mann and Associates
  Nix, Mann and Associates Office (Mitchell King House), 112m, **131**, *131*
  Emory University Hospital, 218m, **228**, *228*
  Theaters, Lenox Square, 264m, **272**, *272*, *273*
  Saint Andrew Catholic Church, 308m, **313**

Noguchi, Isamu
  Play Scapes, 138m, **145**

Norrman, Gottfried L., xxvi
  The Mansion Restaurant (Edward C. Peters House), 86m, **91**, *91*
  Fountain Hall (Stone Hall), Morris Brown College, 162m, **164**, *164*
  Woodruff-Burrus House, 186m, **190**
  Inman Park Elementary School, 186m, **191**

Ohlson Lavoie Corporation
  Athletic Club, Concourse at Landmark Center, 296m, **303**, *303*

Olmsted, Frederick Law, xxii, 42, 137, 146, 185, 207, 242
  Olmsted Brothers, xxii, 145, 146, 181, 207

Palmer, Charles F., 153

Palmer, Hornbostel and Jones
  Michael C. Carlos Hall (Lamar School of Law), Emory University, 218m, **222**, *222*
  Pitts Theology Library (Candler School of Theology), Emory University, 218m, **223**

Pardue, Tom
  Coca-Cola North Avenue Tower, 148m, **152**, *152*

Parker and Scogin
  High Museum at Georgia-Pacific Center, 20m, **38**, *38*

Parkins, William H., xxvi
  Shrine of the Immaculate Conception, 2m, **7**, *7*
  Gaines Hall (North Hall), Morris Brown College, 162m, **164**

James Patterson and Associates
  Baltimore Row (Baltimore Block), 86m, **88**, *88*

Pauley, William C., 154
I. M. Pei and Partners
  Wildwood Plaza, 282m, **291,** *291*
Perkins and Partners
  Odd Fellows Building, 72m, **77,** *77*
Perry, Heman, xxii, 172
Perry, R. Kennon
  Academy of Medicine, 86m,
    107, *107*
Peters, Edward C., 91
Peters, Richard, xxv, 85, 95
Peters Land Company, 52
Porter Associates
  Crestwood, 236m, **243,** *243*
Portman, John, xxvi, 45
  Charles A. Dana Fine Arts Center,
    Agnes Scott College, 316m,
    322, *322*
John Portman and Associates. *See also*
  Edwards and Portman
  Westin Peachtree Plaza Hotel, 46m,
    51, *51*
  Peachtree Center Mall, 46m, **53,** *53*
  Atlanta Merchandise Mart, 46m, **54**
  Atlanta Apparel Mart, 46m, **54,** *55*
  Inforum, 46m, **54,** *55*
  Atlanta Gift Mart, 46m, **54**
  Hyatt Regency Atlanta Hotel
    (Regency Hyatt House Hotel),
    46m, **56,** *57*
  Atlanta Marriott Marquis Hotel,
    46m, **58,** *58*
  Marquis One and Marquis Two
    Towers, 46m, **58**
  One Peachtree Center, 46m, **59,** *59*
  George W. Woodruff Physical
    Education Center, Emory
    University, 218m, **224,** *225*
  R. Howard Dobbs University Center,
    Emory University, 218m,
    225, *226*
  Alumni Memorial Hall, Emory
    University, 218m, **225,** *226*
  Riverwood 100, 282m, **287,** *287*
  400 and 500 Northpark Town
    Center, 296m, **301,** *301*
Portman-Barry Investments, 287, 301
Post, George B.
  Georgia State Capitol, 2m, **9,** *9*
Powell, Warren C.
  Samuel M. Inman Middle School,
    196m, **204**
Preacher, G. Lloyd
  Atlanta City Hall, 2m, **10,** *10, 11*
  Carnegie Building (Wynne-

Claughton Building), 20m,
    35, *36*
  Atlanta Transitional Center (332
    Ponce de Leon Apartments),
    196m, *196,* **198**
  Briarcliff Summit (Briarcliff
    Apartments), 196m, **202,** *202*
Pringle and Smith
  William-Oliver Building, 20m,
    23, *23*
  Rhodes-Haverty Building, 20m,
    33, *33*
  W. W. Orr Building, 86m, **89**
  Days Inn Hotel-Peachtree, 86m, **101**
  H. W. Beers House, 236m, **255,** *256*
  Ryburn Clay House, 236m, **257**
  Bolling Jones House, 236m, **257**
Prybylowski and Gravino
  The Omni, 64m, **66,** *66*
Public Works Administration, 153, 154

Rabun Hatch and Associates
  Biltmore Hotel, 105
  GLG Grand, 112m, **120,** *120*
  Swissôtel, 264m, **272,** *273*
Ramsey, Tom
  Hartsfield Atlanta International
    Airport, 326m, **329,** *329*
Richard Rauh and Associates
  Peachtree Post (Micro Mart
    Computer Product Showroom),
    236m, **238,** *239*
Reagan, John, 178
Reid, Neel, xxvi, 207, 310
  Steiner Building, Grady Memorial
    Hospital (Albert Steiner Ward),
    72m, **78**
  Brookwood Station (Peachtree
    Southern Railway Station), 112m,
    135, *135*
  David Black House, 138m, **140**
  Robert Crumley House, 138m,
    140, *140*
  Stephen S. Lynch House, 138m, **140**
  The Sisters Chapel, Spelman
    College, 162m, **167,** *167*
  Will Campbell House, 208m,
    211, *212*
  Sigmund Montag House, 208m, **211**
  Louis Regenstein House, 208m, **211**
  Frank Adair House, 208m, **212,** *213*
  Oscar Strauss House, 208m,
    214, *214*
  Joseph Neel Reid House, 208m, **214**

Walter Rich House, 208m, **215,** *215*
Emory University Hospital, 218m,
   228, *228*
Luxemburger House, 236m,
   238, *238*
Henry B. Tompkins House, 236m,
   244, *244*
C. C. Case House, 236m, **245,** *246*
Winship Nunally House, 236m, **250**
James Dickey House, 236m,
   252, *252*
Joseph D. Rhodes House, 236m,
   252, *252*
T. M. Watson House, 236m, **256**
Livingston Wright House, 236m,
   256, *257*
William F. Manry House, 236m, **256**
Philip McDuffie House, 236m,
   257, *258*
Jesse Draper House, 236m, **257**
Henry Newman House, 236m, **257**
Robert Alston House, 236m,
   259, *259*
Stuart Witham House, 236m, **259**
Vaughn Nixon House, 236m, **259**
Community Center of South Decatur
   (Scottish Rite Hospital for
   Crippled Children), 316m,
   323, *323*
East Lake Country Club, 316m,
   324, *324*
M. Garland Reynolds and Partners
   MARTA Civic Center Station, 46m,
   61, *61*
Rhodes, Amos Giles, 33, 132
Rich, Morris, 15, 176
Rich, Walter, 215
Rickey, George, 151
Rivers, E., 235, 240
Robert and Company
   United States Eleventh District Court
      of Appeals (Federal Courthouse
      and Post Office), 20m, **28**
   Margaret Mitchell Square, 20m, **34**
   Atlanta Civic Center, 46m, **62**
   Grady Memorial Hospital, 72m,
      78, *79*
   Price Gilbert Memorial Library,
      Georgia Tech, 148m, **157,** *158*
   Emory University Hospital, 218m,
      228, *228*
Robinson, Arthur Neal
   First Church of Christ, Scientist,
      112m, **126,** *126*
   Avondale Estates, 316m, **320,** *320*
J. W. Robinson and Associates

Herndon Plaza, 72m, **76**
Robert W. Woodruff Library, 162m,
   166, *166*
Kevin Roche, John Dinkeloo and
   Associates
   NationsBank Plaza, 86m, **93,** *93*
   One, Two, and Three Ravinia Drive,
      296m, **298,** *298*
Rosenthal, R. S.
   Baltimore Row (Baltimore Block),
      86m, **88,** *88*
Rosser Fabrap International. *See also*
   FABRAP
   Fulton County Government Center,
      2m, **12,** *12*
   SciTrek, 62
   Georgia Dome, 64m, **69,** *69*
   O. Wayne Rollins Research Center,
      Emory University, 218m,
      231, *232*
Roswell Historical Society, 307
Emory Roth and Sons
   Wachovia Bank of Georgia Building
      (First National Bank Building),
      20m, **22,** *22*
Richard Rothman and Associates
   Underground Atlanta, 2m, **4,** *5*
   Biltmore Inn (Biltmore Apartments),
      86m, **104**
   Hotel Peachtree Manor (696
      Peachtree Apartments), 86m,
      105, *105*
Rouse Corporation
   Underground Atlanta, 2m, **4,** *5*
Rudolph, Paul
   Pitts Theology Library, Emory
      University, 218m, **223**
   William R. Cannon Chapel, Emory
      University, 218m, **223,** *224*
Ruff, Solon Z., 137

Salzman, Allan
   The Mansion Restaurant (Edward C.
      Peters House), 86m, **91,** *91*
Sargent, Terry
   Manufacturing Research Center,
      Georgia Tech, 148m, **159,** *159*
   Trinity School, 236m, **249,** *249*
Sasaki, Dawson, DeMay
   Georgia Plaza Park, 9
   Lenox Square, 264m, **272,** *272, 273*
   Executive Park, 264m, **277**
Sayward, William J. *See also* Edwards
   and Sayward
   Pythagoras Masonic Temple, 316m,
      318

Schwartz, Marta
Rio Shopping Mall, 86m, **90,** *90*
Scogin, Elam and Bray. *See also* Parker
and Scogin
New Visions Gallery, 112m, **116**
Turner Village and D. Abbott Turner
Center, Emory University, 218m,
232, *233*
Buckhead Library, 264m, **267,** *267*
Herman Miller Showroom, 264m,
269
Bridge, Concourse at Landmark
Center, 296m, **303,** *304*
Clayton County Headquarters
Library, 326m, **328,** *328*
Scogin, Mack. *See also* Parker and
Scogin
Georgia Power Company Corporate
Headquarters, 46m, **62,** *62*
Bridge, Concourse at Landmark
Center, 296m, **303,** *304*
Herman Miller, Roswell Facility,
308m, **313,** *313*
Shultze, Leonard
Biltmore Hotel, 86m, **104,** *104*
Shultze and Weaver
Biltmore Hotel, 86m, **104,** *104*
Biltmore Inn (Biltmore Apartments),
86, **104**
Shutze, Philip, xxvi, 243
Rich's Department Store, 2m, **15,**
15, 16
NationsBank Building (Citizens and
Southern National Bank Building;
Empire Building), 20m, **24,** *24, 25*
Muse's Building (George Muse
Clothing Company Building),
20m, **30,** *30*
Macy's Department Store (Davison-
Paxon Department Store), 46m,
48, *49*
Goddard Chapel, Grady Memorial
Hospital, 72m, **78**
Hotel Peachtree Manor (696
Peachtree Apartments), 86m,
105, *105*
Academy of Medicine, 86m,
107, *107*
Phelan Apartments, 86m, **108**
Spring Hill Mortuary, 112m,
114, *114*
Reid House (Garrison Apartments),
112m, **130,** *130*
The Temple, 112m, **133,** *133, 134*
The Villa, 138m, **142**
Piedmont Driving Club, 138m, **146**

Glenn Memorial United Methodist
Church, 218m, **220,** *220*
Education Building and Little
Chapel, Glenn Memorial Church,
218m, **220,** *221*
Rich Memorial Building, Emory
University, 218m, **220**
Emory University Hospital, 218m,
228, *228, 229*
Harris Hall (Florence C. Harris
Memorial Nurses' Home), Emory
University, 218m, **228**
North Fulton High School, 236m,
242
Andrew Calhoun House, 236m, **250**
Patterson-Carr House, 236m,
250, *251*
Joseph D. Rhodes House, 236m,
252, *252*
Southern Center for International
Studies (James J. Goodrum
House), 236m, **253,** *254*
Harry L. English House, 236m, **253**
Knollwood (W. H. Kiser House),
236m, **254,** *255*
Albert E. Thornton House, 236m,
254
Floyd McRae House, 236m, **255**
Edward Van Winkle House, 236m,
255
Swan House (Edward H. Inman
House), 236m, **260,** *260, 261*
East Lake Country Club, 316m,
324, *324*
Shutze and Armistead
Academy of Medicine, 86m, **107,**
107
Education Building and Little
Chapel, Glenn Memorial Church,
218m, **220,** *221*
Rich Memorial Building, Emory
University, 218m, **220**
Emory University Hospital, 218m,
228, *228, 229*
Sineway, Ronald
Peachtree Summit, 46m, **61,** *61*
Skidmore, Owings and Merrill
Equitable Building (1968), 20m,
32, *32*
Georgia-Pacific Center, 20m, **36,** *37*
Southern Bell Center, 86m, *97*, **99**
The Terraces at Perimeter Center,
296m, **300,** *300*
Smallwood, Reynolds, Stewart, Stewart
and Associates
Georgian Terrace Apartments

(Georgian Terrace Hotel), 86m,
101, *101*
Eleven Hundred Peachtree Street
Building, 112m, **118,** *118*
Mayfair, 112m, **119**
The Peachtree, 112m, **131**
Federal Home Loan Bank of Atlanta
(Lincoln Pershing Building),
112m, **131**
Atlanta Financial Center, 264m,
271, *271*
Resurgens Plaza, 264m, **275,** *275*
Atlanta Plaza, 264m, **276,** *276*
Overlook III, 282m, **285,** *285*
The Galleria, 282m, **288,** *289*
Wildwood 2500 Building, 282m,
290
Perimeter Mall, 296m, **298**
Smith, F. P.
Clark Howell Homes, 148m, **153**
Smith, Hamilton
Atlanta–Fulton County Public
Library, 20m, **34,** *34*
Smith, Henry Howard
Shrine of the Immaculate
Conception, 2m, **7,** *7*
First Church of Christ, Scientist,
112m, **126,** *126*
Smith, Hinchman and Grylls
Hartsfield Atlanta International
Airport, 326m, **329,** *329*
Smith, Keller
The Galleria, 282m, **288,** *289*
Smith, Robert Hiram, 261
Smith and Jones
All Saints Episcopal Church, 86m,
95, *95*
Snyder, Kit Tin
Margaret Mitchell Square, 20m, **34**
Spencer, Samuel, 135
Stang and Newdow
Garnett Station Place (Southern
Belting Company Building), 2m,
18
Walton Place (Georgia Railway and
Power Building), 20m, **27**
Healey Building, 20m, **28,** *28*
Odd Fellows Building, 72m, **77,** *77*
Stankus, Roman
7000 Central Park, 296m, **302,** *302*
Starrett and Van Vleck
Macy's Department Store (Davison-
Paxon Department Store), 46m,
48, *49*
Steinichen, John
The Counsel House (Bass Furniture

Building), 2m, **13,** *13*
Stevens and Wilkinson. *See also* Burge
and Stevens
Rich's Store for Men, 2m, **15**
Atlanta–Fulton County Public
Library, 20m, **34,** *34*
North and East Wings, Georgia
Baptist Medical Center, 72m, *82,*
83
Professional Building, Georgia
Baptist Medical Center, 72m, **83**
East Professional Building, Georgia
Baptist Medical Center, 72m,
83, *83*
First Baptist Church, 86m, **102**
Robert W. Woodruff Arts Center
(Atlanta Memorial Arts Building),
112m, **127,** *127*
Gambrell Hall, Emory University,
218m, **227,** *227*
E. Rivers Elementary School, 236m,
240, *240*
The Tower at Tower Place, 264m,
268, **269**
Atlanta Financial Center, 264m,
271, *271*
Executive Park, 264m, **277**
MARTA Decatur Transit Station,
316m, **318,** *319*
Hartsfield Atlanta International
Airport, 326m, **329,** *329*
Stoddart, William L.
The Suite Hotel at Underground
Atlanta (Connally Building), 2m, **4**
Winecoff Hotel, 20m, **35,** *35*
The Ponce (Ponce de Leon
Apartments), 86m, **98,** *98*
Georgian Terrace Apartments
(Georgian Terrace Hotel), 86m,
101, *101*
Surber, Barber and Mooney
Academy of Medicine, 86m,
107, *107*
D. Lurton Massee Jr. House, 236m,
244, *245*
Lawrence P. Klamon House, 236m,
246, *247*
Surber and Barber
Campbell-Egan Educational
Building, 2m, **8**
The Castle, 112m, **123,** *123*
The Roosevelt (Franklin D.
Roosevelt High School), 174m,
179, *179*
Sustata and Associates
Lakewood Amphitheatre, 326m, **332**

SWA Group
  Promenade Two, 112m, **124,** *124*
  7000 Central Park, 296m, **302,** *302*

Taylor, John Knox
  United States Eleventh District Court
    of Appeals (Federal Courthouse
    and Post Office), 20m, **28**
Taylor, Richard
  American Security and Insurance
    Company Building, 236m,
    248, *248*
Taylor and Collum. *See also* Taylor
    and Williams
  American Security Insurance
    Building, 236m, **248,** *248*
Taylor-Anderson. *See also* Tippett,
    Taylor and Anderson
  Atlanta Transitional Center, 196m,
    198, *198*
Taylor and Williams
  Piedmont Arbors, 138m, **145,** *146*
  Stillwood Chase, 208m, **210,** *211*
Thompson, Ventulett and Stainback
  The Omni, 64m, **66,** *66*
  CNN Center (Omni International),
    64m, **66,** *67*
  Georgia World Congress Center,
    64m, **68,** *68*
Thompson, Ventulett, Stainback and
    Associates
  The World of Coca-Cola Pavilion,
    2m, **6,** *6*
  Georgia Dome, 64m, **69,** *69*
  Herndon Plaza, 72m, **76,** *76*
  Campanile, 112m, **118,** *118*
  Colony Square, 112m, *118,*
    119, *119*
  Promenade Two, 112m, **124,** *124*
  Promenade One (AT&T
    Communications, Southern
    Regional Headquarters), 112m,
    125, *125*
  1275 Peachtree at the Circle, 112m,
    126
  1315 Peachtree Building, 112m,
    128
  Ronald McDonald Childhood
    Cancer Clinic, 218m, **228**
  Buckhead Plaza, 264m, **266,** *266*
  Phipps Plaza, 264m, **274**
  Honeywell Office Building, 264m,
    277
  IBM U.S. Marketing and Services
    Headquarters, 282m, **284,** *284*

Georgia U.S. Corporate Center (Life
    of Georgia Corporate Center),
    282m, **288,** *289*
  HBO & Company (Perimeter 301),
    296m, **299,** *299*
  Concourse at Landmark Center,
    296m, **303,** *303, 304*
  Decatur Town Center, Buildings
    One and Two, 316m, **318**
Thompson Hancock Witte
  Cyclorama, 174m, **180,** *180*
Tiffany Studio, 95, 128
Tippett, Taylor and Anderson
  William R. Cannon Chapel, 218m,
    223, *224*
Tippett and Associates
  South Clinic Building (Eye Center
    and Emory Clinic Addition),
    Emory Clinic, 218m, **228**
  Scarborough Memorial Building
    Addition, Emory Clinic, 218m,
    228
Tippett and Taylor
  Rich Memorial Building, Emory
    University, 218m, **220**
Tomberlin and Sheetz
  Forty Marietta Building (First Federal
    Savings and Loan Association
    Building), 20m, **26,** *26*
Toombs, Amisano and Wells
  Forty-One Marietta Building
    (Standard Federal Savings and
    Loan Building), 20m, **27,** *27*
  Grant Building (Grant-Prudential
    Building), 20m, **28,** *29*
  MARTA Peachtree Center Station,
    46m, **48,** *48*
  Peachtree Summit, 46m, **61,** *61*
  Robert W. Woodruff Arts Center
    (Atlanta Memorial Arts Building),
    112m, **127,** *127*
  Robert W. Woodruff Library, 162m,
    166, *166*
  Second Church of Christ, Scientist,
    264m, **271**
  Lenox Square, 264m, **272,** *272, 273*
  D&B Software Building (Cities
    Service Building), 264m, **274,** *274*
  Corporate Square Office Park,
    264m, **277,** *277*
  John Knox Presbyterian Church,
    282m, **293,** *293*
  One West Court Square, 316m, **318**
Toombs and Creighton
  Rich's Bridge and Store for Homes,
    2m, **15,** *16*

Totten, George O., Jr.
  Villa Lamar, 236m, **250,** *251*
Trammel Crow Corporation, 288
Tucker and Howell
  Garden Hills School, 236m, **242**
  Morris Brandon School, 236m,
    247, *247*
Turner, Ted, 67
Turner Associates
  Underground Atlanta, 2m, **4,** *5*
  Fulton County Government Center,
    2m, **12,** *12*
  Cornerstone Building (J. P. Allen
    Building), 46m, **52,** *52*
  The Coca-Cola Company Corporate
    Headquarters, Central Reception
    Building, 148m, **150,** *150*
  Coca-Cola USA Building, 148m,
    150, *151*

Urban Design Associates
  Decatur Town Center, Buildings
    One and Two, 316m, **318**

Vintage House Renovations
  Shellmont Bed and Breakfast Lodge
    (William P. Nicholson House),
    86m, **106,** *106*

Wachendorff, Eugene C.
  Booker T. Washington High School,
    162m, **171,** *171*
Wagoner, Harold A.
  Evangelical Lutheran Church of the
    Redeemer, 86m, **102**

Walker and Chase
  Old DeKalb County Courthouse,
    316m, **318,** *318*
Warnecke, John Carl
  Neiman-Marcus Department Store,
    Lenox Square, 264m, **272,**
    272, 273
Weidlinger Associates
  Georgia Dome, 64m, **69,** *69*
Whatley and Partners
  Courtyard by Marriott, Cumberland
    Center (Compri Hotel), 282m,
    286, *286*
Wilburn, Lila Ross
  Atlanta Transitional Center (The
    Rosslyn), 196m, **198,** *198*
Wilkins, Grant, 146
Williams Russell and Johnson
  Margaret Mitchell Square, 20m, **34**
Willis, George R., 320
Wilner and Millkey
  Bank South Building (Fulton
    National Bank Building), 20m,
    27, *27*
Winecoff, William Fleming, 35–36
Woodruff, Ernest, 191, 217
Woodruff, George, 217, 224, 231
Woodruff, Robert W., 127, 128, 151,
    166, 230
Wylie, James
  Equitable Building (1968), 20m,
    32, *32*

Zion and Breen
  One Atlantic Center (IBM Tower),
    112m, *120,* **121**